AF323205

The European Union, the United Nations, and the Revival of Confederal Governance

**Recent Titles in
Global Perspectives in History and Politics**

United States Foreign Policy at the Crossroads
George Schwab, editor

The Press and the Rebirth of Iberian Democracy
Kenneth Maxwell, editor

Macro-Nationalisms: A History of the Pan-Movements
Louis L. Snyder

The Myth of Inevitable Progress
Franco Ferrarotti

Power and Policy in Transition: Essays Presented on the Tenth Anniversary of
the National Committee on American Foreign Policy in Honor of its Founder,
Hans J. Morgenthau
Vojtech Mastny, editor

Perforated Sovereignties and International Relations: Trans-Sovereign Contacts of
Subnational Governments
Ivo D. Duchacek, Daniel Latouche, and Garth Stevenson, editors

The Pure Concept of Diplomacy
José Calvet de Magalhães

Carl Schmitt: Politics and Theory
Paul Edward Gottfried

Reluctant Ally: United States Policy Toward the Jews from Wilson to Roosevelt
Frank W. Brecher

East Central Europe after the Warsaw Pact: Security Dilemmas in the 1990s
Andrew A. Michta

The French Revolution and the Meaning of Citizenship
Renée Waldinger, Philip Dawson, and Isser Woloch, editors

Social Justice in the Ancient World
K. D. Irani and Morris Silver, editors

The European Union, the United Nations, and the Revival of Confederal Governance

Frederick K. Lister

Contributions in Political Science, Number 371
Global Perspectives in History and Politics
George Schwab, Series Editor

GREENWOOD PRESS
Westport, Connecticut • London

Library of Congress Cataloging-in-Publication Data

Lister, Frederick K.
    The European Union, the United Nations, and the revival of
confederal governance / Frederick K. Lister.
        p.   cm. — (Contributions in political science, ISSN 0147–1066
; no. 371. Global perspectives in history and politics)
    Includes bibliographical references and index.
    ISBN 0–313–29890–4 (alk. paper)
    1. Confederation of states.   2. European Union.   3. United
Nations.   I. Title.   II. Series: Contributions in political science
; no. 371.   III. Series: Contributions in political science. Global
perspectives in history and politics.
JC357.L57   1996
327.4—dc20   95–47183

British Library Cataloguing in Publication Data is available.

Library of Congress Catalog Card Number: 95–47183
ISBN: 0–313–29890–4
ISSN: 0147–1066

First published in 1996

Greenwood Press, 88 Post Road West, Westport, CT 06881
An imprint of Greenwood Publishing Group, Inc.

Printed in the United States of America

The paper used in this book complies with the
Permanent Paper Standard issued by the National
Information Standards Organization (Z39.48–1984).

P

In order to keep this title in print and available to the academic community, this edition
was produced using digital reprint technology in a relatively short print run. This would
not have been attainable using traditional methods. Although the cover has been changed
from its original appearance, the text remains the same and all materials and methods
used still conform to the highest book-making standards.

Contents

Foreword

At this moment in history, when the world is groping its way through the uncertainties of the post–Cold War period in search of new international governance modalities to replace the overbearing dominance of bi-polarism, Frederick Lister's book on confederal governance, with particular attention to the European Union and the United Nations, is a most welcome addition to the debate. Despite the shrill cries from the partisans of isolationism and "going-it-alone," the realities of the world are that the inhabitants of planet earth are interconnected and interdependent. They are confronted by the common problem of existence in the face of the continued threat of mass destruction posed, even without the Cold War, by the continued existence of stockpiles of nuclear, chemical, and biological weapons. In addition, they are all part of a global economy which makes inordinate demands upon them to subordinate their freedom of action as they form social and political institutions to cope with the new economic and technological facts of the still rapidly evolving era of the globalization of information and communication. All this has to be accomplished by a humanity that is composed of a myriad of peoples divided racially, culturally, socially, economically, religiously, and linguistically that add up to a composite of incompatability resulting in a difficult and challenging task.

Over the course of millennia, humanity has evolved an answer to the problem of social organization and governance that has taken the form of the sovereign political state, usually driven by strong feelings of patriotism qua nationalism in the modern era. But few of these states lived in hermetically sealed cocoons isolated from other states. During the last several centuries, the world of states has become increasingly interdependent through trade and scientific discoveries. This growth of interdependence has generated needs for new political and legal institutions to cope with the changed circumstances. In recent times, it has become abundantly clear that the sovereign nation-state is being undermined by an array of national problems, such as security, economic welfare and growth, unemployment, the environment, population movements, currency and monetary policy, and health, that do not respect national boundaries and are beyond the grasp of states acting alone. Unless harnessed, these problems have the propensity to cause conflict among states, even widespread war, and over the course of time there has been a search for political institutions under which disparate peoples can live together harmoniously.

The search has been for institutions that go beyond the nation-state. Among such institutions is that of confederal governance. The more favored supra-national institution of governance since the adoption of the United States Constitution in 1789 has been federalism. Since then, federations have appeared, and disappeared in some cases, on almost every continent— Canada, Mexico, Brazil, Germany, Russia, Indonesia, Nigeria, South Africa. The failure of the Articles of Confederation among the thirteen American colonies all but consigned the confederal pattern to the dust bin. However, federalism has not worked out satisfactorily in all cases and the need for a political institution bringing states together, short of integrating them into one single sovereignty—the distinctive mark of a federal system, has not been obviated.

Fred Lister, a long-time international civil servant in the United Nations and a keen student of its institutions, has been intrigued by this problem of finding suitable political institutions to cope with the interdependence of states and people and yet preserve a semblance of their individuality. Confederal governance, he argues, may provide the answer. His curiosity has led him back to the ancient Greeks and across the centuries of history during which examples of confederal governance have functioned. He has found that, in our day, the European Union and the United Nations are living examples of institutional arrangements that have utilized many of the concepts of confederal governance. In his carefully argued, meticulously researched, and insightful study he provides us with an important perspective from which to examine the conditions of the persistent problem of interstate governance. This book serves the very useful purpose of alerting us to the saliency of the confederal model as a practical alternative to more utopian, but unattainable, plans for world government.

Benjamin Rivlin
Ralph Bunche Institute on the United Nations
January 1996

Preface

This book is part of a much longer work, *Confederal Governance, Its Long History and Modern Revival,* which remains tucked away in my word processor. That work is in its turn the product of more than five years of research on confederal-type governance as it has evolved over the centuries. The three chapters in this book have been excerpted from the longer work and adapted so as to constitute a self-contained introduction to the wider subject.

I became interested in confederal governance when I realized that only one other person (at least so far as I have been able to discover) has studied the topic in depth, Murray Forsyth, in his *Unions of States,* published in 1981. Thus, although the term is widely used by political scientists and by writers generally to refer to a loose form of political association, as if it were something too well known to require definition or further study, the reverse is true. I also came to realize that confederal-type governance is the "missing link" between our many intergovernmental organizations like the IMF and the United Nations, on the one hand, and federal-type governments like those of Switzerland and the United States, on the other.

Like federal and unitary (centralized) states, confederal "unions of states" refer to a broad class of polities that have certain characteristics in common, but that differ from one another in many ways depending upon the time and the circumstances in which they emerged. The primary goal of my research has been to open up the process of discovering which polities belong to this class and the nature of the characteristics required for membership.

I say "open up" because what I have found is a new field for study, and a single individual working alone can only scratch the surface of that field!

My search has taken me back to Ancient Greece, the cradle of political inventiveness, and to its "sympolities," which may well have been the earliest confederations. It has also taken me to Swiss, Dutch, American, and German history, each of which had its "confederal" period. I have approached my task by investigating how confederal-type governmental institutions came to integrate peoples and states in new and larger entities, and how those larger entities fared under confederal governance. To do so, I had to tell the story of each confederation being studied. This involved linking its form of governance with its evolution as an association of states and peoples. There is one example of this technique in the present book, the brief summary of the history of the European Community/Union in Chapter 2.

Since they have been mostly ignored until now, confederal governmental institutions are in need of a closer scrutiny in their own right. In that sense, this book has a relatively narrow focus. No attempt has been made to integrate its findings with the wider concepts (e.g., the interdependencies of states and regime theory), which have been developed in recent years in some of the scholarly writings on international relations.

At the same time, it should not be supposed that this book is focused only on obsolete forms of government that have little or no relevance to our contemporary problems. On the contrary, confederal governance, retaining its essential characteristics yet adapted to contemporary conditions, is making its reappearance on the world scene. In fact, it is possible that it may be revived on a larger scale during the twenty-first century, and that it may prove helpful in dealing with some of the very serious problems that have been emerging in the second half of this century. This possibility is enlarged upon in the Opening and Closing Arguments, which frame the more detailed analysis of confederal governance in the three main chapters of the book.

In my investigations, I have been fortunate in having a lot of help. Helena Stalson, lately of the staff of the Council on Foreign Relations in New York, has reviewed every chapter of this book. I have benefited particularly from her long experience and knowledge in the field of international economic relations. She has also given me unstinting encouragement when I needed it most.

Many others have contributed by giving me the benefit of their comments on earlier drafts of various chapters in the book. They include some of my former UN colleagues, Abraham Bargman, Juergen Dedring, Blaine Sloan, James Sutterlin, and Wiebe Van der Heide; also Professor Charlotte Patton of York College (CUNY) and Christopher Matthews of the European Commission's New York office. I thank them all while retaining sole responsibility for whatever flaws and shortcomings may be found in the pages that follow.

I am also deeply indebted to the Ralph Bunche Institute of the City University of New York and to its Director, Benjamin Rivlin, as well as to its Director Emeritus, Seymour Maxwell Finger, both as friends and as long-time colleagues. The supportive atmosphere of the Institute and its weekly seminars have helped me greatly in writing this book. I wish also to register my special indebtedness to Professor George Schwab of CUNY.

Finally, I should like to thank my dear wife, Beatrice Bassi Lister, who has also been a lifelong student of the ways of government and the political process. She has not only filled in for me in many ways when so much of my attention was focused on books, articles and my word processor, she has also given me the benefit of her comments on almost all of my drafts. I am more grateful than I can say for her continuing love and support.

Frederick K. Lister
Rye Brook, New York, January 16, 1996

The European Union, the United Nations, and the Revival of Confederal Governance

The Opening Argument

The stockpiles of nuclear, chemical, and biological weapons of mass destruction and the raw materials from which they are made continue to present an ominous backdrop to humanity's growing and spreading material prosperity. While there is no longer much risk of a cataclysmic nuclear exchange between two superpowers, the research and development of nuclear, chemical, and biological weaponry systems still go on, though doubtless at a much slower pace than during the Cold War. Probably, nothing can stop this accumulation of knowledge and of our capacity to use it in ways that could devastate the surface of the earth in the twenty-first century. Pandora's box has been opened, and humanity has been condemned to live forever with the terrible secrets that it contains. Our species has been presented with the alternatives of changing its warlike ways or of ultimately suffering an unenviable fate. And the time left for us to act on the first alternative may be much less than we have been hoping for.

The end of the Cold War has, in fact, increased the dangers we face because it has helped the least responsible governments and terrorist groups to enter the arms race. Middlemen from developed countries seem quite ready to send rogue governments like those of Iraq, Iran, Libya, and North Korea the industrial equipment needed to produce such weapons. And some unemployed scientists can always be induced to place their technological skills at the disposal of such governments and groups.

Worst of all, in Russia, the former rigid control systems over large stockpiles of weapons-grade uranium and plutonium seem to have broken down completely in many of the depots. The frequent discovery of samples of pure plutonium and enriched uranium on the black market, and what appears to be a terrorist experimentation with chemical weapons in the Tokyo subways, constitute ugly omens of what the twenty-first century may have in store for the human family. If they do accurately foreshadow our future, governments will, sooner or later, face crises far graver than those of the two world wars.

In August 1995, Senator Richard Lugar focused attention on this problem in public hearings held in Washington. His opening statement contained the following warning: "As a consequence of the collapse of [the Soviet totalitarian] command and control [structure], a vast potential supermarket of nuclear weapons and weapons-grade uranium and plutonium is becoming increasingly accessible." He added that "the probability that one, two or a dozen nuclear weapons [will] detonate in Russia, or Europe, or the Middle East, or even the United States has increased," and that in his view "Americans have every reason to anticipate acts of nuclear terrorism against American targets before this decade is out." He concluded that "because this new threat comes in a form so unfamiliar, indeed so radically different from prior experience . . . the American political leadership, the Congress and the American people have great difficulty in awakening to this fact" (Lugar 1995, pp. 1–3).[1]

Senator Sam Nunn, in his turn, pointed out at the same hearings, "Today, weapons of unthinkable destructive power appear near the grasp of those willing and unafraid to commit the unthinkable." He continued: "Never before in history has an empire disintegrated while in possession of some 30,000 nuclear weapons, at least 40,000 tons of chemical weapons, significant biological weaponry capability, and thousands of weapons scientists and technicians unsure how long they will receive salaries with which to feed their families . . . I believe this threat is the number one security concern facing our nation today" (Nunn 1995, pp. 1–2).

John Holdren, one of the expert witnesses, informed the senators that, until recently, the main obstacle to building nuclear bombs has been the unavailability of plutonium and enriched uranium and that if these substances become readily available, a third-world bomb program might be shortened "from a decade to months—or even less." He went on to explain, "the amounts required are small. . . . A few kilograms of plutonium or roughly three times that amount of highly enriched uranium is enough for a nuclear bomb." Without proper safeguards, a worker "could simply put enough material for a bomb under his overcoat and walk out." There have been reports that 80% of the nuclear facilities in Russia lack the electronic monitors that could detect such thefts (Holdren 1995, pp. 3, 5, 6).

These Senate hearings are a wake-up call to a serious gap in the world's security. They also indicate that the former superpower rivals are cooperating, for the time being at least, in a number of steps to deal with it. The extent to which these steps are likely to be successful is far from clear, but, presumably, some of the nuclear materials no longer under Russian control may have already reached those who will begin to use them in making military devices.

Certain broad conclusions would seem to emerge from the foregoing information: (1) A crisis stemming from the leakages from these stockpiles of enriched uranium and plutonium may be coming sooner than had been expected; (2) When it comes, such a crisis will probably consist either of threats to use nuclear or other weapons of mass destruction or of their actual use; (3) The crisis is more likely to involve, at least in its first stages, only one or a few such weapons, not the large numbers that might have been involved if the Cold War had suddenly turned hot; (4) The world community may therefore have a "window of opportunity" to get itself into a survival mode by adopting whatever emergency measures may be deemed necessary; (5) The repercussions of the crisis will be global, and the response to it will, of necessity, require the leaders of the world community to cooperate through political institutions capable of exercising an effective global authority.

Much will doubtless be written in the near future on the emergency measures that will need to be taken if the fears expressed at the Senate hearings prove to be well founded. I am not competent to write on those aspects. This book is concerned with the long-term ways of preserving civilized life in the next century. We are moving more rapidly than we would like towards a world in which weapons of mass destruction will be available to rogue states and terrorist groups, and where the need for other states and other groups to find ways of protecting themselves is therefore likely to become ever more imperative. A principal obstacle to meeting this need is the division of the world's peoples into ethnic and racial groups, many of which are deeply hostile to one another. This problem will be explored next.

ETHNIC TENSIONS

If the past half-century provides any indication of what the future holds in store, our most serious political problems will stem from the ethnic (that is to say, the racial-cultural-social-religious-linguistic) incompatibilities of peoples living within the many remaining multiethnic states.

In 1991, Thomas Friedman put his finger on the underlying problem in dealing with ethnic tensions when he wrote, "America's brand of federalism aims to forge one nation from people of diverse origins. This is not a realistic aim for multinational societies like the Soviet Union and Yugoslavia. For them, the challenge is to design political societies that can contain many nations—who want to retain their separate national identities—yet remain part of a single political and economic unit" (Friedman 1991, p. 1).

We live in an era when ethnic minorities believe that they are entitled to secede from multiethnic states in which they no longer feel comfortable.

We have entered this era gradually over the past two centuries. Beginning with the English, American, and French Revolutions, a fundamental change in the way in which humanity is governed has, gradually and despite many temporary setbacks, been spreading across the globe. Instead of being ruled as subjects by kings, dictators, or small groups of oligarchs, peoples, one after another, have been conceded their right, as citizens of their nation-states, to choose their own leaders in free elections and to have their laws made in legislatures composed of their own freely elected representatives.

This gradual transition from multiethnic empires formed by force to voluntary unions enjoying the willing participation both of individuals and of the wider ethnic groups to which they belong is an epochal development. It signifies that more and more states are now voluntary political associations. That is to say, they are composed, mainly or entirely, of people who choose to live in them and who are vested by their constitutions with certain basic political rights in the running of those unions. While such a transition may be disruptive in the short term, it is gradually producing more stable states. This may, in turn, produce a more stable world community. Governments elected under these circumstances enjoy what has become known as "political legitimacy."

Not surprisingly, there is a downside to this restructuring of the world community. It has been accompanied by major strains and stresses, indeed by the serious political and economic crises that generally attend the breakdown of multiethnic empires. Further, it has spawned a mounting awareness of ethnic identity, a corresponding intensification of ethnic nationalism, and an increasing tendency of ethnic groups of all kinds to press for full-scale independence.

It does not help that the confrontations to which such demands often lead are now being played out in a world where weapons of mass destruction are becoming increasingly available, and where the indiscriminate use of even conventional weapons often leads to appalling results. These civil wars, and the widespread bloodshed that has always been a part of such transitions, are now more alarming because, with the increasing interdependency of states, there is a greater risk that neighboring states and the world community as a whole may become involved in them.

The states that are or have been involved in recent ethnic-type confrontations include Canada, the United Kingdom (in Northern Ireland), Yugoslavia, Czechoslovakia, Turkey, Cyprus, India (in Kashmir), Israel, Iraq, Russia, Georgia, Azerbaijan, Armenia, Afghanistan, Sri Lanka, Somalia, Sudan, Rwanda, Burundi, and Liberia. If one goes back to the Cold War period, the list would have to be lengthened to include Nigeria, Pakistan, Indonesia, Trinidad and Tobago, Peru, Spain, Zanzibar, Ethiopia, Zaire, Rhodesia (now Zimbabwe), Angola, Mozambique, and South Africa.

Sooner or later, most multiethnic states may find themselves facing this kind of challenge. In the United States, for example, the tradition of forging one nation from peoples of diverse origins is starting to bend to the demands of the cultural pluralists. Now that so many ethnic groups (among them, the Armenians, Georgians, Azerbaijanis, Croatians, Slovaks, Slovenes, Lithuanians, Latvians, Estonians, etc.) have won their independence, the demonstration effect is inspiring numerous other ethnic minorities to entertain thoughts of secession and independence.

Furthermore, as this transition proceeds into its later stages, the law of diminishing returns may be setting in. Under Article 1 of the United Nations Charter,[2] UN members have agreed to respect the right of "peoples" to self-determination. That presumably means that any self-appointed ethnic group may elect to join the ranks of sovereign states. Yet there are inevitable complications in translating that none-too-straightforward concept into practical politics. For example, what happens to secession-minded ethnic groups that are too small or too disorganized to form viable states?[3]

It must be borne in mind that the ethnic substructure of humankind is extraordinarily complex. Although ethnologists differ on the number of distinct human cultures, they agree that they are very numerous. George Peter Murdoch places the number at 1,264 and Ivo Duchacek at "some 3,000" (Murdoch 1980; Duchacek 1977). From his 1,264 cultures, Murdoch identifies 563 distinct "societies." One hundred and eleven of them are in sub-Saharan Africa; 81, in East Asia; 65, in areas adjacent to the Mediterranean; 81, in Central and South America; 124, in North America; and 101, in the insular Pacific. While many of these groups are small, and some may have died out, enough of them remain in sufficient numbers to create the possibility that the world community might conceivably expand to 400–500 states. The extent to which these groups will actually engage in separatist activities remains uncertain, but ethnic nationalism in one form or another has become such a powerful motivating force that it would be risky to underrate its growing potential for disruption.

Ethnic surveys reveal how widespread that potential is. Worldwide, four out of ten countries are composed of more than five ethnic groups, and less than one-third of them are relatively homogeneous, that is to say, less than one in three has a dominant ethnic group making up more than 90% of its total population. Said and Simmons, in their sample of 132 states, found only 12 that could be considered uniethnic. In 39, the largest ethnic group accounted for less than half of the population; in 31, the figure was 50–74%; and in 25 others, between between 75–89% (Said and Simmons 1976, p. 10).

Moreover, our times are characterized by massive migrations of people, sometimes to escape persecution, more often as part of a search for economic opportunity and a better life. These migrations, far from concentrating ethnic groups and thus relieving ethnic tensions, are creating new and larger diasporas of "illegals" who are usually (often for reasons beyond their control) not particularly popular in their new neighborhoods. In many countries, the absence of effective immigration barriers has been allowing the number of aliens to increase more rapidly than they can be socially or culturally absorbed.

The plight of the successor states of the former Soviet Union illustrates how complex the question of self-determination of ethnic groups is. In the 1979 census of that union, more than 100 national groups were listed, 22 of them composed of more than a million persons. The unity of many of these successor states is now being threatened, in turn, by their own minorities. For example, the 1.3 million inhabitants of the "republic" of Chechen-Ingush who live inside Russia's southern border have been asserting their independence. While few would defend the ugly methods that the Russians have used in subjugating them, neither would most states acquiesce in one of their small provinces asserting its independence. For Russia, the potential for similar troubles is alarming, for there are roughly 30 autonomous republics, oblasts, and national "okrugs" in that country alone. These entities together occupy more than half the land surface of Russia, including most of Siberia (Gilbert 1972, pp. 144–145).

The so-called Third World in which most of the human family lives is especially vulnerable to ethnic strife because many of its borders were drawn not to reflect ethnic or cultural differences but to resolve colonial rivalries. African states particularly troubled by their ethnic minorities have included Nigeria (the Ibos), the Sudan (the Dinkas), Ethiopia (the Eritreans and others) and, of course, South Africa with its Caucasian, Indian, and Colored minorities. These are only the obvious ones; the list could easily be lengthened.

It is sometimes supposed that Latin America is free of ethnic incompatibilities. However, in Peru, we have perhaps a foretaste of how serious they may become. James Brooke has written that "the driving force behind the [Shining Path] rebellion is a racism that permeates Peruvian society." He adds that "when Peruvians scrutinize the photographs of arrested guerrillas, few fail to notice their pronounced Indian and mixed-race features, while once again this year Miss Peru looks as if she was plucked off a Spanish beach . . . [the guerrillas] speak Quechua and everyone knows it" (Brooke 1991, pp. A1, A6).

With the break-up of the colonial empires in Asia and Africa, the world's system of sovereign states has been expanding at a rapid rate. Since 1945, the membership of the United Nations has increased from 50 to 186 members. Many of these new members have small backward economies, and some may present tempting targets to aggressive neighbors. Quite a few of them are composed of groups that have little or no experience in self-rule and are thus doubly vulnerable.

The United Nations, under its Charter, has a responsibility for keeping the peace and for promoting the settlement of disputes, but the larger and more prosperous states on whom this burden mainly falls are increasingly unwilling to bear it. If the UN's membership were to double in the next century, the world community would begin to resemble the Holy Roman Empire, which broke up into so many tiny units that it became ungovernable. Should our system of sovereign states follow in its footsteps, it might become impossible to provide the peacemaking and peacekeeping services that would be required to maintain order amongst them.

Thus, the world community faces a serious dilemma. From the political and economic standpoints, it is important to have a manageable number of major political actors of commensurate size instead of hundreds of small states and ministates. On the other hand, the internal stability of every state would in the long run be enhanced if each self-conscious ethnic group of people that wishes to enjoy its own social and cultural autonomy is allowed to do so.

A STRATEGY FOR PROMOTING PEACEFUL CO-EXISTENCE

Summing up, the main challenge of the next century will be to prevent weapons of mass destruction from being widely used, indeed, if possible, to prevent such weapons from being used at all. And the main obstacles to attaining that goal are likely to be twofold: the warlike proclivities of nation-states and their leaders; and the ethnic divisions that compartmentalize humanity into so many incompatible groups. Accordingly, there is a great need to find ways of blocking those warlike proclivities and of moderating ethnic incompatibilities.

The first of the two obstacles may prove the lesser problem. Even during the Cold War, the prospect of widespread nuclear devastation was enough to keep most world leaders from pursuing overtly expansionist policies. Even irresponsible leaders, unless they are madmen, are not likely to be tempted in that direction, especially after seeing what has been happening to Iraq under Saddam Hussein. Thus, the greater danger will probably not come from governments *per se*. Rather, it is likely to come from ethnic groups, working either within or outside government, that are ready to risk all on behalf of their nationalist goals.

Thus, what is most urgently needed now is to moderate the intensity of the various ethnic confrontations and to persuade ethnic leaders to move their many followers in the opposite direction, that is, towards interethnic reconciliation and co-existence, if not out of love (that would be expecting too much!), at least by yielding to the simple imperatives of survival. In fact, it is not necessary that they love one another, only that they refrain from carrying their hatreds to the point of mutually destructive warfare.

But, of course, convincing ethnic leaders of this is more easily said than done. Putting international relations and relations among ethnic groups into a survival mode involves altering ingrained human attitudes and patterns of behavior, not just in one country but in all countries. This obviously cannot be achieved by admonitions alone. It requires some form of broader political union with an accompanying framework of global political institutions. In addition, the form of political union must moderate, not inflame, the hatreds that ethnic groups often feel for one another.

Of course, all this is not new; the search for international peace has been conducted unsuccessfully for many years. The only new element is that we shall now be under increasingly intense pressure to take timely action. As long ago as 1957, a leading political scientist, Karl Deutsch, deeply concerned by the risk of war in a nuclear age, sought to devise an "integration theory" that would clarify the circumstances in which the various nation-states would find it possible to join one another in forming much wider unions dedicated to keeping the peace, perhaps eventually a union that would include all the world's peoples. On the basis of some three dozen case studies, Deutsch and his colleagues elaborated six "essential requirements" for peoples who aspire to form economic or collective security unions.

These requirements included compatibility of values and expectations; adequate administrative capabilities and communications; mobility of persons; multiplicity and balance of transactions; mutual predictability of behavior; and capacity of participating units to respond to one another's needs and actions in a timely way. Other political scientists carried out similar exercises (Deutsch et al. 1957, pp. 46–59; Haas & Schmitter 1964; and Nye 1971).[4]

Unfortunately, most peoples who satisfy requirements of this kind have already been living together in the same state under a common government. Furthermore, events seem to be moving too rapidly for us simply to sit back and await the moment when ethnic groups may ultimately decide to form wider unions with one another.

In any event, political union has usually anteceded and has probably been a major factor in producing closer social and economic ties rather than the other way around. Up until recently, conquerors created multiethnic states with polyglot populations without worrying about their compatibility. Yet when the ethnic differences among them were not too great or exacerbated by mistreatment of minorities, a few decades spent under a common political umbrella often led, in a natural way, to a growing homogeneity among the peoples living in them.

In fact, if the goal is to find a basis for regional unions or a global union within which the world's peoples might learn to act together to eliminate war, it does not help to set preconditions that usually cannot be met. It would seem better to devise a loose form of governance under which diverse peoples would be able to coexist peacefully with one another despite their diversity, in the expectation that this will lead gradually to an increasing sense of solidarity among them.

Thus, what we seem to need is a form of governance that may prove viable for peoples who lack the same values and expectations; who cannot predict one another's behavior patterns, needs, and actions; who have not been in daily contact; and who do not speak the same language or share the same social mores or espouse the same religion. In short, what is required is a form of governance that will permit quite heterogeneous peoples to embark upon the road to economic, sociocultural and political coexistence.

In focusing on form of governance rather than prerequisites for integration, this book sets off in a new direction. Instead of investigating the conditions that peoples must satisfy in order to form broader unions, the approach will be to find a form of governance that might enable diverse groups of peoples (who, after all, share the same deep-seated interest in their own survival) to live together in peace and to achieve economic prosperity.

Let us now enquire into the criteria that such a form of governance should satisfy. First of all, matters would be simplified if it does not seek to replace our present system of "sovereign" states, but merely introduces a new order of political relationships that could be grafted onto that system. Second, this form of governance should have the option of focusing on security needs alone. Third, it should be extendable to various economic or other general welfare functions. Fourth, it should be "minimalist," that is to say, it should win the acceptance and support of the citizenries of its members by intruding as little as possible into their daily lives. Fifth, it would need to have assured sources of revenue that would enable it to carry out the functions assigned to it. Finally, this form of governance should pave the way for the peoples living under it to form the limited ties of human solidarity that are a condition of their survival in a world where weapons of mass destruction will be readily available.

As it happens, we may not need to invent new forms of governance to satisfy these six criteria. Two already exist that might be combined and adapted for that purpose: intergovernmental organizations (IGOs) and confederations. Each one will be briefly described in the next two sections.

INTERGOVERNMENTAL ORGANIZATIONS

The IGO, invented in the nineteenth century, is already a familiar feature of the global and regional political landscapes. In fact, there are now more than a hundred IGOs. They have been assigned a wide variety of tasks that run the gamut from postal to peacemaking services, which they carry out on behalf of their member states. They are, in effect, laboratories in which national governments and international secretariats are learning how to work together in performing the broad spectrum of functions that are better carried out jointly. In this process, governmental delegates are under pressure to acquire attitudes and working habits that are oriented towards cooperation rather than confrontation.

However, IGOs operate under certain limitations. First, the powers delegated to them do not usually include those of the greatest importance. For example, they seldom include those associated with the exercise of sovereignty.

Second, when IGOs do have mandates that involve the exercise of important powers, their authority is usually limited to making recommendations rather than to taking action. In such cases, if there is a need for joint action, it is usually achieved through the adoption of multilateral treaties requiring ratification by the governments that are to be bound by them, with the IGOs' role, if any, limited to secondary support such as helping to implement the agreements reached. The treaties on the law of the sea are a good example of this way of proceeding.

A third major limitation of IGOs is that they are mainly "functional" bodies, that is to say, most of them are merely vehicles or conveniences that governments have created to help them carry out certain functions that are best handled transnationally. It would seem to follow that if IGOs are only "vehicles" and "conveniences" for governments, they will not be able to generate the kind of popular support and allegiance necessary to pave the way for a wider transnational social integration or solidarity.

The principal IGO in the realm of collective security is, of course, the United Nations. All three of the foregoing limitations apply to it. Whereas the absence of popular support may not matter much for technical IGOs such as the Universal Postal Union, the International Civil Aviation Organization or the International Monetary Fund, the UN's mandate is too ambitious to be carried out successfully without the full backing of the peoples of its member states. In the light of 50 years of experience, and especially of its performance in post–Cold War conditions, it is becoming clear that a political association with only a traditional IGO-type framework (and the very limited public support that goes with it) is too weak either to act as a reliable guardian of international peace and security or to impose adequate controls on the manufacture, storage, and use of weapons of mass destruction.

Yet the grave threat posed by the increasing availability of those weapons cannot be dealt with by any state acting alone. It has to be tackled internationally. It may be presumed that, some time not too far in the future, the United Nations—or some alternative entity—will have to be turned into a political body that is capable of exercising the effective global authority necessary to deal with the impending crisis to which the evidence revealed in Senator Lugar's hearings points. That body should have a mandate to prevent the use of these weapons (to the extent that this is possible) and to manage the situations that we shall all face if and when they are actually used. In the framing of such a stronger mandate and the procedures by which it will be carried out, the experience with various confederal models, past and present, will be most useful.

A FIRST LOOK AT CONFEDERAL GOVERNANCE

The confederation, or union of states, little known today, is essentially an IGO with teeth that has been empowered to carry out, with the joint participation of its member states, a limited range of sovereign functions on their behalf. Its decision-making bodies do not merely produce recommendations that member governments are free to ignore. Instead, they reach agreements on joint actions that member states are legally obligated to carry out. And, when they work properly, the centralizing aura of their unions generates enough popular support and allegiance to create nascent communities among the peoples living in the confederated states. Governments can usually form or dissolve IGOs without risking public outcry, but confederal-type communities, once they take hold in the public consciousness, are not so readily terminated.

Though confederalism, as a generally recognized form of governance, has been obsolete for more than a century, there are signs that it may be in a stage of quiet revival. Daniel Elazar, for example, has asserted that "with the emergence of permanent multinational communities, of which the European Community is the prime example, . . . we are now witnessing a revival of confederal arrangements" (Elazar 1987, pp. 50–51). And other political scientists, such as Ivo Duchacek, have recognized the Community's predominantly confederal character (Duchacek 1982, p. 131). The framers of the Treaty of Rome (the Community's treaty-constitution) seem to have drawn, consciously or unconsciously, upon many procedures of a kind that had been employed in the nineteenth century German Zollverein or customs union, which defined itself as an "economic confederation" in the treaties establishing it. The International Atomic Energy Agency, the International Monetary Fund, and the new World Trade Organization are IGOs that might at some stage be upgraded to confederal status. The United Nations Charter, too, contains important confederal features that remain unimplemented or even widely recognized for what they are. The creation of a new class of confederal-type IGOs would provide political vehicles that could unite, for certain carefully defined purposes, large groups (or all) of the nearly 200 separate polities that now compose our network of sovereign states.

What is a confederation and how did this form of governance come about? These questions will be covered in greater detail in Chapter 1, but we shall begin to answer them here. Historically, interstate alliances have always been a standard feature of state systems. Mostly, these alliances are no more than instruments of high-level politics. They are formed or abandoned as they are perceived as serving or no longer serving national interests.

But, sometimes, it has served national interests to turn long–standing alliances into loose permanent unions of the allied states. This has happened when a number of smaller states have a more or less permanent common enemy that is both strong and militant and that threatens all of them. Such unions are voluntary in the sense that their member states have joined them freely, each in pursuit of its own security. There are several examples of this phenomenon: the Aetolian and Achaean Leagues of Ancient Greece were formed to counter Macedonian and Roman threats; the first Swiss Confederation to fend off the Austrian Habsburgs and other invaders; the Dutch Republic to free its provinces from the Spanish Habsburgs and later to keep out the French; the United States Confederation, in response to the British attacks; and the Germanic Confederation, in part anyway, as a permanent alliance against the post-Napoleonic French.

These were all "collective security" confederations. They were formed because their member states faced a long-term threat to their independence and perhaps to their very existence. But these loose political unions had one unintended consequence that went far beyond their professed goal. They opened up a process of social integration that, in each instance, eventually led to the emergence of a new people living in the closer union of a federal or of a centralized "unitary" state. Thus, in many cases, confederal governance allowed groups of states that lacked many of Karl Deutsch's essential requirements to form enduring political unions.

An example will serve to show how unintegrated, even initially incompatible, member states could come to coexist peacefully within a confederal political framework. In the late sixteenth century, the western provinces that formed the Dutch Republic (Holland, Utrecht, and Zeeland) were far from being closely akin, ethnically, culturally and religiously, to what became its eastern provinces of Gelderland, Groningen, Overyssel, and Friesland. The latter were mostly composed of practicing Catholics, who shared with the westerners only a common dislike of the Spanish Habsburg overlord, Philip II. In the 1580s, the easterners were forcibly incorporated in the republic, mainly because Holland and Zeeland needed a territorial barrier to shield them from overland invasions.

But the resulting hostility of the easterners soon disappeared as the republic flourished, and their provinces were treated as full members of the States-General, the republic's legislative body. Moreover, being part of the republic brought them status and benefits that set them above their other neighbors. In fact, the Flemings of Flanders and Brabant, who in the sixteenth century had been close kin, ethnically, linguistically and culturally, of the Zeelanders and Hollanders and who had enthusiastically signed the Pact of Utrecht creating the republic, were compelled by military and political developments to break off their ties with it. Those ties were never restored. The subsequent history of the Netherlands and Belgium shows how peoples that leave a political union become dissociated from those who remain within it and that the homogeneity of the two groups gradually disappears.

(Incidentally, in 1945, a similar abrupt breaking off of ties between the people living in East and West Germany resulted in these people growing apart and has complicated their reunion after less than 50 years of separation.)

Today, the situation of the two groups has long since been reversed. The inhabitants of Gelderland, Groningen, Overyssel, and Friesland are loyal Dutchmen, while the Flemings, who together with the Walloons founded modern Belgium, are now the outsiders. There could be no better example of how political and military developments often determine the evolution of ethnic and social ties.

When they were formed, none of the other confederations was composed of ethnic groups that had gone very far down the road to integration. For example, the mountain and city-state cantons of Switzerland were originally disparate entities whose citizenries did not have much in common beyond the need for security against external enemies. In the United States of the confederal era, there were many cross-currents of hostility among the various states (e.g., between the New Englanders and the Virginians). The peoples of the 13 states had differing religious and social origins, and each had acquired a distinct identity of its own during the long colonial period.

In post-Napoleonic Germany, there were important ethnic differences among Prussians, Saxons, Rhinelanders, Austrians, and Bavarians, even though the peoples of the German states had long shared a name and a vague sense of ethnic unity that went with that name. For example, we are told that when the young Goethe moved from Frankfurt to Leipzig, his clothes, speech, and manners marked him as a foreigner (Sheehan 1989, p. 72). Germans' sense of belonging to a common ethnic group certainly grew stronger during the half century spent under the confederal umbrella (1815–1866) and, ironically, helped Bismarck achieve German unification while destroying the union that had been fostering it!

In each case, a loose political union came first, and popular communities were formed afterward. Might not long-term alliances, also designed to serve an "overriding" need—survival in a nuclear age—produce in our era the same permanent unions of states that they did in times gone by? Might not this confederal "halfway house" (the term used by Murray Forsyth) make the same contribution to political integration in the late twentieth century that it did in earlier centuries? (Forsyth 1981, p. 6). Assuming that basic human behavior patterns tend to change very slowly if at all, would it be too far-fetched to expect confederal governance to produce the same kind of outcome that it did in the past?

THE LONG HARD ROAD AHEAD

The twenty-first century is likely to be the most crucial in human history. As already noted, the omens are not good. Our post–Cold War brew of ethnic conflict, religious fundamentalism, national egocentricity, and just plain banditry bodes ill for the survival of civilization in an age when a whole spectrum of lethal weaponries is becoming increasingly available. It is only prudent to expect that the next century will see these weapons being used as instruments of blackmail (or worse) by the leaders of rogue states or by ethnic groups with their backs to the wall.

It would be absurd to suppose that the mere introduction of confederal institutions will prove a panacea for solving problems such as these. Even if we can put them in place, their capacity to help the world community to weather serious crises remains untested. However, as shown, such institutions did seem to work passably well in Ancient Greece, Switzerland, and the Dutch Republic. And their failure to work equally well in the United States and Germany is attributable, in part at least, to the much greater size of those lands combined with the inferior state of transport and communications in pre-industrial times. Moreover, as will be shown in Chapter 2, modern confederal institutions seem considerably more promising than those of their predecessors. They will be operating in a much-changed political environment and can call upon more sophisticated structures and procedures to enhance their effectiveness.

On the downside, in the case of the world community as a whole, there is no longstanding common enemy against whom popular anger and determination can be mobilized, as there was in the earlier confederations. It will surely be asked, will confederal-type institutions prove strong enough, in the absence of such an enemy, to deal successfully with complex and desperate situations for which there are no simple, clearcut solutions? While this question is unanswerable, it does seem likely that our odds would improve if we had available a confederal rather than the present weak IGO-type world organization. Moreover, once the member states of such a stronger body learned how to deal with lesser problems, they might be able to handle the more serious crises if—or more probably when—they are confronted with them.

The present book explores the possibility that confederal institutions may provide part of the answer to the question, How can human beings learn to act together to save their civilization from the war that would destroy it? Its three chapters focus successively on: (1) The main characteristics of little-known confederal governance; (2) The potential of that form of governance in modern times as revealed in the evolution of the European Community/ Union (the first and only full-scale example of what a modern confederation might be like); and (3) The possibility of applying confederal institutions to the elimination of war on a worldwide basis through the United Nations. A final Closing Argument offers brief concluding comments.

NOTES

1. The hearings were also sponsored by Senators Sam Nunn and Joseph Biden. Witnesses included Graham Allison, former Assistant Secretary of Defense; Bruce

Blair of the Brookings Institution; Thomas Cochran, Director of Nuclear Programs, Natural Resources Defense Council; John Gibbons, Assistant to the President for Science and Technology; John Holdren of the President's Council of Advisers on Science and Technology; Fred Ikle, former director of the Arms Control and Disarmament Agency; and Lt. Gen. William Odom, former director of the National Security Agency.

As Fred Ikle wrote recently, "If just one or two nuclear bombs should explode somewhere—whether by accident, because of a terrorist act, or as part of a military campaign—the international order would be transformed more profoundly than by the collapse of the Soviet Empire" (Ikle 1996, p. 8). See also William C. Porter's article "Before the Deluge? Assessing the Threat of Nuclear Leakage from the Post Soviet States" (Porter 1995).

2. All references to the UN Charter are to the *Charter of the United Nations and the Statute of the International Court of Justice,* published by the United Nations Office of Public Information, undated but including the amendments of 1965. Future references will be to "Charter" plus the chapter or article involved.

3. Buchheit (1977) contains a comprehensive account of the many complications, legal and political, stemming from proclaiming a right to self-determination, which carries with it an implicit right to break up an existing state.

4. The establishment of the European Economic Community and other common markets inspired an outpouring of studies on regional integration. A handbook of political science published some years later included a long chapter dealing with this approach to which a 12–page bibliography was appended (Keohane & Nye, 1975). However, cold water was poured on this avenue of scholarship as the common markets in Latin America and federal-type unions in East Africa and Southeastern Asia broke down, and even the surviving European Community limped along in a way that disappointed those who looked forward to its becoming a United States of Europe (Wallace 1982, p. 57; Franck 1968).

REFERENCES

Brooke, James. "Marxist Revolt Grows Strong in the Shanty Towns of Peru." In the *New York Times,* November 11, 1991, pp. A1, A6.

Buchheit, Lee C. *Secession: The Legitimacy of Self-Determination.* New Haven, CT: Yale University Press, 1977.

Deutsch, Karl, et al. *Political Community and the North Atlantic Area: International Organization in the Light of Historical Experience.* Princeton, NJ: Princeton University Press, 1957.

Duchacek, Ivo. "Antagonistic Co-operation: Territorial and Ethnic Communities." In *Publius,* 7 (4), 1977, pp. 3–31.

———. "Consociations of Fatherlands: The Revival of Confederal Principles and Practices." In *Publius,* Fall 1982, vol. XII, no. 4, pp. 129–77.

Elazar, Daniel J. *Exploring Federation.* Tuscaloosa, AL: The University of Alabama Press, 1987.

Forsyth, Murray. *Unions of States.* Leicester: Leicester University Press, 1981.

Franck, Thomas M., ed. *Why Federations Fail: An Inquiry Into the Requisites for Successful Federalism.* New York: New York University Press, 1968.

Friedman, Thomas. "For the Nations of Eastern Europe, the U.S. Is More Symbol Than Model." In the *New York Times,* June 30, 1991, Section 4, p. 1.

Gilbert, Martin. *Russian History Atlas.* New York, Macmillan, 1972.

Haas, Ernst B., and Philippe C. Schmitter. "Economics and Differential Patterns of Political Integration: Projections about Unity in Latin America." In *International Organization,* 18, 1964, pp. 705–37.

Holdren, John P. Testimony, U.S. Senate Committee on Foreign Relations, Sub-Committee on Europe, August 22, 1995.

Ikle, Fred. "Facing Nuclear Reality." In *The Wall Street Journal,* January 2, 1996, p. 7.

Keohane, Robert O., and Joseph S. Nye, Jr. "International Interdependence and Integration." In *Handbook of Political Science,* edited by Fred L. Greenstein and Nelson W. Polsby. Andover, MA: Addison Wesley, vol. 8, 1975, pp. 363–414.

Lugar, Richard G. Opening Statement, U.S. Senate Committee on Foreign Relations, Sub-Committee on Europe, Hearings on "Loose Nukes, Nuclear Smuggling, and the Fissile-Material Problem in Russia and the NIS," August 22–23, 1995.

Murdoch, George Peter. *Atlas of World Cultures.* Pittsburgh, PA: University of Pittsburgh Press, 1980.

Nunn, Sam. Opening Statement, U.S. Senate Committee on Foreign Relations, Sub-Committee on Europe, Hearings on Nuclear Smuggling and the Fissile Material Problem in Russia, August 22–23, 1995.

Nye, Joseph S., Jr. *Peace in Parts: Integration and Conflict in Regional Organization.* Boston: Little Brown, 1971.

Porter, William C. "Before the Deluge? Assessing the Threat of Nuclear Leakage from the Post-Soviet States." In *Arms Control Today,* October 1995, pp. 9–16.

Said, Abdul A., and Louis R. Simmons, eds. *Ethnicity in an International Context.* New Brunswick, NJ: Transactions Press, 1976.

Sheehan, James J. *German History, 1770–1866.* Oxford: Clarendon Press, 1989.

United Nations Charter, published by the United Nations Office of Public Information, undated and including amendments of 1965.

Wallace, William. "Europe as a Confederation: The Community and the Nation-State." In *Journal of Common Market Studies,* XXI, Nos. 1–2, Sept.–Dec. 1982, pp. 57–68.

Chapter 1

The Nature of Confederal Governance

The purpose of this chapter is to provide readers with the background that they will need to grasp the nature and the significance of the unheralded revival of confederal-style governance. It is "unheralded" because its revivers either do not recognize it for what it is or are not anxious to acknowledge a form of government that has never been very highly regarded.

The chapter is composed of four sections: (1) The place of confederations in a typology of governments; (2) A reevaluation and defense of the confederal approach to governance; (3) An analysis of the common features of confederal-style governments; and (4) An examination of three possible applications of confederal-style governance that may both safeguard the right of ethnic, religious, and linguistic groups to equal treatment and serve the need for peace in a world in which so many of these groups are hostile to one another.

(1) THE PLACE OF CONFEDERATIONS IN A TYPOLOGY OF GOVERNMENTS

Strictly speaking, every government and every community over which it holds sway is *sui generis.* However, it is the task of scholarship to find the patterns and similarities among them that help us understand the nature and potential of the various forms of governance. In this chapter, the focus will be on the centralization and decentralization of governmental authority and power within various types of political association. More particularly, it will be on the centralization and decentralization of what has long been called "sovereignty," and might be better described as the *ultimate* governmental authority. As Carl Friedrich has written, "The issue of sovereignty is the issue over who has the last word, that is to say, who makes the final decision" (Friedrich 1968, p. 76). This would seem to include the supreme power to exercise and to delegate various governmental functions, including the power to reclaim them for the center or to relocate them within the state concerned.

There are four levels of community and four levels of government to match them—local, regional, national, and supranational.[1] In larger states, there may be even more levels, but the fact that there are many interlocking levels of this kind is well known.

In most states, the power to delegate, reclaim, and relocate governmental authority and functions among these several levels has been centralized in one place, the national capital. The authority to exercise them, whether constitutionally based or not, generally resides with relatively small groups of governmental officials who constitute the nucleus of the central government. In most cases, the power of delegation is not exercised very often, because the basic allocation of functions among the various levels is of long standing and has been found to work satisfactorily. The political entities where such arrangements prevail are generally known as "unitary states," and most states fall in this category. In such states, as K.C. Wheare has written, "there is no doubt that the power to legislate must be with the general legislature, no matter how much it may decentralize that power to provincial councils or legislatures. It will always be able to exercise an ultimate controlling power in the last resort" (Wheare 1964, p. 145).

In some polities, however, ultimate governmental authority has been divided between the national and the regional levels. The prototype for this type of governance is the federal system that was set up in the United States in 1789. Efforts to replicate it in other countries, with the necessary adjustments, have led to many variations of federal-type governance, some of them successful and others less so. However, it must be added that the American federal system was an outgrowth of its earlier experience with confederal governance. The Swiss and German federal systems can also be traced back to their respective confederal roots.

Since the last confederal union, that of Germany, disappeared in 1866, the theory and practice of divided government have been focused on federal models. As a type of government, federalism is used in two very different senses. In one, it is an umbrella concept that covers all situations in which ultimate governmental powers are shared between two or more levels. In this sense, confederations are merely one of several subtypes (others would be consociations, condominiums, and "federacies") that fall under that umbrella. But, in this book, federalism is not used in this broader meaning.

More narrowly, federalism refers to the prototype set up in the United States in 1789, which was later adapted to the situations of a number of other countries. This definition fits the concept into an older and still widely used typology that divides polities into three main classes—unitary states, federations, and confederations. In this classification, confederal governance is not a subtype, but constitutes a class of its own. The differences between it and the more narrowly defined federal governance are far-reaching and seem to justify a return to this older typology, especially now that confederalism may be in a state of revival.

Let us begin our comparison of the main features of federal and confederal governance by mentioning a few that they have in common. Both have written basic laws in which the allocation of functions between center and regions is set forth. In both, power is divided on the basis of territorial units, with independent powers being exercised both by the central authorities and by the "regions" or homelands that have been united in the larger polity. In each case, this involves some decentralization (or noncentralization) of ultimate authority. At the same time, both federations and confederations face (or are supposed to face) other polities and the outside world as unified entities (see Elazar 1987, pp. 157–68; Friedrich 1968, *passim*).

Federal Governance

The differences between the two classes of governance are, however, greater than the similarities. The main features of federal governance will be described first. It employs a detailed constitutional framework setting forth what Wheare describes as the division of the field of government "between a general authority and regional authorities which are not subordinate one to another, but co-ordinate with each other" (Wheare 1964, p. 2). As Sawer points out, federalism provides for "an area of guaranteed autonomy for each unit of the system" (Sawer 1969, p. 127).

Although federal constitutions may start out as interstate treaties requiring ratification as was the case with the United States and Switzerland, successful federal unions soon assume the characteristics of a state. The treaty aspects of their constitutions atrophy as the integration of the regions progresses. At the same time, the complex constitutional arrangements involving co-ordinate governments operating at two levels present a special challenge to those charged with implementing them and sometimes provide pressure groups with an opportunity to play off one level against the other.

Wheare recognizes only four full-scale federal states (the United States, Australia, Canada, and Switzerland), but many writers include others that have federal-type constitutions, for example, Austria, Germany, India, and Nigeria. Indeed, Lemco identifies as many as 44 while Elazar lists 14 "federal systems" and 21 "political systems with federal arrangements" (Lemco 1991, p. 77; Elazar 1987, pp. 43–46). These include many that never became fully operative or were never taken seriously by national leaders. Wheare's four federations, taken together, provide a good model for federal governance, four "prototype federations," that will be used in this book in comparing and contrasting the main features of federal with confederal governance.

People living in federations usually have double allegiances and loyalties to the nation and to the region or homeland with which they identify themselves within their federal state. Since the central and regional governments both operate directly upon the people, each citizen is subject to two governments.

Thus, in such polities there are federal and regional communities as well as federal and regional governments superimposed upon one another. Since each community has its own government, there must also be a sharing of ultimate authority between the national and regional peoples on the basis of the constitutional allocation of primary functions to their respective governments. In Wheare's coordinate relationship, each government becomes supreme in the sphere assigned to it.

But while the two levels of government may be coordinate, Sawer observes that "the secular trend is toward the increase of the authority of the Center" (Sawer 1969, p. 127). Many aspects of federal governance make it easy for the central government, if its leaders so wish, to gain the upper hand over the regional governments. For example, its sphere almost always includes the most crucial sovereign functions. Thus, it is the federal government that controls relations with other sovereign states and has the power to declare war and to conclude peace. If there is to be a unified economy (and usually this is a principal goal of federal unions), it is the central government that is (and must be) given the primary role in managing it. Further, when the federal and regional laws are in conflict, it is the federal laws that usually prevail, and the judges who decide such cases usually are (and almost have to be) the federal, not the regional judges.

The centralizing tendencies of the four main federal states have been presented in detail by Wheare, while Friedrich goes so far as to speak of "the predominance of the nation and its government." Duchacek explains that "the national power is clearly favored . . . because the purpose of the . . . federal structure is either to create one nation out of many or to preserve a nation by a timely recognition of its inner diversity" (Wheare 1964, pp. 127–41, 147–50, 205–8; Friedrich 1968, p. 22; Duchacek 1970, p. 233).

Federal bureaucracies have an interest in expanding the scope of the activities for which they are responsible. In the four prototypal federations, the central governments have become collectors for major sources of revenue, such as the income tax. This makes the regions (e.g., the states, provinces, or cantons) dependent upon them for grants to help finance activities in the spheres assigned to them. Accordingly, in federations, the trend is for the central government to intrude into the spheres assigned to the regions, not the other way around (Friedrich 1968, pp. 23–24).

Most important of all, as a federation becomes widely accepted by its citizens, the new federal community may begin to loom larger in people's minds than their respective regional communities. In the United States, for example, under federal governance, the primary allegiance of most people in 1789 was to their home states, while nowadays most think of themselves, first and foremost, as Americans and only secondarily as citizens of one or another of those states.

Accordingly, under successful federations, new and broader communities emerge within which the regional communities may gradually be absorbed. Federal government evolves steadily to take these new circumstances into account. Its coordinate governments at the lower level, which originally enjoyed equal standing, tend to drift into a situation in which they find themselves, in practice if not in law, in a somewhat inferior position vis-à-vis the central government. This trend, a notable feature of federalism, has been a main focus of federal scholarship and has led to the establishment of a number of subtypologies of federal governments.

While this aspect does not need elaboration in a book on confederations, one of these subtypologies may be mentioned briefly as a prerequisite to comparing confederalism with federalism. Wheare's definition, cited earlier, is known as "coordinate" or "dual" federalism. His is a theoretical definition of federalism never fully achieved in practice; yet, it has remained a kind of standard. In certain federal states such as the United States and Australia, coordinate constitutional provisions have led the central and regional governments to find their way to something called "cooperative" federalism. This involves an intertwining of governmental functions between the two levels, in which the regional governments have maintained their own autonomous sphere even though they no longer enjoy full equality in practice.

Germany and Austria have a third subtype, known as "organic" or "integrated" federalism, involving an even closer interlocking of governmental functions. In those countries, though some functions continue to be reserved for the regional governments, the legislative power has been, to a greater extent, centralized, while the responsibility for administration has been mainly delegated to the regions. In the comparisons that follow, coordinate theory/cooperative practice (but not organic federalism) is used as the basis for comparing the main features of federal and confederal governance.

A main issue faced by federal states is whether the autonomy of the regional governments in the spheres assigned to them can be sustained in practice. This is primarily a political question. Where the people of each constituent unit continue to attach great value to its separate existence, as for example the Swiss to their cantons, the issue may become moot. In the United States, on the other hand, the popular attachment to states' rights has been in a long secular decline.

At the same time, some observers have perceived a trend away from centralization since the 1960s. Even for some unitary states, the devolution of certain functions to regional or local levels has become increasingly attractive. The fact that the extreme centralization characteristic of totalitarian states now seems incompatible with economic prosperity and social well-being has strengthened federalism and encouraged its revival in countries such as Mexico and Brazil that have federal constitutions that have long amounted to "window dressing" (Elazar 1987, pp. 201–3).

Confederal Governance

There are also four prototypal examples of confederal governance (i.e., the Swiss, Dutch, American, and German Confederations mentioned in the Opening Argument) whose principal features will now be described.

When sovereign states come together to form confederations, the balance is tilted towards the constituent states. In these "unions of states," the relationship between central and regional governments is reversed since confederal treaty-constitutions are designed to protect the latter from the risk of subordination, and the treaty aspect of the basic law is strictly maintained. In confederal unions, the central authorities are kept subordinate to those of its member states; hence any devolution of functions to those authorities must be approved by those states. This stronger position of the member states is likely to make the confederal model more acceptable than the federal model to ethnic groups that would become minorities in the larger union that is being formed.

At the same time, the member states are committed to helping the central authorities exercise the powers granted to them in the treaty-constitution because, if they do not do so, confederal unions cannot serve the purposes for which they were created. To this end, their member governments and peoples comprehend that, in enabling the central authorities—which at the legislative level are their own representatives—to carry out their confederal mandate, they are merely serving their own interests.

Confederal-style unions do not raise any question of the transfer of ultimate authority, which remains firmly fixed with the national governments of the confederating states. Instead, these states merely exercise it jointly in the various confederal decision-making bodies. It should be noted that these differences between federal and confederal governance, far from being minor ones, are fundamental and far-reaching in their scope and effect.

The peoples living in confederated states maintain their own separate communities, which are affected minimally by the new political union. At the same time, as in the Dutch Republic, merely being under a confederal umbrella tends to multiply the economic, social, and cultural ties among these several peoples and to open up the process of creating a new and broader community composed of them. Moreover, all confederal treaty-constitutions have contained *some* provisions that are directly binding on the individuals who live in their various member states. For example, of very great importance in creating such confederal communities is wartime co-operation in staving off a common enemy and public involvement in a broad spectrum of less intrusive general welfare functions, ranging from standardization of coinages, weights, and measures, to regulation of international and interstate trade and coordination of transport and communications facilities.

There is one important difference, however: In a confederal setting, the principal loyalty of individuals remains focused on their home region, state, province, or canton. Thus, it is harder to develop popular pressures to transfer authority and power from regional governments to the central government. Harder, but far from impossible! In the long run, the political culture of all four of the prototypal confederal communities evolved in ways that made it possible for them to become highly stable federal or unitary states. Also, the development of substantial public support for confederal institutions puts pressure on the various regional leaders, when they act as confederal legislators, to make those institutions function effectively.

The spheres of responsibility allocated to the central authorities and to the member states are surprisingly similar in federal and confederal unions though, of course, more powers and more exclusive powers are usually allocated to federal central authorities than to confederal ones. Also, they tend to exercise the powers allocated to them in ways that are in line, respectively, with central government or member-state predominance. In the highly complex division of functions between the two levels, more key legislative and financial powers are exercised from regional capitals by the various member governments in confederations and from the national capital by the federal authorities in federations.

In the next chapter, it will be shown how in the European Union, confederal governance has been establishing itself through European governments' readiness to delegate a number of important powers to its various institutions. Elazar regards the emergence of such permanent multinational "communities" as a revival of confederal governance both in Europe and elsewhere. He sees the European Union as a union of specific functions though one without any "general act of confederation."

On other continents, he cites the Association of South East Asian Nations (ASEAN), Senegal/Gambia, and the Caribbean Community in this connection. These communities were organized in "such a way as to minimize the threat to the existing states," which seek to remain independent, while enabling the establishment of "sufficiently energetic government in certain limited spheres with the means to attain the ends for which it was constituted" (Elazar 1987, pp. 50–54). In effect, confederal-type governance has been sneaking in through the back door, and economic pressures may accelerate that process as well as enhance its effectiveness.

As noted, federalism has not been very good at preserving the rights of its constituent entities. Instead, it seems to lead to a fluid relationship between center and regions that results in the subordination of the latter. Confederal governance, on the other hand, by allowing each member state to keep its sovereignty, establishes a more clearcut and stable situation that can be altered only when the member states are agreed that they want to create a closer union.

One final point. While collective security confederations are quite different from economic ones, both involve structures, institutions, and relationships of the kind that have just been discussed. The following observations may be made in this regard: (1) Collective security confederations address the personal safety of the people who live in them, clearly an overriding concern when they feel threatened; (2) Economic confederations have as their goal an enhancement of the material well-being of the people who live in them, a less urgent and precise goal, but one that is capable of being sustained over the long term; (3) Integrating a number of modern economies is, as the EU has been discovering, a very complex and somewhat intrusive process; (4) Coordinating military capabilities and foreign policy, functions of the highest importance, involve mainly governments and, in peacetime, do not usually intrude directly in peoples' daily lives; and (5) There is nothing to prevent a confederation from having a joint economic and collective security mandate (the EU is currently moving in that direction).

The purely technical process of forming a collective security confederation is less complicated than that of forming an economic confederation. In both cases, however, the main obstacle is not technical. Rather, it is the difficulty of creating the corresponding community of human beings without which no confederation can become a durable political association. At the same time, entrusting very important sovereign political functions to a broader partnership is no small matter; it is usually done only when peoples and governments feel an overriding need for it. Historically, all four of the prototype security confederations were formed in such circumstances. Indeed, it is difficult to imagine this type of confederation being formed in the absence of intense pressures. On the other hand, the EU provides an example of an economic confederation being formed in a situation where the pressures were considerably weaker.

To the threefold typology for polities mentioned earlier, the new category of intergovernmental organizations (IGOs) may or may not be added. As already pointed out in the Opening Argument, IGOs resemble confederations in some ways, but there are very significant differences between them. Specifically, IGOs are solely associations of states; they ordinarily do not create communities of individuals from which they can derive significant popular support. And if they legislate at all, it is in technical areas where their member states have much to gain and little to lose by cooperating with one another; that is, in "win–win" situations. Instead, it is far more common for them to adopt recommendations to their respective governments, which may be carried out only when those governments find it useful and convenient to do so.

As a fourth type of political association, IGOs may be thought of as a much weaker form of confederation. But they may be dropped entirely from this typology on the ground that they do not involve the exercise of sovereign powers. At the same time, they are important as training grounds where sovereign governments learn to plan and carry out jointly a wide variety of activities. As such they may sometimes be way stations on the road to closer unions of the confederal or federal type.

All typologies are somewhat artificial, and the threefold (or fourfold) typology just outlined is not without its critics (see King 1982). Yet all such conceptual devices are designed to serve specific purposes. This one helps us understand what is happening in Europe and the United Nations. Even so, it must be kept in mind that they are very broad classes, and that political associations falling under each of them are characterized by numerous structural and procedural variations. Most polities that are primarily federations, confederations, or IGOs will include some hybrid institutions that do not conform to the boundaries that have been drawn between the several classes. As already noted, federal subtypes have been identified to reflect some of the main structural and procedural differences that are found among federal states. Because confederal-type governance has been little studied in recent years, a similar process has yet to take place among confederal bodies. In addition, there are gray areas in which major distinctions between confederal and federal governance remain vague.

Even the prototype unions contain features that are not in full conformity to the class to which they belong. For example, the American constitution retained until 1913 a typical confederal-type arrangement that senators should be chosen by the various state legislatures.[2] On the other hand, the European Union, though its structure and procedures remain primarily confederal in character, includes a number of federal features, for example, a parliament composed of members elected popularly throughout the Union's member states and an executive that can exercise a number of independent powers. Similarly, the framers of the United Nations Charter, though mainly providing for an IGO-type relationship among its member states, vested it with a confederal-type collective security system.

However, these aberrations are often not as important as they might seem at first. Confederal features incorporated into a federal state tend to be adapted to the union's basic structure, which in turn tends to presume a relatively high degree of homogeneity among the peoples living in its constituent states. And, as will become clear in Chapter 2, federal features incorporated in a primarily confederal entity also tend to be adapted to that structure, which has to be compatible with the somewhat lower degree of homogeneity among the peoples living in its member states.

Finally, a major distinction must be made between the political unions that form new states (unitary states and federations) and those composed of affiliated states (confederations and IGOs). In the first two, the central power is organized, in whole or in large part, vertically, with ultimate authority being exercised independently by the federal or unitary governments. In the second two, power is exercised horizontally by collegiate bodies, with ultimate authority remaining in the hands of the governments of the member states in their various capitals.

There is also a difference in geographical scope between the two groups. Most IGOs and the European Union are global, continental, or at least transnational in their geographical scope, while the member states of those unions, usually unitary states or federations, are correspondingly smaller in area. If it were to continue to its logical conclusion, this process would produce an upper level of IGOs and confederations, strictly limited in the power and authority delegated to them by their member states, conjoined with a lower level of unitary states and federations exercising sovereign powers for some purposes exclusively within their own borders and for other purposes jointly in these higher-level forums.

(2) THE BAD REPUTE OF CONFEDERAL GOVERNANCE

It is necessary at this early stage to address the extremely negative reaction that confederal governance often evokes among students of government and the educated public. Its bad reputation may be traced to the vast improvement in the central governance of the United States when the 1787 constitution replaced the Articles of Confederation. During the next 60 years, confederal-style governance was also abandoned in Switzerland and the Dutch Republic, the two states that had clung to it the longest. However, a reputation formed more than two centuries ago needs to be reviewed in the light of the enormous changes that have taken place in the character of all governance over such a long period of time. Such a reappraisal of the potential of confederalism, as one of the three main classes of government, is overdue, and is the main purpose of this book.

Let us begin this reappraisal by responding to the exaggerated criticism that confederalism evoked more than two centuries ago. In the *Federalist,* Hamilton and Madison launched a vitriolic attack on it from which after all this time it has still not recovered. In the days before it was replaced by a federal government, Hamilton wrote of "the imbecility of our [present] government," and termed it "a system so radically vicious and unsound, as to admit not of amendment" but to "require an entire change in its leading figures and characters." He added that the country had "reached almost the last stage of national humiliation" and was on the brink of anarchy (*Federalist,* 1937 edition, Paper No. 15, pp. 87–88 and No. 22, p. 140).

He similarly castigated the Swiss and Dutch confederations. He dismissed the Swiss union by writing that "the connection among the Swiss cantons scarcely amounts to a confederacy" (*Federalist*, Paper No. 19, p. 118). He denounced the Dutch Republic in unmeasured terms: "What are the characters which practice has stamped upon it? Imbecility in the government; discord among the provinces; foreign influence and indignities; a precarious existence in peace, and peculiar calamities from war" (*Federalist*, 1937 edition, Paper No. 20, p. 121).

So much for confederations that had survived for five and two centuries, respectively!

Such a sweeping condemnation flies in the face of the facts. In Switzerland, loose confederal governance was not only long lived (1291–1798 and 1814–1848), it united the Swiss cantons and allowed them to develop and exercise a military power that was respected throughout Europe in an age when such a reputation was needed for survival. Indeed, in the fifteenth century, the Swiss under their confederal arrangements briefly achieved great-power status. In the centuries following the Reformation when Catholic and Protestant cantons coexisted uneasily, the union suffered from the schism but survived five brief civil wars that were notable for their lack of serious bloodshed. The cantons' long-standing confederal ties proved strong enough to weather these crises. When, in 1814, the German Swiss revived their confederation after the Napoleonic interlude, they demonstrated its broad potential by creating the first voluntary multiethnic union: it incorporated French- and Italian-speaking cantons on equal terms with the German-speaking ones.

In its golden age in the seventeenth century, the Dutch Republic (1589–1795) was managed by its confederal States-General. By the end of that century, the Dutch Republic had successfully warded off the armies of Philip II and his successors, defeated the English navy in the Thames, and defended the country against an invasion by Louis XIV. Sir William Temple, England's seventeenth-century ambassador to the Republic, wrote favorably of the country's institutions, political as well as economic, social and cultural, which were at that time highly regarded and even studied as a model (Temple 1972).

The Germanic Confederation (1815–1866) was on the rise when Bismarck decided to finish it off, but it might have provided a sounder foundation for German union than did his autocratic Prussia.

Even the United States, under confederal governance, was able to win independence from the strongest power on earth. And, in 1787, while the new constitution was being written, the much-maligned Continental Congress adopted the Northwest Territories Ordinance, a brilliant plan that paved the way for the country's subsequent expansion from 13 to 50 states after being taken over by the new Federal Congress. Needless to say, achievements such as these were not mentioned in the pages of the *Federalist*.

Modern historians such as Merrill Jensen paint a more balanced picture of the American confederal period and regard the *Federalist* as propagandistic. Among political scientists, Friedrich calls the confederal period "a significant beginning," and writes of the "much maligned and little studied Articles of Confederation." Elazar, when he studied the Articles, reached the conclusion that the authors of the *Federalist* were engaged in a "polemic" against them, and that this "behooves us to question the accuracy of what they did" (Jensen 1948, pp. 3–15; Friedrich 1968, p. 14; Elazar 1982, pp. 1–2).

Even so, it must be allowed that Hamilton, with Madison's help, did make a cogent case that confederation was not a viable form of government for the United States in peacetime, given the conditions of the late eighteenth century. To mobilize support for the new constitution, he marshalled four main arguments against it.

First, he denied that a central government could successfully legislate for state governments in their corporate capacities, for experience had shown that they would treat these laws as mere recommendations that, in practice if not in law, they were free to ignore whenever they chose.

Second, he argued that a central government must be able to pass laws that directly bind the people living in those states, and be entrusted with its own separate administrative and judicial arms to compel them to abide by those laws rather than having to rely on the state legislatures and state enforcement authorities to perform those functions.

Third, he felt that government must have its own sources of revenue rather than depend on assessments that the state legislatures, again in practice if not in law, would refuse to provide on one pretext or another.

Finally, Hamilton argued that the central government must be given the authority to regulate the union's international trade and interstate commerce.

It is clear that Hamilton (and Madison) had concluded that the basic premise of confederal governance, namely, that the leaders of the governments of confederated states could exercise a limited range of sovereign powers jointly rather than separately, was totally impractical. It is true that confederal governance can function effectively only if the various leaders "identify" with their common government and take seriously their duty of seeking consensus on the actions to be taken and the laws to be adopted. In a well-functioning confederal union, it is ordinarily their representatives, provided with formal instructions or cognizant of their wishes, who carry out this function in a plenipotentiary council of the member states. Thus, when member-state leaders are persuaded that their confederal union is needed, they have it within their power to ensure its effectiveness. When they are not so persuaded, they can also ensure its breakdown. For example, in the aftermath of the Revolutionary War, the state leaders and legislatures were allowing, and some of them may have even been promoting, the disintegration of their wartime union.

On the other hand, while the outcome of the Revolution was in doubt, the state governments often operated their jerry-built union in confederal fashion. For example, the Declaration of Independence was adopted only after those sitting in Philadelphia had received the requisite authority from their state capitals, and the Articles of Confederation came into force only after Maryland, the last hold-out, belatedly ratified them. But it proved nearly impossible to follow the procedure of "government by instruction" for lesser matters. And those who wrote the Articles seem not to have understood the main premise of confederal governance when they made it possible for delegates from the same state to the Continental Congress to cancel out one another's votes, thereby demonstrating that they were voting as individuals rather than as the instructed delegates of their state governments.

Nonetheless, in the United States, a quasi-confederal regime existed during the Revolutionary War at least so long as the state leaders were keenly aware that, in Benjamin Franklin's words, they had to hang together if they did not wish to be hanged separately by the English. These leaders knew that they could not wage a successful war or form alliances with foreign powers without machinery for central coordination of the kind provided by the Continental Congress. Once the war was over, however, most of them showed by their actions that they had little intention of continuing to exercise jointly the sovereign powers that they had acquired as a result of winning that war. In peacetime, in the absence of any serious external pressures, they came to regard the Continental Congress as a nuisance that kept bothering them with its demands for funds. Even while the Revolution was underway, at least one member of the Congress claimed that there had never been any agreement to retain that body once the war was over.[3] Without it, of course, the Union would have become a hollow shell.

Accordingly, it was not so much that confederalism, as a system of governance, proved wanting, but that those with the responsibility for properly operating it chose to ignore that responsibility. That is, in fact, the substance of Hamilton's first and third arguments. However, these same leaders had behaved more responsibly in response to the intense pressures they faced during the wartime years. And the leaders of the Swiss cantons and the Dutch provinces must have been more willing to take the basic premise of confederal governance seriously, or their respective confederations would not have lasted as long as they did.

It must be added that even if the American state leaders had been willing to retain their confederal union, they would have faced great difficulties. The United States of that day was simply too far-flung and communications and transport still too slow to permit the leaders of 13 state governments spread out over more than a thousand miles of coastline to concert their positions in a confederal way once the special exigencies of wartime were past. Only small and compact confederations, like those of the Swiss and the Dutch, could function adequately without modern communications such as the telegraph and the telephone, and rapid transport such as the railroad and the airplane.

As regards Hamilton's second argument, that governments must be able to legislate for individuals, all confederations *did* pass a limited range of laws that were binding on the citizenries of their respective states in the sectors for which they had been given responsibility. In the United States, for example, the Continental Congress had "the sole and exclusive right and power . . . of establishing rules for deciding in all cases, what captures on land or water shall be legal." It had a similar exclusive right and power to regulate "post-offices from one state to another, throughout all the United States, and exacting such postage on the papers passing thro' the same as may be requisite to defray the expenses of the said office" (Article IX of the Articles of Confederation, 1948, first and fourth paragraphs).

Furthermore, if a confederation is functioning properly, its laws will be adopted by its central decision-making body, with each member voting on the basis of instructions from his or her state government. Thus, even if they do not come into force immediately, their reenactment by state legislatures should not pose a problem.

In many cases, confederal laws, enacted centrally, did not even need to be reenacted by member states. As Christopher Hughes points out:

In [the Germanic Confederation], the states had a duty of publication, but confederal law went into effect *ab initio* and of its own force independently of state publication: the state of Baden on one famous occasion [in connection with an 1832 Press law] attempted to deny this, to its cost . . .

I found that [Swiss] confederal legislation was, as a matter of course, bound up with cantonal legislation wherever it affected the duties of the citizen. It was clear that such legislation went into force of its own: the canton printed it, but did not add to the law the canton's command that the confederal law must be obeyed. (Hughes 1963, p. 13)

Hughes discovered the old Swiss practice by browsing in the official library of a small court in Berne; it would be interesting to learn how postal laws were handled during the confederal period of American history. In any event, all of this proves that Hamilton was wrong in supposing that the central authorities of confederations could not legislate for the peoples of the various member states.

Hamilton's insistence that central governments must have the power to administer their own laws is undermined by the modern practice of the governments of Germany and Switzerland where the administration of federal acts is mainly entrusted to the governments of the *länder* and cantons. It works well, and there are many advantages to be gained therefrom (see

Friedrich 1968, Chapter 8, "The Theory and Practice of Delegated Administration," pp. 70–75).

As regards Hamilton's fourth argument, the need for the central government to regulate international and interstate trade, the Confederation had very nearly adopted an amendment incorporating such powers in the Articles of Confederation. Later economic communities, such as the German Zollverein and the European and Benelux Unions, had or have these functions as their principal raison d'être, and have demonstrated that they can indeed be carried out by unions with confederal-type institutions.

It would appear, therefore, that Hamilton and Madison were too sweeping in their blanket condemnation of confederalism. Under some circumstances, say, when interstate cooperation is perceived to be crucial for resisting a common enemy or for promoting economic well-being, it has often worked passably well. In other circumstances, say, when member states do not feel threatened, militarily or economically from abroad, its chances of success depend on the inclination of the leaders of its member states to cooperate with one another within the framework of established confederal institutions as well as on the extent of public pressures on them to do so.

After 1783, the leaders of the American states gradually became disinclined to use the Continental Congress to maintain their union. And should the present leaders of, say, the European Union become similarly disinclined to use its institutions, that political association would face a similar decline. However, as will be seen, there are forces in play that make it unlikely that the EU will lose its leaders' support.

The bad repute of confederal governance is an obstacle in the way of any group of states that desires to form a closer union, but one that remains under the control of their respective governments. It makes those who have been reviving confederal-style institutions in the twentieth century reluctant to acknowledge their origins. If, on the other hand, confederalism were to become an acceptable option, it would be easier for groups of states for whom federal ties are not yet feasible to weigh the pros and cons of establishing these alternative unions.

It may be added that the successful functioning of many IGOs also suggests the need to reevaluate confederal governance. The IGOs have, in fact, been utilizing a confederal approach in carrying out several of their functions. Hamilton's four main arguments could be used to suggest that IGOs could never carry out their mandates. Yet the Universal Postal Union (UPU), for example, in a round-about way, legislates for governments, and its postal regulations are widely honored by them. At the same time, this occurs without its legislative powers being directly extended to the individuals who benefit from these arrangements, mostly without even knowing of their existence. Moreover, the governments of its member states, for the most part, do pay their assessments. Thus, for more than a century, the UPU has been a success story of international cooperation. The same could be said for many other IGOs: for example, the International Telecommunication Organization, the International Civil Aviation Organization (which regulates air safety), the International Maritime Organization (which regulates safety at sea), the World Health Organization (especially with respect to its epidemiological responsibilities, now needed more than ever!), and the International Monetary Fund.

Moreover, whatever the limitations of confederal governance, it is far stronger than any IGO-type relationship. Now that IGOs have shown their potential by providing so many common services, the time may be at hand for like-minded groups of states to form more ambitious confederal-type unions to promote their joint security or economic prosperity or both simultaneously.

(3) AN ANALYSIS OF CONFEDERAL GOVERNANCE

Because few political scientists are interested in obsolete forms of government, confederal governance has not given rise to much scholarly study in this century. There are, however, a few exceptions. Murray Forsyth's interest in the confederal cast of the European Community's institutions inspired him to write *Unions of States: The Theory and Practice of Confederation* (Forsyth 1981). Christopher Hughes's studies of Swiss history led to his provocative lecture on *Confederacies* (Hughes 1963). Two German works must also be mentioned, Carl Schmitt's *Verfassungslehre* (Schmitt [1928] 1970) and Ernst Huber's multivolume, *Deutsche Verfassungsgeschichte* (the early volumes of which cover the Germanic Confederation and the Zollverein) (Huber 1957 *et seq.*). S. Rufus Davis's *The Federal Principle: A Journey Through Time in Quest of Meaning* completes this list.

At the periodical level, my review of such journals as *Publius,* which is devoted to federalism in the broad sense, and *Telos,* which has occasional issues focusing on federalism, reveals relatively little scholarly interest in confederal governance. The main exception is Volume XII (4) (1982) of *Publius,* which celebrated the 200th anniversary of the entry into force of the U.S. Articles of Confederation. However, in recent years, political scientists such as Elazar and Duchacek have been giving confederalism a little more attention than the brief notices that it had been receiving from their federalist predecessors (See, for example, Elazar 1982, 1987, 1991; Duchacek 1970, 1982, 1988; Jillson 1988).

The interest in confederal-style government was not always so limited. In earlier centuries, the existence of functioning confederations led European political observers such as Pufendorf, the Abbé St. Pierre, Rousseau, Kant, Seydel, Le Fur, and others to study confederations as a separate class of governance to which attention needed to be paid. The analyses of these observers (and the later work of Schmitt and Huber) are well summarized in Forsyth's *Unions of States* (Forsyth 1981, pp. 73–159).

But most of this work relates to state regimes and international relations so remote and so different from those of the contemporary world that they have only limited modern relevance. Now that confederal governance may be coming back into the limelight, the features that characterize its modern reincarnation need to be examined more closely.

Forsyth has called attention to what may be the most basic difference between IGOs and confederations:

A treaty of [confederal] union founds a body that possesses personality, but it is more than merely the technical, "legal" personality of the typical international organization . . . The personality formed by [such a] union is an original capacity to act akin to that possessed by the states themselves . . . the permanence accorded to a confederation is more than merely the standing "disposability" of the institutions of the typical international organization, it is a profound locking together of states themselves as regards the exercise of fundamental powers. The same words may thus be used to describe the two kinds of body—the typical international organization and a union of states—but their meaning is quite different. (Forsyth 1981, p. 15)

This alliance/partnership approach is built into confederal governance at every level, in the direct relations of the partners with one another, in the multinational governing bodies that conduct their common decision-making and in the auxiliary bodies that may be set up to support the confederal structure and to promote common confederal goals.

Confederation, moreover, may be seen as an undertaking by a group of states to create a special order among themselves that is superior to that of the international order (or disorder) to which all states belong. It follows that all confederations, even economic ones not involved in collective security arrangements, such as the European and Benelux Unions, are obliged to ensure peaceful relations among their members because war would frustrate the very purposes for which they were created. That is why even the most primitive confederation, the one established by the Swiss cantons in the late thirteenth century, made elaborate provision for the compulsory arbitration of intercantonal quarrels. Of course, to the extent that it shared this feature, global confederation would either greatly reduce the incidence of interstate wars or perhaps even eliminate them entirely.

Confederalism and Its Defining Features

Confederalism as a class of governance is characterized by the following 15 features:

1. It unites states without depriving them of their statehood;
2. It can unite states whose populations are too heterogeneous to form viable federal-type unions;

3. It requires a written basic law in the form of treaty-constitutions that are legally binding upon the various confederal allies;

4. It presupposes a raison d'être of overriding importance such as a powerful common economic interest or the need of the confederating states for protection against a great power that threatens them all;

5. It provides for a minimalist mandate that leaves most governmental powers to be exercised independently by its member states;

6. It provides for two quite different types of mandate involving collective security and/or economic union. The security mandate always includes the same functions (foreign affairs, war and peace, military integration or coordination). The economic mandate also always includes the same functions (e.g., regulation of external trade and internal commerce, standardization of such things as weights and measures, and the establishment of common or single markets);

7. Confederations require a wide measure of support among the peoples of their member states based on the belief that such ties will enhance their country's security and/or its economic growth and prosperity;

8. As a corollary to this, relations among the member states need to be of a kind that will engender the gradual growth of popular support for, and allegiance to, the confederal union;

9. This popular support and allegiance, however, are subordinate to peoples' primary allegiance to their homelands (otherwise, the union is likely to "graduate" to federal or unitary status);

10. In a confederation, all member states must be ready to settle their quarrels through arbitration or adjudication rather than force;

11. In a confederation, member governments exercise the powers to be confederalized in a joint council that meets regularly and operates under mutually agreed rules of procedure;

12. This council has (i) a voting system in which state representatives vote on behalf of their countries; (ii) a decision-making system whose decisions are legally binding on its member states and are usually based on consensus or broad support rather than simple majorities of those member states; and (iii) a decision-implementing system that delegates the major burden of implementation to its member state governments;

13. Confederal governance presupposes a willingness on the part of the member states to furnish the funds that enable the union to carry out the tasks assigned to it;

14. It also provides for the conduct of the executive and judicial functions of government in ways that are unthreatening to the sovereignty of its member states; and finally

15. It embodies mutually acceptable working solutions to hegemonic and other problems that may emanate from any inequalities of power and resources among its larger and smaller member states.

Let us briefly probe these 15 features to bring out some of their more important ramifications and also to discover how confederal governance differs from IGO governance, on the one side, and federal governance, on the other. This will be done by comparing and contrasting how each of the 15 features is handled in the three classes of governance.[4]

Unions of States. An IGO does not normally unite states (much less the people who live in them), at least not in any fundamental way. As previously indicated, it is best described as a functional convenience by means of which states cooperate for certain carefully defined and usually secondary purposes. There can never be any question of an IGO exercising sovereignty in the sense of having final authority over important decisions. This power always remains with its member states.

At the other extreme, under a federal system citizens directly elect the persons who will represent them in the federal legislature; thus, such systems involve full-scale unions of peoples as well as of states. A federation is treated by the world community as a state, and its constituent states are soon treated as former states. In federal systems, it usually becomes quite clear that in practice ultimate sovereignty rests with the central government (because of the nature of the functions assigned to it) even though the regional governments may continue to have the final say on the functions assigned to them.

In both IGOs and confederations, all sovereign powers remain in the hands of their member states. However, there are many basic differences between these two classes. For example, in contrast to IGOs, confederal governance involves a far-reaching structural union of a group of sovereign states as well as the development of growing ties amongst the peoples living in them. On the other hand, its unique feature is that it unites states without depriving them of their statehood. While those states retain their sovereign powers, they have agreed to exercise some of them jointly and, occasionally in situations where they find themselves alone, or almost alone, to allow themselves to be outvoted. In such circumstances, their sovereignty and statehood are preserved by their inherent right (as states) to denounce the confederal treaty-constitution and to secede from the union, should their partners adopt decisions that they find intolerable. For some categories of "major" decision, the possibility of such a dilemma arising may be excluded by requiring unanimous approval.

Accordingly, in confederations, decision-making must seek to steer clear of crises that may break up the alliance, on the one hand, and of the gridlock that may make it ineffective, on the other. Negotiations among confederal partners resemble those among sovereign states, except that the partners are aware that if their talks break down with regard to crucial matters, their union may be placed in jeopardy. A confederation is not a state, because sovereign powers are exercised through it at one level removed by entities that are states. On the other hand, it is not merely a functional convenience of those states because it is a union that embraces (to varying extents) their peoples as well as their governments. Accordingly, Forsyth's concept of the confederal halfway house coincides rather closely with the political reality.

Hetereogeneity. If the states wishing to form a wider union have sufficiently homogeneous populations, they may be able to form and sustain a stable and effective federal relationship. At the other extreme, our experience with IGOs has shown that states with the most heterogeneous populations and forms of government can work together successfully within their confines. In between are the states with populations that are not homogeneous enough for a federal union, but might be able to maintain a confederal-style relationship. As a general rule, the looser the form of union, the greater its capacity to tolerate heterogeneity among the populations of its member states.

Hetereogeneity has many overlapping dimensions, racial, ethnic, linguistic, religious, cultural, social, ideological, and political. The greater capacity of confederal-type governance to unite heterogeneous states is shown by the capacity of the Germanic Confederation of princely states to accommodate city-states run by merchant oligarchies, and of the Swiss Confederation to unite rural cantons with many democratic features, urban cantons run by oligarchies, and one canton ruled by a royal house (Neuchâtel). The member states of the European Union are heterogeneous in many of the dimensions listed above, but this has not stood in the way of their developing confederal-type institutions.

On the other hand, federal unions require a higher degree of homogeneity among their member states. Though not for lack of trying, European countries remain unable to form a full-scale federal union, and the list of failed federations since 1945 includes those undertaken by states in the Commonwealth Caribbean, East Africa, and the Malay peninsula. There are also the cases of Quebec, which finds itself uncomfortable in Canada's federal framework, and of Puerto Rico, which is unwilling to become the 51st American state.

Constitutions or Basic Laws. All three forms of governance may be based on pacts that also qualify as their constitutions or basic laws. IGOs are almost always established under treaty-type agreements adopted (and sometimes amended) by their member states. These instruments are not constitutions for communities of people.

Federal constitutions may orginate, as did that of the United States, as a long-term pact among the constituent states, but they quickly become the constitution, or political rulebook, for the people who live in those states as well as for their governments. Over the years, any status that such constitutions may have had originally as a pact between their member states generally disappears.

Confederations, again, occupy the middle ground. They also have treaty-constitutions. But, in this case, the treaty relationship among the member states does not wither away. When, for example, the EU's member states rewrite the provisions of the Rome Treaty, the revisions do not enter into force until they have been ratified by *all* of that Union's member states, that is to say, the normal procedure for amending multilateral treaties must be followed.

Should such revisions be put into force despite the objections of a member, that member might secede from the union, or it might be allowed to retain its membership without, however, being bound by the additional duties and without benefiting from any new privileges that derive from these revisions. It must be added that confederal pacts are binding not only upon the constituent states but also, to the extent that they may be involved, upon individuals and corporate enterprises within those states.

The situation regarding secession is usually left in a state of deliberate ambiguity. For example, the right of self-determination of peoples, set forth in Article 1(2) of the UN Charter,[5] is nearly the same as a right of secession. In federations, however, it may be argued that there is no right of secession because its citizens comprise a single people joined politically by a basic law that has become more constitution than treaty. In confederations, on the other hand, it may be argued that the right of secession and self-determination remains because it is composed of several peoples who continue to be joined together by a pact that is as much treaty as constitution. However, since secession is very often the product of mass emotion, with a readiness to resort to force lurking in the background, legal or political rationales may not greatly influence the course of events. In principle, federations may not allow the right of secession; in practice, as with confederations, constitutional provisions prohibiting it sometimes do not prove an effective deterrent.

Nature of the Mandate. The functions assigned by its member states to an IGO are usually set forth in the pact that sets it up, though, of course, they may be altered from time to time in the light of experience. They are almost never of "overriding importance."

The basic raison d'être of a federation is much more fundamental than the need to solve certain problems of overriding concern; it is the formation of a permanent union composed of the federation's constituent states and peoples. It involves a basic change of status on two levels: a group of states is replaced by a new federal-type state, and a new people is formed through the integration, for certain major functions, of the various peoples living in those states. Moreover, the new state carries out the functions assigned to it in an authoritative way. Wheare describes in some detail how federal government works in the financial, economic, social, foreign policy and military sectors in what he calls the "federal bargain" in which wartime needs and social welfare concerns have led to the increasing centralization of many functions (Wheare 1964, pp. 93–208).

Here again, the confederation occupies a middle ground. It creates a new and far-reaching *union* of states, which involves their respective governments in a complex and demanding relationship with one another. Usually, they need to be under some sort of pressure to embark upon such a relationship. The desire of governments and peoples to retain their countries' political independence *and* their separate communities underlies the formation of most collective security confederations. The desire of governments and peoples to flourish materially underlies the formation of most economic confederations.

The primary concerns of the founders of a confederation are made clear in treaty-constitutions where the functions to be carried out in common are usually listed. In carrying out these provisions in a cooperative way, there is also an implicit "confederal bargain," but it is one among member governments rather than one between a national government and its respective regional governments.

Minimalist Mandate. The mandates of IGOs are minimalist in two senses. First, their capacity to adopt decisions that are binding upon their member states is ordinarily confined to carefully delimited functions of secondary importance. Second, to the extent that their mandates extend beyond those functions, they are usually empowered only to adopt recommendations to their member governments.

The mandates of federal states can seldom be described as "minimalist." On the contrary, as we have seen, the central government's sphere of activities tends to be expanded, on a legal or *de facto* basis, at the expense of those of its constituent regions or states.

While entrusted with primary functions, confederal unions have mandates that are usually intended to be, like those of IGOs, minimalist. They seem based on the implicit assumption that only those activities that can benefit substantially from being carried out jointly should be centralized. Recently, the concept of "subsidiarity" embodying this concern has been incorporated in the Maastricht revisions of the Rome Treaty. It reassures the members of the EU that its central authorities will not intrude upon areas where policies and activities are better carried out at the national level. The promise is credible because its member governments are not likely to surrender powers to the union's central authorities unless there are sound reasons for doing so.

The principle of subsidiarity is in line with another reality of confederal governance: The less the central government interferes in their daily lives, the greater the likelihood that it will win and retain the support of the more heterogeneous populations of its member states.

Functions Usually Centralized. The secondary functions delegated to IGOs for joint decision-making span the full spectrum of governmental activities but usually occupy niches, such as the postal, communications or police services of, respectively, the Universal Postal Union, the International Telecommunication Union, and Interpol. The functions assigned to such

IGOs are focused on those spheres in which governmental activities regularly cross national boundaries and therefore stand to benefit from a carefully orchestrated coordination.

In both confederations and federations, the kinds of primary function that are usually centralized are the same. They include foreign relations, the power to declare war and conclude peace and to regulate economic and technical activities. Control over social, educational, public health, and cultural activities, i.e., those that impinge most directly on the daily lives of individuals, are usually left wholly or mostly within the spheres allocated to their regional states.

But the responsibility for most functions usually has to be shared between the two levels, and the basis on which they are shared may be tilted in favor of either the national or the regional governments.

In federations, the tilt is towards the former, that is to say, most of the functions that fall in the central government's sphere are assigned exclusively to it, whereas those assigned to the regional governments are, to varying extents, shared between the two levels. For example, in the United States, the state governments are not commonly involved in foreign policy negotiations or questions of war and peace, while the federal government regularly adopts legislation that affects educational, health, social welfare, and cultural matters.

In confederations, the areas in which the central authorities tend to be involved (while, of course, differing between security and economic ones) are much the same, but the tilt is now towards the member states. The reason for this is clear: Representatives of the regional governments are the decision-makers at the central as well as the regional level. Thus, it is for them to decide, within the overall confederal basic law, which categories of decision will be taken jointly by the confederal partners, and which will be taken separately by each national government. Since they are directly involved at both levels, it may not matter as much to them which way the decision goes. At the same time, many of these representatives are likely to have a certain bias in favor of keeping such decision-making at the national level where it will be under their government's exclusive control.

Degree of Popular Support. IGOs, involved to a large extent in technical activities, do not require the same kind of popular support as federal or confederal unions. For example, the Universal Postal Union and many other IGOs carry out their much-needed functions with little fanfare or without arousing much interest on the part of the people of the world whom they serve. Thus, the beneficiaries of mail deliveries or of patent or trademark protection (regulated by the World Intellectual Property Organization) are not likely to form political communities based on their sharing of those services.

With federations, the situation is totally reversed. Abraham Lincoln's famous phrase "government of the people, by the people and for the people" well expresses the essence of federal governance. The regional governments may still play a role, but it is the people who as voters and as constituents are the ultimate determiners of the policies adopted at both levels of government.

In this sphere, too, the confederation is again a halfway house. Unlike IGOs, no confederation can prosper for long without a substantial measure of support on the part of the peoples of its member states. All confederations require their active participation—whether as soldiers in confronting a common enemy, or as manufacturers, traders and consumers in a common market. Many confederal decisions and laws, if they are to become effective, must bind the citizenries as well as their governments. At the same time, it is the representatives of those governments, and not the directly elected representatives of those citizenries, who take those decisions and adopt those laws. However, if the member states are representative democracies, those who sit in confederal councils must look over their shoulders at the wishes of their respective electorates. For example, those who sit in the European Union's Council of Ministers, and their superiors in national capitals, are likely to be swayed by their assessment of whether particular decisions and laws will please or annoy their domestic constituencies.

Federations have popular support because their leaders are the persons chosen by their electorates. Confederations need such support, too, as a counterweight to the tendency of governmental leaders to become bogged down in rivalries and petty quarrels. Popular pressures may sometimes reduce the risk of confederal decision-making bodies being paralyzed by gridlock among their member states.

Degree and Focus of Allegiance. These questions do not arise for IGOs since, as mentioned, the Universal Postal Union or similar bodies are not likely to evoke popular allegiance. On the other hand, federal governments need to inspire the same kind of primary allegiance as unitary states. In federal states, after a few generations, many people may have little more than residual feelings of allegiance to their home states, particularly if they have been moving from one to another of them at regular intervals.

In confederations, on the contrary, primary allegiance remains focused on the member states, and feelings of allegiance to the wider entity are acquired only gradually, possibly as a result of comradeship on the battlefield or of the political and economic interrelationships that may be generated by confederal ties. Such a secondary allegiance constitutes a necessary popular infrastructure that underpins confederal institutions and helps them to work more effectively. Once this secondary allegiance turns into a widespread primary allegiance, a confederal union is ready to graduate to federal status. This is what happened with the Americans in 1783 and the Swiss in 1848, while the Dutch by 1815 had become so closely knit that they were ready to form a unitary state.

Successful confederation goes beyond mere political and economic ties.

It creates, as a kind of by-product, a societal integration that is hard to define. People living under a confederal umbrella, if all goes well, gradually coalesce into a new "in-group" that sets them apart from the rest of humanity without usually breaking up (or even disturbing) the more intimate in-groups that they have long enjoyed in their member state homelands.

Dispute Settlement. When disputes arise among IGO member states over the nature of their activities, their costs or the manner in which they are operating, prescribed procedures for dealing with them are usually available, either in their founding treaties or in international arrangements for arbitration or adjudication. Thus, such disputes seldom jeopardize the functioning of an IGO, much less lead to its disappearance. For example, the United States successively withdrew from its memberships in the International Labor Organization and UNESCO, but soon returned to the former and will probably eventually return to the latter. While these IGOs were inconvenienced by the withdrawal of an influential member state that paid a large fraction of their budget, they continued to perform the functions assigned to them. Over the years, such secessions have not been a frequent or very serious drawback for IGOs.

In federations, internal disputes are seldom serious enough to threaten a union's survival. They can usually be handled by the federal and state courts. However, when such disputes involve issues that cannot be settled by the courts, the consequences may be very serious indeed, as Americans and Nigerians learned during their respective civil wars, and as the Canadians are discovering in their efforts to avert the secession of Quebec from their federal union. But such crises are relatively rare exceptions. Furthermore, even unitary states are far from immune from civil strife.

The situation for confederations is basically different. Disputes among the proud leaders of their sovereign member states are apt to occur more frequently and may have rather serious repercussions. Traditionally, confederal unions have relied more on arbitral procedures than on courts of law for resolving their disputes. All of their treaty-constitutions, beginning with the 1292 Uri-Schwyz-Unterwalden Pact of the Swiss, contain elaborate provisions for dealing with quarrels that may arise amongst the leaders of their member states.

Such disputes were greatly feared because any member state might at any time seek to dramatize its displeasure by threatening to withdraw or by actually withdrawing from the union. Dispute settlement procedures typically involve finding mutually acceptable escape routes from strongly held opposing positions without necessarily focusing on which of the contending member states occupies the legal high ground. However, none of the four prototype confederations was actually broken up by such disputes.[6]

In the European Union, member states have found it possible to deal with most of their quarrels within the framework of the Rome Treaty, as interpreted by the European Court of Justice. However, the de Gaulle crisis which shook the EU in the 1960s and the Thatcher crisis in the 1980s had to be dealt with by the "escape route" procedure (see Chapter 2 for the details).

Historically, confederal partners have seldom gone to war with one another. The American states and the Dutch provinces never did; the German states, only when Bismarck deliberately sacrificed their Confederation in order to unite the other German states with Prussia. The Swiss had five civil wars that were surely the most half-hearted civil wars in history.[7]

Decision-Making Organs. In all IGOs and confederations, the delegated powers are exercised in joint councils that meet regularly and operate under mutually agreed-upon rules of procedure. One of these joint councils is usually supreme. Among confederal bodies, there were the Diets of the two Swiss Confederations, the Continental Congress of the United States, the States-General of the Dutch Republic, and the Bundestag of the Germanic Confederation. In the present-day European Union, there is the European Council composed of the heads of state or government and the Council of Ministers which together fulfil this function.

Similar bodies could be cited for each of the various IGOs. The main difference between IGOs and confederations in this respect is that the latter have been entrusted with certain sovereign powers: Their joint councils are thus involved in a decision-making of crucial importance for their member states. These bodies are the legislative counterparts of the national parliaments of federal and unitary states.

Decision-Making Systems. "Majority rule" is generally regarded as the fairest basis for decision-making in representative democracies and has become the norm in most federal and unitary states. But the fairness of this system is posited on the existence of electoral constituencies having the same (or nearly the same) numbers of people. Even in federations, this is sometimes not the case as, for example, in the United States Senate, where the smaller states exercise a disproportionate influence.

In both IGOs and confederations, the instructed representatives of member governments, not elected representatives, are the voters. Except for several IGOs and confederations with weighted voting systems, each member government has only one vote regardless of its position on the ministate/great-power spectrum. In such circumstances, majority rule cannot guarantee fairness.

But because majority rule is usually the norm in the national legislatures of member states, it has sometimes, rather mechanically, been transferred to the decision-making bodies of IGOs without much thought given to the risks that it involves. In IGOs in which most decisions relate to technical issues, these risks may be minimal. On the other hand, when controversial issues arise, majority rule may lead to the taking of decisions that cannot be carried out in practice, either because no member state is obliged to implement a decision that is merely a recommendation, or because member states are sometimes ready to ignore binding decisions of which they strongly disapprove. Most close observers of the UN General Assembly's procedures soon recognize that its "majority rule" decision-making system suffers from serious limitations of this kind.

Experience has led most IGOs, including the United Nations, to take as many decisions as possible on the basis of consensus or "without objection." This is especially true for decisions having "financial implications," because some countries are unwilling to pay their share of the costs of activities that they regard as inimical to their interests.

The same considerations apply, *a fortiori,* to confederal unions. Whatever the formal voting requirements for decision-making, the members of confederal bodies are usually well aware that a large preponderance of support is required for proceeding with important actions. And in establishing what constitutes a "preponderance of support," the member states do usually weigh the importance of each of their number in the sphere under consideration.

What constitutes a preponderance of support may be spelled out in the decision-making procedures of the confederal treaty-constitution or established on the basis of practice. In the German confederal Bundestag, for example, certain smaller states shared a vote. The member states of the European Union and the International Monetary Fund adhere to complex systems of weighted voting. Under the Articles of Confederation, many important decisions could be taken only "by nine states present and voting," an important impediment since a few seats were almost always empty. But, even in the absence of any formal requirements in the rules of procedure, there is often awareness that decisions taken without a sufficient preponderance of support among the more influential member states will prove to be "dead letters." In such cases, the members supporting a particular decision must include those whose participation will be needed in carrying it out.

As regards the implementation of decisions, in federations, this is sometimes carried out by the central government, sometimes by the regional governments. In confederations, however, it is always carried out by the member states. From the standpoint of uniformity of execution, this may create problems. Therefore, the central government should be empowered to monitor the progress of implementation in the various member states and possess the power to challenge laggards.

On the other hand, this practice avoids duplication and saves money. The local authorities are given the responsibility of executing decisions to which their representatives in the central decision-making body have agreed rather than entrusting outside officials with the invidious tasks of administration and enforcement (see, in this connection, Friedrich 1968, pp. 70–75).

Sources of Finance. IGOs are usually financed by means of assessments on member states, each assessed on the basis of its capacity to pay.

In federations, central and regional governments usually may each tax their citizenries over the full range of direct and indirect taxes. However, it is the central governments that usually control the most lucrative sources of taxation, such as income taxes or value-added taxes, while the regional governments have had either to share these sources or to find other sources. The nature of the relationship is revealed by the fact that the regional governments must generally look to the federal governments for grants in order to cover at least some of their expenses, and never the other way around. Wheare describes the relationship in the following terms:

It has become clear that . . . only the general governments have any important method of taxation confided exclusively to them . . . Do general and regional governments 'live of their own' or do they depend on each other? . . . the general governments have been able to acquire sufficient resources under their own control to perform their functions, but the regional governments have come to rely upon grants from the general government. They have accepted, in varying degree, some measure of financial subordination to the general government. (Wheare 1964, p. 109)

The position of confederal central authorities has been very different. For example, the U.S. Confederation was starved for funds even while the Revolutionary War was still under way, and Congress's continual pleas to the state governments for funds were widely ignored. The Dutch Republic managed a little better, because the wealthy province of Holland came to its rescue when bankruptcy threatened. The old Swiss Confederation had virtually no central government and no central military forces, and therefore did not have to raise large sums of money. The post-Napoleonic new Confederation, on the other hand, finally adopted a scale of assessments like that of contemporary IGOs. The Germanic Confederation followed a similar course, though its central institutions also were modest even in those days of small government. Except in the U.S. Confederation, the common expenses were minimized in security confederations because each member bore the costs of its own armed forces.

The European Union has demonstrated that a modern confederal union need not be starved for funds. It has been able not only to provide for its own needs, but also to render large-scale agricultural support payments to the farmers of its member states. While it has "its own resources," that is, sources specifically allocated to it, it cannot impose direct taxes on the peoples of its member states. Instead, it has persuaded the governments of those states to allocate to it on a long-term basis a small part of the proceeds of the value-added taxes that they collect. In this sense, it is still subordinate to its member states in the financial realm.

Executive and Judicial Institutions. The executive and judicial branches of government have evolved so rapidly during the nineteenth and twentieth centuries that it would serve little purpose to compare confederal arrangements in earlier centuries with contemporary federal or IGO capabilities in these two spheres.

Some insight into the executive aspect is provided by our experience with IGOs. They all have executive heads and well-staffed secretariats to carry out the various functions for which they have been made responsible. It is clear from the EU's experience with its Commission that secretariats capable of carrying out a wide variety of functions can be readily installed in a confederal setting.

On the legal front, the United Nations, as well as the European and the Benelux Unions, also have judicial branches—the International Court of Justice (ICJ), the European Court of Justice, and the Benelux Court of Justice. We have some indications of how modern confederations might fit into this overall picture. The jurisprudence and judicial machinery of the European and the Benelux Unions constitute a new layer that is positioned between the international and national (municipal) legal systems. It is significant that the European Court of Justice, which was provided for in the Treaty of Rome, has had a heavy caseload and performed a role that is comparable to that played by the supreme courts in national governments (for details, see Chapter 2). Much the same can be said of the Benelux Court of Justice.

Their experience dispels any notion that modern executive and judicial institutions may be incompatible with confederal forms of governance. On the contrary, even in some of the later confederations, executive and judicial branches were beginning to emerge. For example, the four main executive departments of the United States Government were formed during the later confederal period, replacing Congressional committees. Almost from the outset, the Dutch Republic had some executive capacity.

In the legal sphere, there were signs that confederal judicial institutions might not be far behind. On the eve of the Federal Convention, Pinckney of South Carolina brought draft amendments to the Articles of Confederation before the Continental Congress that would have given the central government a supreme court (*Journals of Congress* 1786, pp. 494–98). The courts in The Hague, for many decades, did double duty for the Dutch Republic and the Province of Holland, as did the courts of the principal *Länder* for the Germanic Confederation. If the older confederations had not been replaced by federations or unitary states, it seems likely that they would have soon acquired executive and judicial capabilities.

Hegemonic Problems. The legal equality of member states in IGOs and confederations is usually accompanied by some recognition of their real-world inequalities in the spheres in which these political associations have been assigned authority and special powers. In general, of course, the actual importance and influence of great powers tend, in most such spheres, to be far greater than that of, say, ministates or smaller states. At one extreme, there may be IGO and confederal unions in which a great power member is in a position to dominate all the other member states combined. In such circumstances, it is said to exercise "hegemonic powers," that is to say, it is able to exercise a preponderant authority within the union concerned. In the Dutch Republic, for example, the province of Holland enjoyed such a hegemony, and in the Germanic Confederation, Austria and Prussia played the role of joint hegemons. In the Swiss and American confederations, on the other hand, no canton or state was dominant enough to exercise hegemonic powers.

In hegemonic situations, much depends upon the behavior and attitudes of the dominant state or states. The Dutch Republic flourished because Holland was interested in its survival, and generally exercised its hegemonic power with restraint. The Germanic Confederation lasted as long as Austria and Prussia worked in tandem and collapsed only when Bismarck, in effect, expelled Austria from it.

In global IGOs, hegemonic problems, if they exist at all, are of lesser importance. This is both because there is no global hegemon and because the mandates of such IGOs are mainly limited to technical spheres in which the inducements to play such a role are not great.

Hegemonic problems have not arisen in any of the four prototype federations. In the United States and Switzerland, no state or canton could aspire to play such a role. In Canada, Ontario and Quebec, by far the largest provinces in terms of population, have always tended to offset one another, with neither in a position to exercise hegemonic powers. In Australia, New South Wales and Victoria, also the largest states in terms of population, find themselves in a very similar position. In modern Germany, Prussia no longer occupies the dominant position it held in earlier times, hence the hegemonic problem no longer arises.

Even if a federal union contained a member capable of asserting hegemonic powers, the fact that the federal legislature is elected by popular franchise, rather than composed of the instructed representatives of its regional governments, reduces the chances of any state leader entertaining hegemonic ambitions.

The looser confederal union, with the still sovereign member states directly represented in its joint councils, is the form of governance that remains most vulnerable to hegemonic dominance. But, in order for there to be a serious risk of it, the configuration of its membership must include a state that can almost always impose its will on the others *and* the potential hegemon must be willing and able to transform the voluntary confederal union into an empire that it can dominate. Since the present trend is towards greater democracy and self-determination of ethnic groups, it is less likely that hegemonic problems will arise even for confederations.

In conclusion, three other features common to confederations must be mentioned. First, more than other forms of voluntary union, confederations tend to have up-and-down histories. Security confederations generally thrive so long as they are threatened from abroad, and are apt to decay when that challenge has been removed. Like the U.S. Confederation, they have been at their strongest when warding off invaders and at their weakest when adjusting to peaceful conditions. There is always the risk that, when the pressures that led to their formation are removed, the members of the "special order" of a confederation may slip back into the more limited order (or disorder) of the neighborhood of states from which it originally emerged. Still, as noted, the earlier confederal unions all became highly stable federal or unitary states.

Second, a notable feature of confederal governance is its capacity to create a hierarchy of confederations, one within another, like Russian nesting dolls. This capacity was first shown in the Dutch Republic in which the provinces, while being members of the larger confederal union, were each confederations in their own right whose members were the governments of their respective towns. The same capacity is being shown by the European Union within which Benelux has its own three-member confederal-type union. Further, within Benelux, there is the Belgium–Luxembourg economic union formed as long ago as 1921.

Third, as Forsyth has pointed out, the nature of each confederation is a function of (1) the nature of the general interstate relations of the era in which it is formed; and (2) the nature of the states in the area where it happens to be located (Forsyth 1981, pp. 10–16). Since both these variables have been steadily evolving over the centuries, this means that the nature and potential of confederal governance have also been changing, and that a late twentieth-century confederation is likely to differ greatly from the four prototypes. Any modern confederation cannot but reflect the rapidly changing character of contemporary interstate relations and of the governments that are its confederal partners.

Let me conclude this section with the words of a distinguished commentator on federalism: "I differentiate a confederal from a federal system—and the two corresponding political cultures—rather sharply . . . Our understandably reserved reaction to the confederal non-majoritarian formula and its piecemeal and very slow implementation by compromise and consensus is necessarily tempered by the quite disarming and familiar query: 'If not that, what else?' " (Duchacek 1988, p. 31).

(4) MODERN APPLICATIONS OF CONFEDERAL GOVERNANCE

The last step is to tie in this detailed analysis of confederal governance with the role that it might play (1) in dealing with, or even forestalling, the ethnic confrontations that have been plaguing our post–Cold War world; (2) in reconciling the widespread demand for ethnic separatism with our pressing need for some minimal degree of wider political and economic integration for large groups of contiguous states; and (3) in providing the basis for a global collective security system that might enable human civilization to survive the great crises that may arise from the increasing availability of weapons of mass destruction.

It is in the context of the ethnic tensions summarized in the Opening Argument that the confederal capacity to form unions of relatively heterogeneous groups should be arousing special interest. As indicated therein, the prevailing view—that any ethnic group that is able to press its demands hard enough must be allowed to form its own nation-state—has already enlarged the membership of the world community threefold and created the possibility that its numbers may double again in the next century.

The dilemma that this poses has been described. On the one hand, it is desirable to allow each ethnic group to live, if it so desires, in its own homeland where it can enjoy a full measure of social and cultural autonomy. On the other hand, from economic and political standpoints, there needs to be a more manageable number of larger political units of relatively commensurate size that can, as necessary, act on behalf of groups of autonomous small states and mini-states.

In certain situations and in certain ways, confederal institutions might offer some help in dealing with this dilemma. They constitute an option that might keep some multiethnic polities intact. They might also be used to form unions of smaller uniethnic states for the conduct of international relations, including international trade relations, and for the creation of viable economic units. Such unions might come in all sizes and shapes, with some of them, like the European Union, being of continental scope and others, like the Benelux and the Caribbean Communities, being amalgams of small states and ministates.

In this way, (largely) uniethnic homelands might provide the building blocks of the world community with the principle of self-determination governing their creation. Over them, there might be wider multiethnic political and economic unions whose members, (largely) uniethnic homelands, would carry out jointly certain pre-agreed functions and powers. These might include, for example, functions relating to collective security or the broader economy of the kind just described. To the extent that such an approach proves feasible, it may permit inevitable changes in the state system to take place in an evolutionary way with a minimum of confusion and violence.

Daniel Elazar seems to support such an approach. For example, he points out that "for much of the world, group rights—variously defined as national, local or ethnic liberties—are of the essence. For them, confederation may be the most viable way to attain the combination of liberty, good government, and peace which federalism promises" (Elazar 1987, p. 95). Elsewhere, he stresses that confederations preserve the liberties of their constituent polities (Elazar 1982, pp. 2–5). This is the attraction that might make ethnic groups readier to join or remain in larger multiethnic unions where they would be minorities but protected against the discrimination and harsh treatment that minorities have often had to endure.

Elazar has also written of "the serious revival of confederal options around the world since World War II . . . In the post-modern epoch . . . constitutionalized transnational political organization based on shared economic and cultural foundations has been more acceptable, leading to a renewed interest in the possibilities of confederation" (Elazar 1982, p. 1).

The potential applications of confederal institutions must also be weighed against the rather gloomy global situation described in the Opening Argument. The spreading of confederal-type governance seems to represent one way for humanity to enter into a survival mode.

Main Applications of Confederal Institutions

This chapter will conclude by identifying, and giving the current status of, four of the main possible applications of confederal institutions:

1. Some groups of small states and ministates may wish to form confederal-type unions in order to enhance their economic clout. By placing themselves in a position to come forward with mutually agreed positions on specific issues, they would maximize their bargaining power with larger and more powerful entities.

2. Some multiethnic states threatened with break-up may wish to experiment with confederal institutions in the hope that they might provide a viable alternative to dissolving all political ties.

3. Groups of contiguous states, large and small, may contemplate the formation of confederal ties with a view to optimizing the benefits to be derived from an increasingly interdependent world economy. Such groups might also utilize such ties to enhance their collective security in an increasingly dangerous world.

4. Finally, the world community as a whole, in light of the great dangers that appear to lie ahead, will surely be focusing on how it can deal effectively with those dangers. In this wider context, the confederal model also warrants careful consideration.

The main uncertainty, of course, is whether the introduction of confederal-type institutions would, in practice, prove helpful in achieving goals that are doubtless widely shared. The progress made so far with each application is summed up below.

Forming Groups of Small States and Ministates. The prototype is the Benelux Union, which has most of the 15 features outlined earlier and therefore qualifies as a confederal-style economic union. It has been demonstrated that some groups of developing countries (in the Commonwealth Caribbean, East Africa, and the Malay peninsula) could not support federal institutions (Franck 1968). The question now arises whether some of them could form viable confederal-type unions instead. The Caribbean Community, for example, has been actively pursuing that possibility.

Some groups of developing countries are experimenting with looser IGO-type "organizations" in which they try to undertake joint negotiations with larger entities. For example, under the Lomé IV Convention, 45 African, 15 Caribbean and 8 Pacific countries have organized their relations with the European Union.[8] The question that remains is whether some of these IGOs will one day be ready to graduate to confederal status.

It is also conceivable that some form of confederal union might offer reciprocal economic and security advantages to Arab neighbors such as Jordan and the newly emerging Palestinian state on the West Bank. The same might be true for Ireland and Northern Ireland.

Saving Disintegrating Unitary or Federal States. There is, as yet, little evidence to suggest that confederal institutions could save these states. Yugoslavia experimented unsuccessfully with looser institutional frameworks just before it sank into civil war. Canada, which calls itself a confederation, might, if Quebec presses matters, preserve its union by restructuring itself as a true confederation. If confederal unions function tolerably well elsewhere, peoples who find themselves in disintegrating states might be readier to see whether they could reorganize their political ties in a confederal half-way house.

Larger Confederal Unions. Proposals to form large-scale confederal unions are, in effect, proposals to reform the political structure of our present state system. If the European Union is, in fact, the world's first continental-size confederation, the possibility of similar entities being established on other continents arises. For example, Canada, Mexico and the United States now have their North American Free Trade Agreement (NAFTA), the first step on the ladder of economic union. If NAFTA begins to move up the ladder, the presence of two burgeoning continental economic unions might have a demonstration effect on the countries of East Asia. Of course, there are daunting obstacles in North America and East Asia to such an outcome, beyond those already faced by the European Union. But the EU has proceeded far enough down the road to closer union to make it a prototype for jumbo confederations. The close scrutiny that its status receives in Chapter 2 is warranted by these wider implications.

Global Confederation. Far more ambitious and far more problematic is the possibility that a global confederation, composed of all the member states of the United Nations, might be formed, thus realizing the dream of Karl Deutsch and many others of eliminating war as a normal feature of international relations. While we are still a very long way from that goal, the framers wrote into the United Nations Charter a collective security system which, suitably modified, just might make that dream come true. Activating this system would transform the world's armies into police forces and countries that defy the Security Council into rogue states. It would also open up the process of turning our present pseudo "world community" into a real one. These are some of the possibilities explored in Chapter 3.

The present chapter constitutes, *inter alia,* an effort to revive interest in an old, but discredited, class of governance—which now seems to be in a state of modest revival—and therefore to warrant the closer attention of political scientists. In this chapter, I have sought to build on the important pioneer work of Murray Forsyth on unions of states. But before confederal institutions can be confidently recommended to states wishing to form looser political associations, a good deal of further study is obviously required.

In particular, the preceding review of the possible applications of confederal governance has only offered a glimpse of the potential scope of confederal-type governance and the kinds of situation where it might prove useful. If confederal governance emerges as a viable system in its own right, the specific situations where it might prove useful would have to be identified and carefully studied. The examples given were for purposes of illustration only, and did not, of course, constitute concrete proposals. In the next chapter, however, we shall be concerned with one application that seems to have emerged spontaneously, that is to say, without conscious intent, which makes it all the more interesting and dramatic.

NOTES

1. The word *region* may refer to subdivisions of the world or of sovereign states. In this chapter, it will refer to the main subdivisions of federal states (i.e., the provinces of Australia and Canada, the cantons of Switzerland, the *länder* of Germany and the states of the United States). The words "continental" or "supranational" will be used to signify major subdivisions of the world. In Chapter 3, *region* will be used in its wider connotation.

2. Article 1 (3), first paragraph; however, popular elections of senators were already commonplace in the later nineteenth century. In the first half of the nineteenth century, some state legislatures still sought to have their senators carry out their instructions (Riker 1964, pp. 87–91).

3. Thomas Burke, the skillful delegate from North Carolina, expressed his belief that "the end of the war would end all necessity for the continuation of the Congress" (Jensen 1948, p. 186).

4. The analysis that follows is indicative rather than comprehensive. A full-scale, fully documented study of these relationships would require a book of its own. In general, the sources are: (1) for IGOs, the author's first-hand knowledge as a United Nations staff member involved in coordinating the work of the UN, its specialized agencies and other IGOs, as well as his subsequent studies of the way in which IGOs function; (2) for confederations, the sources listed earlier plus the author's unpublished findings on the four prototype confederations; (3) for federations, the author has relied mainly on Elazar's *Exploring Federalism;* Duchacek's *Comparative Feder-*

alism: The Territorial Dimension of Politics; Friedrich's *Trends of Federalism in Theory and Practice;* and Wheare's *Federal Government.*

5. All references to the UN Charter are to the *Charter of the United Nations and the Statute of the International Court of Justice,* published by the United Nations Office of Public Information, undated but including the amendments of 1965. Future references will be to the chapter or article involved.

6. The Germanic Confederation was not broken up by a dispute, but by Bismarck's determination to destroy it.

7. The opposing soldiers sometimes fraternized at lunchtime!

8. The text of the Convention is found in the *UNESCO Courier,* No. 120 of March/April 1990.

REFERENCES

The Articles of Confederation and Perpetual Union. In Appendix 1 of Carl Van Doren. *The Great Rehearsal.* New York: The Viking Press, 1948.

Davis, S. Rufus. *The Federal Principle: A Journey Through Time in Quest of a Meaning.* Berkeley and Los Angeles: University of California Press, 1978.

Duchacek, Ivo D. *Comparative Federalism: The Territorial Dimension of Politics.* New York: Holt, Rinehart and Winston, 1970.

———. "Antagonistic Co-operation: Territorial and Ethnic Communities." In *Publius,* 7 (4), 1977, pp. 3–31.

———. "Consociations of Fatherlands." In *Publius,* 12 (4), 1982, pp. 129–77.

———. "Dyadic Federations and Confederations." In *Publius,* 18 (2), 1988, pp. 5–31.

Elazar, Daniel J. "Confederation and Federal Liberty." In *Publius,* 12 (4), 1982, pp. 1–14.

———. *Exploring Federalism.* Tuscaloosa, AL: The University of Alabama Press, 1987.

———. *Federal Systems of the World: A Handbook of Federal, Confederal and Autonomy Arrangements.* Harlow, Essex, UK: Longman Current Affairs, 1991.

Forsyth, Murray. *Unions of States: The Theory and Practice of Confederation.* Leicester: Leicester University Press, 1981.

Franck, Thomas, ed. *Why Federations Fail: An Inquiry Into the Requisites for Successful Federation.* New York: New York University Press, 1968.

Friedrich, Carl J. *Trends of Federalism in Theory and Practice.* New York: Praeger, 1968.

Hamilton, Alexander, John Jay, and James Madison. *The Federalist.* New York: The Modern Library, Random House, 1937.

Huber, Ernst R. *Deutsche Verfassungsgeschichte seit 1789.* Stuttgart: W. Kohlhammer, 1957 *et seq.*

Hughes, Christopher. *Confederacies.* Leicester: Leicester University Press, 1963.

Jensen, Merrill. *The Articles of Confederation.* Madison: The University of Wisconsin Press, 1948.

Jillson, Calvin C. "Political Culture and the Pattern of Congressional Politics Under the Articles of Confederation." In *Publius,* 18 (1), 1988, pp. 1–26.

Journals of the [Continental] Congress, August 1786.

King, Preston. *Federalism and Federation*. Baltimore: The Johns Hopkins Press, 1982.

Lemco, Jonathan. *Political Stability in Federal Governments*. New York: Praeger, 1991.

Riker, William H. *Federalism, Origin, Operation, Significance*. Boston and Toronto: Little Brown & Co., 1964.

Sawer, Geoffrey. *Modern Federalism*. London: C.A. Watts & Co., 1969.

Schmitt, Carl. *Verfassungslehre*. 1928. Reprint, Berlin: Duncker & Humblot, 1970.

Temple, Sir William. *Observations Upon the United Provinces of the Netherlands*, edited by Sir George Clark. Oxford: The Clarendon Press, 1972.

United Nations Charter, published by the United Nations Office of Public Information, undated and including amendments of 1965.

Wheare, Kenneth C. *Federal Government*, Fourth Edition. Oxford: Oxford University Press, 1964.

Chapter 2

The European Union: Jumbo Confederation

The European Union is the first example of larger and smaller states forming a voluntary economic union of continental scope. Originally a union of six states (Belgium, France, the German Federal Republic, Italy, Luxemburg, and the Netherlands) created by a Treaty-Constitution adopted in Rome in 1957, EU's membership has been gradually expanded to include nine other states (Austria, Britain, Denmark, Finland, Greece, Ireland, Portugal, Spain, and Sweden). It also now embraces all of Germany rather than just the western part of it. Knocking on its door are many of the newly liberated states of Eastern Europe, eager to reenter the European mainstream that they were forced to leave in the aftermath of World War II.

Like all such communities, the European Union reflects the character of its member states. Almost all of them are, economically speaking, leaders rather than laggards. Indeed, the present Community contains an economic superpower (Germany) and three other leading economic powers (Britain, France, and Italy). Nor would anyone characterize eight of its other members (Austria, Belgium, Denmark, Finland, Luxembourg, Netherlands, Spain, and Sweden) as economically backward. Only Greece, Ireland, and Portugal fall slightly below this top level. Thus, the Union is designed to make one of the world's most prosperous regions more prosperous still.

Europeans have always felt some sense of continental unity, and that sense has now been institutionalized in the European Union. In February 1992, the Community once again confounded skeptics by agreeing at Maastricht on a schedule for establishing a common currency and a European Central Bank by the end of this century. Even though, four years later, monetary union seems further off than it did then, it is likely to ride the next lurch forward whenever it comes. In 1996, the members of the Union plan to make a new effort to turn their Union into a full-scale federation.

At the same time, this European Union brings together proud peoples unwilling to see their societies and cultures submerged in any melting pot. The Union is, *inter alia,* an experiment in preserving the sociocultural traditions of each of its members within a broader general welfare union with a politico-economic focus. Like all unions of states, it involves a search for unity in diversity. However, as revealed by several close votes on the Maastricht revisions to the Rome Treaty, many Europeans remain wary of altering their union in any way that increases its scope or the powers delegated to its central authorities. The prospect of a United States of Europe attracts, at most, lukewarm support.

On the homogeneity–heterogeneity axis, the peoples of Europe are much more heterogeneous than the peoples of the four prototype federations, Australia, Canada, Switzerland, and the United States, or of other federal states such as Germany and Austria. This is true whatever yardstick one uses—ethnic, linguistic, religious, cultural, social, or stage of economic development. The difficulties being experienced by Europeanists in forming a federal union spring from an ineluctable reality: The peoples of the continent simply do not provide a human substructure that is sufficiently integrated to support a governmental superstructure like that of the four prototype federations.

Accordingly, this chapter proceeds on the assumption that the peoples of Europe in the closing years of the twentieth century are still too heterogeneous to sustain classic federal-type governance. Two underlying realities support this contention: (1) the primary allegiance of each of these peoples remains, after nearly four decades of union, to their homelands; and (2) the heads of the member governments, unlike their counterparts in federal states, remain the EU's ultimate decision-makers.

The chapter also proceeds on the assumption that the peoples now in the Union *have* reached a stage on the homogeneity–heterogeneity axis that does allow them to sustain confederal-type governance. Elazar and Duchacek both support such a view. Murray Forsyth expands on it:

It is one of the main theses of this study that economic union, of the kind represented by the Zollverein and the European Community, is a subspecies of the genus confederation. Its development as a distinct form alongside confederations for defense and security is largely explicable in terms of the profound changes that have taken place in the structure and needs of the state with the development of the industrial revolution and the concomitant intensification of economic exchange over the boundaries of states. These changes provide a strong added impetus to the "welfare" motive for confederation, sufficient to sustain it on its own. (Forsyth 1981, p. 6)[1]

Finally, contemporary confederal governance is bound to differ in many ways both from that of earlier centuries and from contemporary federal governance. While retaining the 15 basic features described in Chapter 1, it seems in the case of the European Union to be adopting many techniques and devices that are creating a modified "confederal balance." This is a balance that satisfies the need for a minimal level of political, economic, and technical integration while simultaneously conceding as much autonomy as possible to the member states in the spheres where they are heterogeneous. The fact that the heads of government of the member states run the union provides the main guarantee that the confederal compact will be respected and upheld by all concerned. Thus, the tendency in federations for the central government to overshadow the governments of their member states would be blocked by groups with political and personal interests in preventing that from happening.

The purpose of this chapter is to examine how the above-mentioned techniques and devices have been achieving the EU's present level of political, economic, and technical integration within the overall context of a contemporary form of confederal governance. The chapter consists of three sections: (1) A brief narrative summary of the EU's origins and evolution; (2) An analysis of how its institutions, many of which were deliberately cast in a federal mold, have fared in the EU's predominantly confederal environment; and (3) A series of conclusions.

(1) THE EUROPEAN UNION'S ORIGINS AND HISTORY, 1957–1995[2]

The concept of European unity is very old. Its roots go back to the late Roman Empire and the medieval Holy Roman Empire. When the latter went into decline after 1250, there were many proposals to replace it with more effective instruments. As early as the fourteenth century, Pierre Dubois proposed a European Confederation that would be ruled by a European Council composed of "wise, expert and faithful men." In his *Essay Towards the Present and Future Peace of Europe,* William Penn urged the creation of a "European Diet, Parliament, or State." A carefully drawn proposal for European confederation was also advanced by the Abbé St. Pierre, which was clarified and then rebutted by Rousseau. Jeremy Bentham, Henri Saint-Simon, and Victor Hugo each produced his own scheme. As Swann writes, "History is littered with proposals and arrangements which were designed to foster European unity" (Swann 1970, p. 13).

None of these proposals was taken very seriously by political leaders, however. After World War I, the security problem was dealt with on a global rather than a European basis. Nevertheless, in 1923, an Austrian aristocrat, Count Richard Coudenhove-Kalergi, founded a movement for a federalist Pan-European Union with economic as well as security goals. This movement was joined by politicians of current and later fame, such as Eduard Benes, Aristide Briand, Eduard Herriot, Konrad Adenauer, and Georges Pompidou. At the League of Nations in September 1929, Briand proposed a scheme of union that would involve a "confederal" bond between European peoples. Although a "Study Group on European Union" was created in the League of Nations Secretariat, none of these ideas led to governmental action (Urwin 1991, pp. 4–7).

After World War II had left much of Europe in ruins, many national leaders and intellectuals became readier to turn to action. But they differed on whether their union should be an IGO-type entity following the model of the United Nations and its specialized agencies or a stronger federal union that would create a "United States of Europe." The middle road of confederation seems to have been overlooked. As Pinder has pointed out, "many federalists had concentrated on the idea of a federal constitution without giving much thought to the confederal system that was likely to precede it" (Pinder 1991, p. 11). Pinder himself did not go on to give much attention to that system, perhaps reluctant to highlight the extent to which it remained predominantly confederal.

Moreover, the proponents of European unity had originally conceived of a union that would embrace the entire continent, east and west, but the Cold War made that impossible. Thus, the breach between the superpowers not only shattered the hopes for an all-European union, it led to the formation in 1949 of the North Atlantic Treaty Organization (NATO). Militarily, North America and the major states of Western Europe were linked in defense against the Soviet Union and other states of Eastern Europe for four decades. The nature of these links left little latitude for the formation of a separate West European security community.

The states that remained outside the Soviet sphere were themselves divided on the form that unification should take. For example, Britain and the Scandinavian countries disagreed with France, Italy, West Germany, Belgium, Netherlands, and Luxembourg over the extent to which their economies should be integrated on the international trade front. The Six gradually became convinced that, if they wanted meaningful political/economic union, they had to proceed on their own. In 1950, they joined together for the first time to create the European Coal and Steel Community (ECSC). That community had a political as well as an economic purpose, that of making a war between France and Germany not only "unthinkable but materially impossible" (Swann 1970, p. 19).

But its political effect went far beyond that; it embarked the Six on an experiment in which they sought to create the beginnings of a federal state. Indeed, the Schumann Plan for the ECSC declared bluntly that "Europe must be organized on a federal basis" (Urwin 1991, p. 46). It sought to begin this process by endowing a High Authority composed of international officials "with substantial direct powers which could be exerted without the prior approval of the Council of Ministers" (Swann 1970, p. 20).

Much was made of these "supranational" powers of the High Authority, though those vested with them were too wise to exercise them freely. When they ventured to use them at all, they were careful to keep one eye on the reaction of member governments. Nonetheless, Europeanists such as Jean Monnet regarded the ECSC as a significant first step towards federation.

In focusing on a federal goal, the founders of ECSC frightened the British and the Scandinavians deepening the gulf between what became known as the Six and the Seven (Britain, Sweden, Denmark, Norway, Portugal, Austria, and Switzerland). The latter were reluctant to join the Six in establishing a full-scale customs union with a common tariff barrier, but they might have been persuaded to do so if the limited (confederal-type) character of the Union had been made plain from the outset. Instead, they formed a rival European Free Trade Association (EFTA).

The prospect that there might be a supranational authority "that is utterly undemocratic and is responsible to nobody" helped Prime Minister Attlee persuade Parliament that Britain should stay aloof from the ECSC (Swann 1970, p. 20). This is all the more ironical for, as Pinder points out, Jean Monnet seems not to have anticipated how much the ECSC's Council of Ministers "would come to dominate the politics of the Community, as the political structures of member states came to assert themselves against the realization of the federal idea" (Pinder 1991, p. 6).

The practical experience of the ECSC soon showed the extent of its founders' miscalculations. Its member governments were quite willing to transfer unpopular decisions to the High Authority for action, while the latter responded by behaving cautiously and by exploring what steps member governments were ready to accept. Far from handing down orders, that Authority was involved from the outset in mediating conflicts of interest and disputes among its competing members. The limits of supranationality were revealed in 1959 when an overproduction of coal led the High Authority to declare that it constituted a "manifest crisis." But only the Special Council of Ministers could proclaim such a crisis, and it was unable to muster the qualified majority that was required to do so. The High Authority sought to deal with the problem by imposing production quotas and import controls but encountered Italian, Dutch, and German resistance, while in France President de Gaulle denied that supranational bodies had the right to acquire and use emergency powers. Urwin writes,

Out of the disarray into which the ECSC had fallen, the High Authority attempted to move forward to a general agreement on energy, but it was not until April 1964 [i.e., five years later] that the Council of Ministers eventually agreed to a document. While the High Authority hailed it as an energy equivalent of the common agricultural policy to which the new Economic Community was committed, the document essentially confirmed the superiority of national interests. It essentially involved the the coordination of existing national practices, especially on subsidies, and any element of a jointly financed common policy under the direction of the High Authority was simply absent. (Urwin 1991, p. 54; see pp. 51–57 for Urwin's full account of these events.)

Little more was heard of the High Authority's supranational powers.

At the same time, the ECSC paved the way for the European Economic Community (EEC). While it did not internationalize the ownership of the means of producing coal and steel, by removing customs duties and quotas it created a common market in those products. This was an approach that could be extended to other products. The success of this approach generated confidence in its viability among the leaders of the six member states as well as in ECSC's modus operandi of solving specific problems by acting in stages, each of which had a binding deadline.

Moreover, under the ECSC's aegis, a Court of Justice began the long process of establishing a European jurisprudence; governments could appeal to it against the ECSC's decisions affecting them. By rejecting most of these appeals and by gaining acceptance of most of its decisions, the Court offset to some extent the obvious weaknesses of the central machinery. It built up a body of case law, which conferred on that machinery an authority and legitimacy that served as a foundation for the future development of a true community. Although the scope of the ECSC was very narrow, it was the first European body empowered to act in a sphere where its member states had powerful competing interests.

The Rome treaty, adopted in 1958, established the European Economic Community. It set the goal of abolishing all tariff, quota, and other nontariff barriers to trade amongst the Six, with time limits set for removing the trade and quantitative barriers. It also provided for free movement of workers, enterprises, and capital throughout the Community and contained chapters on agricultural, transport, and competition policy. Its modus operandi was patterned after the one employed for coal and steel by the ECSC.

The EEC's institutions also paralleled those of the ECSC. For example, it shared the latter's Assembly (which had mainly advisory powers) and its Court of Justice. But, as Pinder writes: "The significant difference lay, however, in the relationship between the EEC's executive and its ministerial Council. Instead of High Authority, the new executive was called the Commission; and this reflected a weakening of the federalist impulse and a strengthening of the ministers representing member governments over against the independent European executive" (Pinder 1991, p. 8). However, this was widely regarded as a temporary expedient. The Commission, the Assembly, and the Court were still viewed, at least by Europeanists, as nascent federal entities.

The "Ups and Downs" of Political Integration

Paul-Henri Spaak (Prime Minister of Belgium) and Walter Hallstein (the first President of the Commission) were correct in thinking that economic integration could not be achieved unless accompanied by a requisite degree of political integration. Spaak regarded the European Community (EC) "as a stage on the way to political union," while Hallstein went so far as to suggest that "we are not integrating economies, we are integrating politics" (Urwin 1991, p. 76).[3] But they failed to notice that the political relations of the EC's member states were being integrated in a pattern more characteristic of confederal than of federal unions.

That pattern is implicit in the on-again, off-again history of the European Community. It began on an upbeat note in its earliest years, roughly from 1958 to 1962. France, Germany, and Italy, its three large-state members, were led by men who were eager to make the Community a success. The collapse of the fourth republic in France in 1958 and the emergence of the fifth republic with de Gaulle at the helm did not prove an obstacle, at least not at first. On the contrary, France accepted its role as EEC's leader, and West Germany the role of "supporting second" as its ticket to regain European respectability. De Gaulle had a good relationship with Adenauer.

It was also an era of economic prosperity, which made it easier for the Community to meet its timetable of targets for reducing internal tariffs and for building a common external tariff wall. Politically, too, there was a basis for unity in the fact that the Community began as, and for some time remained, a creation of the like-minded Christian Democratic parties in power in its member states. This period reached its high point when Britain applied for membership in 1961. Even though this first application was rejected, EFTA's standing was undermined by the mere fact that its leading member was ready to join the EC.

The Community's first major crisis came with de Gaulle's attempt to remodel it as a *Europe des Patries.* His plan would have turned it into an IGO-type union with France as its hegemon. This was correctly seen by the other five as a step backward, and they consequently rejected it. On the other hand, Hallstein had grandiose ambitions for the Community's executive, the Commission, whose powers he aimed to increase. Moving in this direction, he was seeking to provide the Community (and the Commission) with independent sources of income and to turn the Assembly into a full-scale Parliament to which he would report and which might be more easily managed by the executive. He reportedly even confided to journalists that, as the Commission's President, he could be regarded as a kind of European Prime Minister (Urwin 1991, p. 103). Thus, de Gaulle wanted to turn the Community into an IGO-type body controlled mainly by France, while Hallstein was eager to jumpstart a full-scale federation for which the national leaders, whatever their rhetoric, were not ready.

Not surprisingly, pursuit of these two incompatible goals soon led to a serious crisis. Hallstein sought to bargain with de Gaulle by offering him a package that included both an agricultural plan that favored French farmers financially and his own proposals for strengthening the Commission and the Assembly. At a press conference in September 1965, de Gaulle responded by attacking the Commission for illegally attempting to usurp powers that belonged to national governments and announced that France's seat in the Council of Ministers would remain empty until this package was withdrawn. He denounced the Commission as "some sort of technocratic body of elders, stateless and irresponsible" (Urwin 1991, p. 111). For a time, however, the other five members continued to support the package, which would have entrusted the Assembly with certain financial powers over the budget. The crisis of "the Empty Chair" dragged on for some months.

In the end, the five had to recognize France's de facto veto power, and an agreement called the "Luxembourg Compromise" was worked out. This so-called Compromise was in reality almost a total victory for de Gaulle. It provided that where very important interests of one or more partners were at stake, unanimous decisions must be found. In practice, if not in law, this meant the reintroduction of a unanmity rule in most of the decision-making of the Council of Ministers. Urwin speculates that this safeguard was "almost as welcome to the other five as it was to France" (Urwin 1991, p. 115).

Hallstein's ambitious proposals were not pursued, and his Commission was soon being blamed for provoking the crisis. At the end of his term, he resigned knowing that French opposition would block his reappointment as President. Moreover, the French farmers obtained the subsidies that they had been promised.

The Compromise confirmed the predominantly confederal character of the union that had been created by the Rome Treaty. The primacy of the member state governments was upheld, and the Commission and its President discovered that if they were to lead the Community, it would have to be by pleasing rather than by challenging those governments. They could still produce "packages" to move the Community forward, but not ones involving their own self-empowerment.

In the end, however, de Gaulle could not stop the Community's forward progress or keep Britain from joining it. No more was heard of the French model for an IGO-type community. In January 1963, de Gaulle had bluntly blackballed Britain's application as, under the Rome Treaty, any member was entitled to do. But his manner of doing so, and his obvious vindictiveness towards an important fellow-European state, violated the spirit of that Treaty, which was inclusive rather than exclusive. Moreover, by this time, applications for association by other EFTA members were also pending, and these were likewise stopped in their tracks.

France's five partners were saddened and annoyed by this action which had come upon them unawares. In 1967, Britain reapplied for admission, only to face a second de Gaulle rejection. This time, however, Britain did not withdraw its application, but simply left it pending until the general stepped down from office. Negotiations for the entry of Britain, Denmark, Ireland, and Norway into the Community took place during 1971, and the first three became members on January 1, 1972. Norway stayed out because the proposal to join the Community was voted down in a popular referendum. For the first time, the tenuousness of the EC's popular support was demonstrated.

In the aftermath of the 1965 crisis, the Community resumed its forward progress on the basis of its existing institutional structure as a union of sovereign states. The Six began to act as a bloc in trade negotiations, and the magnitude of their combined economies gave them additional clout in the conclusion of trade agreements, for example, in the Kennedy and Tokyo Rounds of the GATT negotiations. It also gave them a veto power over much of the decision-making of the IMF (Lister 1984, p. 99). In the Third World, they concluded accords giving reciprocal preferences to their former African colonies, a process that was to pick up momentum in the years ahead, especially when Britain became a member. By 1969, 76 countries were represented diplomatically in Brussels, though the Council of Ministers barred the Commission from being represented in foreign capitals.

Foreign policy and external relations were coordinated, if at all, by the Council of Ministers, but at that stage were more often handled at the national level. In the UN, for example, the members acted independently about as often as they adopted a common position (Urwin 1991, p. 131).

As the EC flourished, the leaders of the member states, who had always been involved from afar in its decision-making, wanted to institutionalize their role. The sectoral preoccupations of a Council of Ministers that met with varying sets of ministers (agriculture, transport, finance, etc.) created the necessity for some higher-level authority to deal with problems and to resolve policy conflicts that could not be settled at the ministerial level. This need provided the opening that they sought. Ironically, it was de Gaulle who had earlier suggested that there be regular meetings of heads of government, but his suggestion had been rejected. Now it was revived by his French successors. Such meetings began to be held at irregular intervals but not at first as an institutional part of the EC itself.

At President Pompidou's instigation, an EC summit was held in The Hague in 1969. It was highly successful, paving the way for the EC's enlargement and setting the precedent for a new style of decision-making that would accelerate that community's evolution in the 1970s. It also highlighted the place where power was concentrated in the EC, in the heads of member governments acting in consensus. They obviously enjoyed reaching agreements that had eluded their ministerial subordinates. Their satisfaction was registered in the quick succession of summit meetings that followed: in

Paris in 1972, in Copenhagen in 1973, and again in Paris in 1974. At the first Paris summit, the heads of the three countries due to join the Community were also present.

In 1974, "summitry" was institutionalized by giving it a name, the European Council. Far from being "Prime Minister of Europe," the President of the Commission was merely given the right to attend the European Council's meetings. In a confederal setting, however, he can still exercise leadership if he is both knowledgeable and persuasive. The Council meets twice a year, and its presidency rotates every six months, which enables the leaders of even the EC's smaller members to occupy the office (and thus to become centers of European economic diplomacy) at fairly frequent intervals. However, Margaret Thatcher oversimplified matters when she declared in 1981 that there was no such a thing as a separate Community interest, merely a compound of the interests of separate national states. Europe had common interests vis-à-vis the rest of the world, and its national leaders were as well able to discover them as any other body of legislators.

But these leaders were also given to making resounding pronouncements that pleased their Europeanist constituents but often had little other impact. Giscard d'Estaing, Pompidou's successor, and Helmut Schmidt of West Germany led the European Council towards a more practical and broader approach whereby it dealt with all matters of joint concern both within the EC's framework and outside it.

The European Council operated for its first decade at the heart of the EC, without being formally a part of it. When it was made a legal instrument of the EC by the Single European Act of 1985, no attempt was made to define its powers which remain open-ended though presumably limited by the provisions of the Community's treaty-constitution. This modus operandi is typical of confederal-type unions but atypical of federal ones.

Once established, the European Council became the EC's principal power center. It also became a political court of appeal, and because of its ultimate authority many more matters were passed up to it for final decision. Yet at least one summit was, in the words of James Callaghan "strong on discussion, not so strong on decisions" (quoted in Urwin 1991, p. 178, with regard to the 1977 London summit). National leaders were sometimes torn between defending national interests and honoring their commitment to further European integration. In searching for consensus-type decisions, the heads of government were often no more successful than their ministers.

Moreover, in their capacity as heads of state or government, national leaders tended to pay more attention to political than to legal constraints. This may be useful when political crises arise that threaten the Union's future. On the whole, the involvement of friendly national leaders in the EC's decision-making has advanced rather than set back the cause of European integration.

Problems of Economic Integration

On the economic front, however, there have also been many ups and downs. True integration has been like a chimera in the desert, first appearing within easy reach and then receding behind the horizon. This has been particularly in evidence in the monetary realm. The achievement of any substantial degree of monetary union has so far eluded the EC's member governments.

The breakdown of the Bretton Woods system of fixed exchange rates in 1971, and its replacement by the present global system of floating rates, greatly increased the need to establish stable exchange rates among the currencies of EC member states. In the simpler times of the mid–nineteenth century, the member states of the Zollverein had been able to set fixed relationships among their several currencies almost from the outset of their customs union. But in modern economies where government regulates and manipulates so many key economic variables on the basis of national needs and popular demands, this is much harder to do. Efforts to stabilize exchange rates are now apt to be thwarted by currency speculators and their unending search for quick profits.

In 1970, on the eve of the collapse of the Bretton Woods system, the EC embarked on the first of what turned out to be three successive plans to establish monetary union among its members. It was a simple plan involving the coordination of short-term policies, intensifying central bank cooperation, and developing a capacity to provide medium-term financial aid. Efforts to adapt it to the new world of floating exchange rates involved the creation of the so-called snake in the tunnel, which permitted a maximum fluctuation among Community currencies of no more than 2.25%, or 1.125% in each direction. These efforts proved unsuccessful. Monetary union proved to be incompatible with what Urwin describes as a Western Europe "divided into hard and soft currency groups, each with different problems and looking for different salvations" (Urwin 1991, p 157) The snake worked only for the hard-currency members, while the others had to fall back on successive devaluations.

A second plan, adopted in 1979, set up a "European Monetary System" with a medium-term outlook as a first step towards monetary union. Its framers acknowledged that, from time to time, currency realignments would probably be needed, and the new system was designed to make such realignments less frequent and more orderly. The Council of Ministers was empowered to authorize such realignments for members whose currencies showed persistent weakness. In addition, a limited-purpose European currency unit (the "ECU") was established as a second step towards monetary union. While this scheme did not succeed in solving the underlying problem of intermittent currency crises caused by speculation against weak currencies, there were fewer such crises in the later 1980s, and restrained macroeconomic policies were helpful in maintaining currency alignments (Urwin 1991, pp. 182–85; Pinder 1991, pp. 128–34).

Convergent economic policies are a prerequisite for monetary union and their absence remained a roadblock to further progress. A third plan that reflected the determination and ingenuity of those committed to forward movement was accordingly produced. Adopted as the centerpiece of the Maastricht Treaty in 1992, it involved far-reaching undertakings by 10 of the 12 partners to coordinate closely their economic and monetary policies. It contained transitional provisions that would allow the partners to bring their monetary union into force gradually over the second half of the 1990s. The main elements of this plan are briefly described below (Pinder 1991, pp. 137–44; Articles 105–109m EEC;[4] Treaty on European Union 1993, Protocol No. 3, pp. 517–54).

The difficulties encountered by the EC's partners in coordinating their monetary policies illustrate the problems that confederal bodies face in the realm of policy coordination in general. This is understandable, for it is far easier for them to agree on specific steps whose impact may be weighed in advance than to commit their countries to the long-term courses of action and continuing expenditures needed to reach common policy goals.

The Common Agricultural Policy (CAP) provides another example of this weakness. The EC's customs union needed to cover agricultural products, yet its members were unwilling to leave their farmers at the mercy of world prices. The original price support system was based on a series of complex "package deals" on which the Six were finally able to agree. However, supporting artificial prices soon involved them in skyrocketing costs, for subsidies led to chronic overproduction of such commodities as grains, wine, and dairy products. This in turn led to complex arrangements to deal with surpluses. Inevitably, the benefits and costs of this policy fell unequally upon the various members in accordance with the size and composition of their farm sectors. Also, European farmers were benefited at the expense of European consumers for whom the policy meant both higher food prices and higher taxes to pay for crop subsidies and for storing surpluses.

While unitary states and federations face similar problems, in a confederation, neither the central authorities nor the governmental joint councils may be strong enough to resist powerful pressure groups with crossnational ties in many of its member states. The inability of the EC's states to control the costs of the CAP reveals the inherent risks, in such looser unions of states, of providing large-scale subsidies that may benefit the partners unequally. Those governments that consider their peoples to be net losers in these transfers of resources are likely to complain loudly.

Because the original six all had important farm sectors, these inequities did not emerge very clearly at first. However, the cost of the farm supports was soon consuming about two-thirds of the Community's expenditures. Their steady increase under a European Agricultural Guarantee and Guidance Fund, which set price floors but did not control the rising costs of subsidies, led to repeated budgetary crises. While recognizing the need to impose ceilings on these subsidies, governments were prevented by their farm lobbies from proceeding very far in that direction.

When it joined the Community in 1972, Britain was "odd man out," since its industrial interests had long prevailed over its agricultural ones. Thus, its relatively few remaining farmers had already made the painful transition being faced by European farmers. It was bound to clash with its Community partners on this issue, since the CAP was for the founding members an almost sacrosanct achievement. For the British, on the other hand, CAP was merely a drain on the treasury for payments to countries some of which enjoyed higher living standards than Britain.

Beginning in 1975, the Labor government complained regularly about its financial burden both in terms of the scale of its contribution and of what it received in return for that contribution. It wanted strict limits placed on the CAP subsidies. Britain was more or less alone, and at first its partners tended to ignore its protests and demands.

Matters worsened when the Thatcher government entered into office in 1979. Margaret Thatcher was not interested in token or cosmetic concessions, and angered her German and French colleagues, Helmut Schmidt and Giscard d'Estaing, by bluntly demanding Britain's money back. The dispute led to increasing strains within the European Council. In 1982, the principle of a British rebate was conceded, but was accompanied by lengthy and acrimonious bargaining over the details. In May 1982, the British responded by vetoing a package of target food prices. This was a stern action, because the practice had grown up that the veto power would not normally be used as a method of settling disagreements over secondary matters. In exasperation, its partners set aside the Luxembourg Compromise on the ground that this was a matter that could be decided by a qualified majority vote. This produced the second great crisis in EC's history.

Urwin describes what happened next:

Despite the angry words, the shock of what happened forced the two sides to withdraw somewhat from the brink. The British reaction was muted and philosophical, possibly in part because of its need for EC support for its Falklands policy. For the other side, foreign ministers hurriedly agreed in principle a temporary financial compensation to Britain for the current year, with the additional costs being borne by West Germany. In addition, Britain was promised a review for subsequent years within a few months. (Urwin 1991, p. 203)

These conciliatory moves eventually led in 1984 to a Fontainebleau Compromise to match that of Luxembourg. A long-term annual "corrective mechanism" for a budget rebate to Britain was accepted and immediately implemented. Under its terms, that annual rebate would be based on 66%

of the difference between its value-added tax (VAT) contributions and Britain's share of EC expenditure. In return, Britain agreed that the level of the VAT contribution could be raised to 1.4%. The Fontainebleau Compromise demonstrated anew that, in a confederal setting, only the leaders of the member states, acting outside of Community law, can deal with crises that threaten to break up their union.

All this excitement did not address the problem of an agricultural policy that produced huge surpluses of farm products that had to be stored at Community expense and somehow disposed of. Storage costs rose while farm incomes, particularly of smaller farmers, did not. Even with higher VAT contributions, the EC remained in a state of perennial financial crisis. In 1989, the budget had to be augmented by further contributions of as much as 1.2% of the EC's combined VAT receipts. Finally, there was agreement on a package of more-than-cosmetic reforms produced by Commission President Delors. But a recent article, "Snout Slimmed, Not for Long," indicates that a more far-reaching revision of the CAP is needed. Its annual cost is rising from 31 to 40 billion ECUs in the 1992–1996 period, and upward pressures are expected to grow in the years ahead (*The Economist* 1995a). The EC's one "success" in policy-making may reveal the outer limits of the capacity of looser unions of states to manage activities that involve substantial redistributions of resources.

Such skepticism is reinforced when one looks at the search for common policies in other sectors. Regional policy—the laudable effort to help backward regions within the various member states—has gone furthest, but the shortage of Community funds has greatly limited its scale. Moreover, it raises all of the redistribution problems of agriculture, with each state vying for the limited funds that remain available. Since the amounts received even by the EC's poorer members are relatively small, they tend to be subsumed in national regional programs. Thus the EC's role is limited to supplying grants, leaving it to each state to decide how they will be spent. Also, because most members have been given quotas, the funds do not always go to the poorest areas that need them most. The experience with both agricultural and regional subsidies confirms that in confederal unions it is especially hard to control and rationalize redistributions of resources.

Policy-making in other sectors has also not fared very well. The Community is still without the transport policy that was specifically called for in the Rome Treaty though some progress has been made in lowering transport costs. Also, EC's efforts in the field of social policy have been very limited, focusing on youth employment in backward regions. Progress has likewise been limited in such spheres as fisheries, steel, and industrial policy. One writer sums up the situation, saying that "while there is a policy world within the EC, it is a world of uneven topology" (Urwin 1991, p. 193).

Step-by-Step Expansion of the Community

The EC's founders envisaged a union that would be open to all European states. Yet, this has meant that European integration has been complicated by frequent increases in the number of partners. This "too-many-partners" problem is intensified if the new partners are economic "misfits" in the Community or if they increase its level of sociocultural diversity, thus pushing it down rather than up the homogeneity-heterogeneity axis. The EC's "too many languages" also increases with the admission of new members. No federation or confederation has ever had to cope with such a multiplicity of languages.

Thus, enlargement of the Six to Nine, then to Twelve and more recently to Fifteen has been attended by a number of painful adjustments. This is particularly true with regard to the economically less developed members, Greece (1981) and Spain and Portugal (1986).

The founding members have long been aware of the risks of enlargement. They refused to allow the three southern states to enter the Community so long as they were ruled by dictators. However, once Franco and the others had been replaced by constitutional governments, negotiations for entry resumed, though they were spun out over many years—six for Greece and nine for Spain and Portugal. In the case of Greece, the Commission had to prepare one of its "packages" to deal with the special economic and social problems involved in its integration in the EC. Clearly, the entry of these new members brought new obstacles to the framing of common trade, monetary, and agricultural policies that would be economically sound, politically implementable and financially acceptable.

A further large-scale expansion of the Union threatens to bring even greater problems of adjustment. Pending applicants, mostly central and east European states, have long been isolated from the European economy into which their economies would now have to be integrated. Moreover, admittance of many more partners would further complicate decision-making in the European Council and the Council of Ministers, and would portend further enlargements of the memberships of the Commission, the Parliament and the Court of Justice. There is a clear risk that at some point overenlargement may make the present union unmanageable as well as foreclose any realistic prospect of reaching the goal of an "ever closer union of the European peoples," proclaimed in the Rome Treaty's Preamble.

Pressures For Forming A Closer Union

In the late 1970s and early 1980s, many supporters of European integration felt that the time had come to press forward towards that "ever closer union." The quest for closer political union took the form of proposals to restructure Community institutions in an increasingly federal mold in order to reduce what was felt to be the undue influence of national governments in Community affairs. The goal of Europeanists was to strengthen what they regarded as the "federal" bodies of the EC, that is, the Commission, the Parliament, and the Court. This was to be accompanied by a downgrading of the authority of what they saw as its "IGO" bodies, the European Council and the Council of Ministers.

Many such proposals, beginning with the Tindemans Report in 1976, called for an independent executive responsible to a parliament composed of two chambers, one popularly elected and the other appointed by governments. Although it appeared many times on the agenda of the European Council, this report was never even discussed by the national leaders. Instead, in late 1978, the Council set up a committee of "Three Wise Men," which came up with proposals calling for the Commission to be given more authority, and urging that majority voting be used more often in the Council of Ministers. The national leaders welcomed the Wise Men's report as "a rich source of ideas and suggestions," but by their inaction showed that it was, as Urwin puts it, "a source from which they were unwilling to drink" (Urwin 1991, p. 220).

The proposal for the more frequent use of majority voting made in that report was not incompatible with confederal principles so long as state representatives were the voters and there was weighted voting. The reluctance of national leaders to go even that far showed that they were not yet ready to liberalize the EC's institutions even within a confederal framework.

Still, pressures for progress kept surfacing, and the leaders responded by toying with possible reforms. For example, the foreign ministers of Italy and West Germany came up with another plan in the early 1980s in the form of a draft European Act and a draft declaration on economic integration. This plan called for more progress on the policy front, this time in foreign affairs (an area where the Swiss, Dutch, and American confederations had been able from the outset to present a common face to the outside world). However, they also provided for budgetary increases and majority voting, which frightened some leaders and ultimately led to the entire package being shelved.

However, in June 1983, the European Council was moved to issue "A Solemn Declaration on European Union," in which it recognized its own responsibility for providing a general political impetus to the construction of Europe by defining the approaches needed to further that construction, and by issuing general political guidelines for the European Communities and for European Political Co-operation (EPC). This proclamation of their joint authority did not foreshadow the readiness of the national leaders to be replaced by a popular parliament! Instead, by emphasizing its own political centrality, the European Council seemed to be ruling out any major overhaul of the EC's institutions or any enhancement of the Commission's powers (Urwin 1991, p. 223).

Next, under the veteran Europeanist Altiero Spinelli, a draft treaty on European Union was produced for adoption by the European Parliament. It would have greatly expanded the powers of the EP and the Commission while correspondingly limiting those of the European Council and the Council of Ministers. The latter would have become a Council of the Union and would have shared legislative responsibility with the EP. The Parliament would have been given the power to raise revenue and to adopt the budget jointly with the Council, whose powers to control the passage of legislation would have been substantially reduced.

This draft treaty was overwhelmingly endorsed by the EP, but was never seriously considered by the two Councils. There was clearly insufficient political support for such far-reaching changes in the Community's institutions. However, it remains the best available summing-up of the goals being pursued by the Europeanists.

Nonetheless, while rejecting what they saw as the EP's over-ambitious initiative, the European Council was again impelled to take seriously the political pressures behind it. Thus, what had happened persuaded the national leaders to return to the question of political union and to consider how the Rome Treaty might be updated in the light of a quarter century's experience. The Council established two groups for this purpose, a Committee for a People's Europe and an ad hoc group of "personal representatives" of the heads of government.

The Committee for a People's Europe tackled for the first time the underlying problem: The EP's supporters were handicapped by the poor voter turnout for EP elections and public apathy (and among some groups antipathy) towards European integration. So long as this was true, federalization was out of the question. The Committee's task, therefore, was to develop practical symbols that would help nurture the growth of a European identity and feelings of allegiance among the peoples of its member states. While it was recognized that this was bound to be a long-term process, it remained a precondition for the formation of a federal-type union.

The other Committee was composed mainly of persons who looked at matters from a European, rather than a national, viewpoint. Not surprisingly, they repackaged many of the suggestions that had been rejected earlier, proposing to strengthen the Commission and the EP and to relegate the European Council to a strategic (i.e., marginal) role in which it would focus on external affairs and be kept aside from the mainstream decision-making of the EC. Also, not surprisingly, the national leaders were not eager to occupy the back seats being offered them.

This time, however, the reform of the Community became, in an unprecedented way, the central issue at their June 1985 meeting in Milan. While the Committee's proposals were rejected, the national leaders decided to convene a special conference on EC reform in September 1985. This conference finally produced politically viable reform proposals, which were adopted by the European Council in December 1985 as the Single European Act (the SEA). This Act opened the second stage of the long-term process of establishing meaningful union among the European states. It signalled an uptick in the Community's affairs that has continued through the adoption and ratification of the Maastricht Treaty.

The SEA refocused attention on the original goals of the Rome Treaty, which were primarily economic in character. A customs union and the abolition of quantitative quotas in internal Community trade had long been in place. But a number of nontariff and nonquantitative barriers to trade remained largely intact. These barriers had not only prevented the development of a true common market; they had increasingly offset the benefits derived from the customs union. The main thrust of the SEA was the launching in 1985 of an all-out campaign known as "Europe 1992" to root them out. (For details, see Calingaert 1988; Cecchini 1988; Crouch and Marquand 1990.)

The SEA committed the member states to creating a fully integrated internal market by the end of 1992 in which persons, goods, and capital would move freely throughout the Union under conditions identical to those existing within a member state. It was agreed that such an integrated market would benefit consumers and put Europe in a stronger competitive position vis-à-vis American and Japanese competition, goals on which all the EC's member governments and peoples could agree. In fact, attainment of those goals would require concerted action by the partners in many spheres, such as taxation, exchange rates, industrial, labor and environmental policies, and standard-setting. It would require them to find a line where the needs of a common economic union left off and the residual right of each member state to go its own social and cultural way took over.

The SEA was not particularly helpful in finding this line, for it was largely silent on how to achieve fixed exchange rates, which are essential to any economic union. At the same time, it did involve the EC in spheres such as health policy, which are not essential. In this respect, the SEA was, like so many Community documents, an uneasy compromise between the Europeanists who supported the transfer of many sovereign powers to Brussels, and the nationalists who wanted as many as possible of them to be exercised solely in national capitals.

The revitalization of the campaign for economic union was accompanied by modest changes in the institutional arrangements of the EC. The European Council remained firmly in the driver's seat, but it was agreed that the practice of decision-taking by qualified majorities should be widened in the Council of Ministers. Unanimity would henceforth be required only for the most important decisions such as admission of new members and for the enunciation of general principles for new policies. Most other nonprocedural matters were to be decided upon by the weighted voting system, which gave the five larger members 48 of 76 votes, with 54 votes required for the adoption of any proposal.

This trend to replace the unanimity requirement by weighted voting and special majority requirements had already been set in motion in the Rome Treaty. These modest revisions in the decision-making system were designed to keep a single large state from blocking legislation. They were in line with the typical confederal decision-making provisions set forth in Chapter 1. These provisions are designed to require a preponderance of support before major decisions are taken while at the same time preventing hold-out states from blocking all progress.

The SEA contains many concessions to the Europeanists. Specifically, the EP's powers were extended by installing assent and cooperation procedures that involved it more deeply in the enactment of certain categories of legislation. It also confirmed the Commission's powers to implement the regulations and directives laid down by the Council of Ministers, in cooperation with the national authorities in countries affected by them. It extended the jurisdiction of the European Court of Justice, and the busy judges were assisted by the creation of a Court of First Instance. At the same time, it gave the European Council a treaty status although it failed to define its powers.

Finally, the SEA codified the informal arrangements whereby the partners sought to formulate and carry out a common European foreign policy. A permanent secretariat was given to the 12 foreign ministers for that purpose, and they were supposed to meet regularly within the framework of the Council of Ministers. It was also provided that the partners should collaborate more closely on defense and security issues. The foregoing measures, taken together, did constitute a major step towards closer union.

The Single European Act was followed by the adoption in February 1992 of the "Treaty on European Union," the so-called Maastricht Treaty, which constitutes a landmark in the history of Europe's unification. Anyone who has ventured to read and digest the 253–page treaty realizes that a very complex political entity is in the process of formation.

The Treaty comprises a legal framework within which federal and confederal features are again mixed together in an unprecedented way. The terms of the Treaty constitute yet another uneasy compromise between Europeanists and nationalists. Only the barest outline of its provisions can be given here.

Like the SEA, the Maastricht Treaty is primarily directed towards attainment of a fully integrated internal market. The key addition is its plan for a comprehensive economic and monetary union. The economic union provides for a "closer coordination" and a convergence of national economic policies on the basis of "broad guidelines," which are to include specified ceilings on the rate of inflation, long-term interest rates, and government deficits. It empowers the Council of Ministers to impose a wide range of sanctions on member states that do not adhere to these guidelines (Article 104c EEC).

Successful economic policy coordination would in turn provide the basis for price stability and monetary union, which would soon enable the member states to establish exchange rates at which the various national currencies will be "irrevocably fixed and at which irrevocably fixed rate the Ecu shall be substituted for these currencies (Article 109 1 (4) EEC). A European System of Central Banks, comprising a European Central Bank and national central banks, would manage the new monetary system. It would have the exclusive right to authorize the issuance of banknotes; it would also hold and manage official reserves, conduct foreign exchange operations, and promote the smooth operation of payments systems.

The Treaty provides for these reforms to take place in stages over six to ten years, with the Council determining which member states meet the economic criteria and are, therefore, ready to join the monetary system and when there are a sufficient number of member states to allow that system as a whole to be activated. The Treaty indicates that this may be as soon as early 1997 and not later than January 1, 1999. Britain, Denmark, and Sweden are likely to stand aloof from the new monetary union. The Treaty was scarcely adopted when some community members underwent a number of exchange rate crises and devaluations, confirming that national economic policies need to be better coordinated before a monetary union of this kind will become feasible.

It also remains to be seen whether a Governing Council composed of independent central bankers will be allowed to run a "European System of Central Banks" with wide monetary powers without (following the precedents of the German Bundesbank and the U.S. Federal Reserve Bank) either national or central political supervision.

Once again, the Treaty widens the scope of the Community in spheres where the linkage to economic union is nonexistent or at best ambiguous; for example, in such areas as education, consumer protection, justice, and "home affairs." In these fields, the new functions being assigned to it seem, on the whole, to have more of an IGO than even a confederal character. But these entries into areas outside the Union's original economic sphere raise complex questions of where the borders between European and national governance should be. If they are eventually elevated into binding legal obligations, they would bring the EU's regulatory powers into what might be regarded as the last strongholds of member-state self-governance.

In an effort to lay such fears to rest, the Maastricht Treaty offers the concept of "subsidiarity." This is defined as limiting the Community's capacity to act in areas that do not fall within its exclusive competence to situations where the objectives of the proposed action can be better achieved by the member states acting together. However, it may prove anything but easy to apply this definition to specific cases!

The Maastricht Treaty did not alter in any fundamental way the ultimate authority that the two councils have over the policies that the Union adopts and over the activities that it carries out jointly. The European Council is now legally empowered to provide the necessary impetus for the Union's development and to define its political guidelines (Article D). Despite many provisions designed to enhance Parliament's decision-making powers, it is difficult to imagine the national leaders voluntarily subordinating themselves (or their ministers) to elected parliamentarians from their own countries or to the persons whom they have selected to take part in the work of the Commission.

It is still much too early to predict how the European Union will evolve in the years and decades ahead, and there are likely to be many unexpected twists and turns. On the whole, Europeanists were disappointed by the concessions that had to be made to nationalists in the Treaty. They will, however, have another chance to move the Union in a direction more to their liking at still another intergovernmental conference in 1996.

The adoption of the Treaty has been followed by a sense of malaise with regard to the future evolution of the Union. This letdown is only partly attributable to the narrow margins by which it won the approval of the French and Danish electorates, the foot-dragging of the British, and the monetary crises that quickly cast doubt on the proposals for creating a single currency. The optimism of the previous eight years has been followed by feelings of disillusionment.

For example, Cavazza and Pelanda conclude, sadly, that "the final destination of Europe will be something more than an alliance but something less than a union. We are not about to see a United States of Europe." They worry over whether what "the European people" want is "a *strong alliance* between the European nations, with the right of vote and veto, or a real and proper *fusion* of these states" (Cavazza and Pelanda 1994, pp. 68–69).

Stanley Hoffman writes that "a year and a half later, deep pessimism prevails." He complains that the Treaty, "while marginally increasing the powers of the EP, consolidated the preeminent position of the Council." He wonders why the progress towards more effective and powerful central institutions remains so slow and halting, even though de Gaulle and Thatcher are no longer around to thwart it. He points out "the somewhat Byzantine setup of the Union," which is "a compromise between the inadequate [a strictly intergovernmental operation] and the impossible [a leap to a federal system]" (Hoffman 1994, pp. 1, 2, and 18).

In their prolonged and intense struggle, Europeanists and nationalists alike seem to have overlooked the fact that the SEA and the Maastricht Treaties constitute in their own right seminal developments, though ones that have necessarily had to rely upon a confederal rather than a federal base of popular support. While the structure of the regime now emerging remains more confederal than federal, Cavazza and Pelanda are correct when they describe it as a Union that is hard to categorize (Cavazza and Pelanda 1994, p. 54). Like the men in Philadelphia two centuries earlier (who faced a similar battle between those who wanted and those who feared a greater centralization of power), the framers of the SEA and the Maastricht Treaties have produced a hybrid compromise that is probably the most that can be hoped for, given the degree of popular support that the Union has been able to evoke.

While the present marriage of federal and confederal governmental components may not have been made in heaven, it may prove to be one that both Europeanists and nationalists will be able to live with, and perhaps even come to like, once they get to know it better. At the same time, its translation from treaty text to working reality is bound to take time.

Meanwhile, patience will prove more helpful than a rush to harsh judgments. The complex functions that will have to be carried out by the Council of Ministers working in close tandem with Parliament and Commission go far beyond anything attempted in the classic confederations. The Court of Justice and the Commission remain empowered to enforce the measures that the Council has enacted in a way and to an extent that no previous confederal body could do. As yet, however, we do not know whether the complex and ingenious compromises adopted in Maastricht can be made to work effectively in the various arenas of national and European politics.

Nonetheless, it appears that this novel track is the only one open to Europeanists and to nationalists who support the notion of European Union. Sooner or later, both sides will probably come to terms with the idea that the future of their Union, at least for some years to come, lies in finding ways of reconciling what seem incompatible instruments of governance. This means that down-to-earth Europeanists will need to work in close cooperation with national governments. The SEA and Maastricht Treaties are interesting precisely because they reveal an unexpected potential for federal-type institutions to be incorporated in what is fundamentally a confederal setting. Whether one describes the result with Pinder as "neofederalism" or with the present author as "modern confederalism" may not matter that much if, like the American Constitution of 1789, the revised Treaty of Rome proves an effective vehicle for European governance.

(2) ANALYSIS OF THE MAIN FEATURES OF THE EUROPEAN UNION

The Maastricht Treaty testifies to the extent to which the Europeanists have succeeded in incorporating federal-type arrangements in the Treaty of Rome and its successive revisions and additions. In form, three of the four main institutions of the Union, the Commission, the Parliament, and the Court of Justice have been given many federal features and, increasingly, federal-type powers. But, like the High Authority of the ECSC before them, they must exercise these powers with discretion in a situation where the member states still retain sovereign authority, albeit jointly, in the spheres designated by the Rome Treaty. If seriously challenged by government leaders acting together in either of the two Councils, neither Commission nor Parliament would be likely to prevail, while the judges of the Court of Justice must take care not to peg their prestige to decisions that will undermine the goodwill that they now enjoy in the legislative and judicial organs of the member states. This goodwill testifies to the restraint of those concerned and to the desire of most players to make an innovative and much-needed system of governance work effectively.

In this section, an effort is made to evaluate how well these federal-type institutions have been able to accommodate themselves to the constraints imposed by the confederal-type union in which they carry out their respective functions.

Political Allegiance and Social Integration

Democratic polities are composed of two elements, an infrastructure of popular support or allegiance and a superstructure of governing institutions. As indicated in Chapter 1, unitary states have the sole allegiance of the people living within their borders; federations, their primary allegiance; and confederations, their secondary allegiance. Depending upon the nature of their mandates, intergovernmental organizations can get by with only minimal popular support or even with none at all. It is a plausible assumption that the governmental superstructure of any political association must be adjusted to the popular foundation of support on which it rests, rather than vice versa. Accordingly, let us first examine the infrastructure of popular support available for European Union, and then the governmental structures that have been erected upon it.

In basic matters, people tend to be conservative: They are deeply attached to their language, their religion, their social mores, and their cultural heritage. Above all, they cling to their homeland, which provides them with the security of a familiar terrain and of a larger family in a world overcrowded with strangers.

Therefore, the transition from a familiar "old-shoe" nation-state to a wider European Union is bound to be for many an unwelcome and even a traumatic process. While some Europeanists may hope for a United States of Europe, the mass of Europeans seem instinctively wary of pursuing a goal that might submerge the lives of their children and grandchildren in an American-type homogenized society and culture, even one with a pan-European cast to it.

While collective popular feelings are an elusive subject, few would argue that the European Union now commands the primary allegiance of the great majority of those who live within its borders, or that its 15 peoples form part of a single integrated society and culture. Only dedicated Europeanists are likely to meet the primary allegiance standard, and they are still a relatively small (though growing) elite group that, fortunately for the cause of European unity, has an influence far beyond its numbers.

At the same time, the rank-and-file of Europeans have long had significant transnational ties. For example, Western and Central Europeans have, at least since the time of Charlemagne, formed a distinct group with common religious and political ties springing from the Roman Catholic version of Christianity and the Holy Roman Empire. For centuries, literate Europeans shared a common mode of expression in medieval Latin as well as common cultural origins and products visible to everyone in the architecture, painting, and sculpture in the western and central parts of the continent. In this sense, the peoples of those parts of Europe long enjoyed a degree of cultural homogeneity and a certain social homogeneity as well. Thanks partly to this and to the institutions of the European Community/Union that they have seen springing up around them, Europeans have begun to recognize that they are part of a political in-group that sets them apart from the peoples who live outside it.

What the majority of Europeans are coming to feel, however, is more of a secondary than a primary allegiance. This is confirmed by a recent poll conducted by the EU itself, which indicates that only about one European in seven feels closer allegiance to the Union than to his or her homeland. On the other hand, roughly half the population feels a secondary allegiance to it (*The Economist* 1995c). While it is risky to predict how rapidly popular feelings may evolve in the years ahead, it is only prudent to assume that most Europeans are unlikely to transfer their main allegiance from their respective homelands to the Union any time soon.

Two observers describe the outlook of the European public in the following terms:

A careful reading of European polls over the years conveys the distinct impression that Europeans are aware of the usefulness of living in a great, institutionalized European economic space within which it is possible to work, travel and sell products without barriers and controls at borders, protected and administered by a homogeneous and reciprocally recognized system of sanctions and norms. . . . [The EU is] based far more on banal utilitarian values than on old-fashioned national values. (Cavazza and Pelanda 1994, p. 69)

Thus, what most Europeans want is an economic confederation.

If this is true, popular attitudes are moving part-way in the direction sought by the proponents of European political unity. But the infrastructure of popular support probably has a long way to go before it can sustain a traditional federal-type union with its propensity for increasing political centralization.

By creating a Committee for a People's Europe in 1984, the European leaders recognized that closer political union requires a wider and deeper level of popular understanding and support. And the Treaty on European Union contains many provisions that emanate from that concern. Not the least among them is the pledge by the heads of state in the Preamble of the Treaty, that they desire to "deepen the solidarity between their peoples while respecting their history, their culture and their traditions." This seems to promise that the EU will be a limited union in which each member state would be allowed to retain its individuality and a large measure of control over the main steps to be taken in common.

Beyond that, the Treaty provides that aid may be provided to promote culture and heritage conservation for purposes not in conflict with the common interests of member states (Article 92 (3) EEC). In the provisions on education, it is stipulated that "the responsibility of the Member States for the content of teaching and the organization of education systems and their cultural and linguistic diversity" must be fully respected (Article 126 (1) EEC). Finally, the following statement of cultural policy should reassure national patriots: "The Community shall contribute to the flowering of the cultures of the Member States, while respecting their national and regional diversity and at the same time bringing the common cultural heritage to the fore" (Article 128 (1) EEC).

A modest degree of cooperation among the member states is foreseen in carrying out this policy, though any action on the part of the Union is hemmed in by constraints. The Council of Ministers must act unanimously; incentive measures must not call for any harmonization of the laws and regulations of member states; and other measures must be drafted in the form of recommendations (Title IX "Culture," Article 128 (2) and (5) EEC).

The boldest effort to promote popular support for the Union is found in the sphere of citizenship. Eight new articles establish a citizenship of the Union. Every national of a member state is now ipso facto a citizen of the Union and has rights and duties conferred on him or her by that citizenship. The rights that the Union confers on its citizens are emphasized in these Articles. They include the right to move and reside freely anywhere within its borders; the right of any European citizen to stand in EP and national elections in any member state where he or she happens to reside, under the same conditions as the nationals of that state; the right to petition the EP on matters that fall within its competence; and the right to appeal to an ombudsman, a new office created under the Treaty. The ombudsman was finally appointed in July 1995 (Articles 8–8e, 138d/e all EEC; *The Economist* 1995b).

The European Parliament has always been viewed by Europeanists as an instrument for mobilizing popular support in their sparring with national governments. This goal has been pursued by empowering the peoples of the member states to elect their Euro-MPs by direct universal suffrage in accordance with procedures to be established centrally. The Council, acting after receiving EP's assent, is called upon to recommend such procedures to member states "for adoption in accordance with their respective constitutional requirements." So far, however, the Council has not been able to agree on what those procedures should be (Article 138 (3) EEC, and the 1976 Elections Act).

The involvement of member-state electorates in choosing members of the EP may not be as good a method of engendering popular support for the Union as it must have seemed at first. So far, turnout at the elections has been rather low and tending to move even lower. Moreover, the voting results are often distorted by the ebb and flow of internal party relationships in each country and by those activist groups that can get their supporters to the polls. The Euro-MPs, therefore, sometimes take positions that may be unresponsive to the wishes of national electorates.

Moreover, the fact that (except in Britain) Parliamentarians do not "represent" any constituency or even the country from which they come weakens the standing of what they do as a corporate body. Article 4 of the Elections Act, for example, provides not merely that Euro-MPs cannot be bound by instructions or by any binding mandate, but that they "shall vote on an individual and personal basis." In the absence of close ties with well-defined constituencies, such a parliamentary process is unlikely to promote popular integration. Indeed, it may even retard it if large voting interests within national electorates become offended by positions taken by those whom they consider "their representatives" in Strasbourg.

The development of a secondary allegiance among the peoples of the 15 member states to the European Union seems to be proceeding about as fast as can be expected. It may be helped along by the steps that have been taken to address the worries of those who fear an excessive intrusion of EU regulations and directives in their daily lives. People need to feel that their governments can still protect them against any unwarranted interference on the part of the Brussels officialdom. On the other hand, they will probably support, maybe even enthusiastically, the development of an effective economic and monetary union with a fully integrated internal market so long as they believe that it is enhancing their material well-being.

General Structure of the Union

The general governmental structure of the Union will be dealt with first. The ways in which that structure interacts with its mandate and financing will be analyzed in subsequent sections, followed by brief analyses of the Union's legislative, executive, and judicial arrangements.

In its formal structure, the EU conforms to earlier confederal models. It is a voluntary union of states formed by governments for an unlimited period of time on the basis of a *treaty*-constitution. Even the text adopted at Maastricht is still called a "treaty," which establishes its status as an accord among sovereign states. Like any treaty, it must be ratified by the states that consent to be bound by its provisions. This requirement is also a part of the amendment process: Amendments do not enter into force until they have been "ratified by all the Member States in accordance with their respective constitutional procedures." While membership in the Union is open to any European state, "the conditions of admission and the adjustments to the Treaties . . . which such admission entails shall be the subject of an agreement between the Member States and the applicant State." Of the six earlier confederations, only the Swiss added many new members, and applicant cantons were admitted, if at all, only after the same protracted negotiations and long delays that have exasperated states wishing to join the Community/Union (Articles N, O, Q, and R).

While neither the Rome Treaty nor the revisions made to it in subsequent treaties provide for secession, there is little doubt that a member state wishing to secede from the Union would be allowed to do so. Indeed, an outlying part of a member state, Greenland, has already seceded from it, reducing the Union's territorial extent rather considerably. In this respect, too, the EU falls more in the class of confederations than in that of federations.

But, in its modus operandi, the EU does not resemble any of the earlier confederations. Cavazza and Pelanda contend that the Union "is the potential terrain for the construction of a novel political organism. Since it can not be a federation or a confederation, and not even a free trade zone because of the need to harmonize and direct complex unified markets, it will be a Union difficult to describe, one without clear precedents in history" (Cavazza and Pelanda 1994, p. 54).

Cavazza and Pelanda's perplexity, and that of other observers, is understandable because the EU is a confusing political association. Some of its features appear to be federal, others confederal, and still others seem to be on the level of IGO-type voluntary cooperation. While its Europeanist founders looked forward to the EC becoming a full-scale federation on the model of existing federal states, the leaders of its member states were not prepared to treat the central authorities in Brussels as equal partners. Decades later, they retain sovereign powers that the governors of American states and the princely leaders of the German *länder* quickly lost when their countries moved from confederal to federal status.

A federal-type transfer of power usually does not come about easily. In Canada and Australia, it took place under the aegis of the British Government. In the ill-fated East African, Caribbean, and Malayan Federations, the component states acknowledged failure and soon abandoned their experiments in constructing federal-type unions. In Europe, as we have seen, there has been instead a prolonged contest over the power structure of the union being created. This contest has been confused, because most of those involved on both sides have lacked any clear idea of the nature of the intermediate confederal track along which they have actually been traveling.

The ambivalence of leaders who promote unions of states is striking. They, and usually large segments of their peoples, have what appear at first glance to be incompatible desires. In Europe they want union, but they want to keep their homelands, too. The institutional structure provided for in the Rome Treaty allows them to do this, as do the modifications in that structure hammered out in the SEA and Maastricht Treaties. But the apparent contradictions within that structure have been, if anything, reinforced by these successive revisions. On each level, certain institutions seem primarily European while others seem primarily national, and these institutions seem positioned for confrontation rather than cooperation.

For example, on the legislative level, there is both the national Council of Ministers and an aspiring European Parliament. At the executive level, there is a European body, the Commission, 20 independent persons heading a 13,000-member supranational secretariat, and a national entity, the 3,000-member secretariat of the Council of Ministers. To add to the confusion, there is still another supranational secretariat that serves Parliament. Finally, on the legal/arbitral plane, there is a European organ, the Court of Justice, which has jurisdiction over legal disputes, and a preeminently national organ, the European Council that, *inter alia,* arbitrates serious political disputes among member states.

But the incompatibilities between these institutions may be less than they seem. If, as has been stated, the Union is at a confederal stage of its evolution, all its institutions have to be compatible with that state of affairs, at least in their operation if not in terms of their legal powers. To the extent that some of the EU's institutions have been deliberately cast in a federal mold, the ways in which they actually interact with one another have had to be adapted to the political realities of a confederal setting.

Some of the confusion may disappear if the relative positions of the EU and its member states are viewed in their true light. In a confederal setting, the primary political power centers in which conflicting interests are resolved, common policies hammered out, and governmental activities agreed upon and carried out are still the member-state governments. In the Union, the two Councils are the principal forums that the various member governments use to oversee and manage the functions that they have agreed to carry out jointly. The Union's capacity to raise this integrating process to the European level remains quite limited because its political power center is still dependent on those of its member states. No constitutional juggling or institutional sleight of hand can alter this fundamental reality of the European scene. Over the past decades, the institutional framework created by the Treaty of Rome and its successive revisions has been repeatedly compelled to take this underlying power structure into account.

Disappointed Europeanists speak as if there has been a dramatic turnback to the national approach. If anything, the reverse is true. The influence of the European political power center has been steadily growing in importance but at a much slower tempo than they had hoped for.

In a confederal setting, the central institutions are both the agents of the member states and the instruments that enable those states to attain the degree of political union that is provided for in their treaty-constitutions. For example, even though the Council of Ministers is the agent of member-state governments, it is also a European institution. In its second capacity, it has had to become increasingly adept in responding to European needs, in formulating Union policies and in organizing, overseeing, and managing Union activities. The other main Community institutions, Commission, Parliament, and Court, have been given independent mandates that make them "European institutions," but they act within the framework not only of the Rome Treaty but also of what is likely to be acceptable or unacceptable to most of the member states.

Each of them assists the Council of Ministers in its own way to carry out its central responsibilities: the Commission, by drafting most legislation and by ensuring that the acts adopted by the Council are faithfully carried out; the Parliament, by keeping it aware of popular wishes and now in some cases vetoing acts deemed to be in conflict with them; and the Court, by ensuring that all institutions, member states, and natural and legal persons abide by the EU's expanding rulebook. Each of the three institutions has other functions that it carries out independently, but in these areas, too, they indirectly help member governments to enhance the effectiveness of the union that they voluntarily created or joined.

These "services" that Parliament, Commission, and Court provide to the central Union also counterbalance the centrifugal pressures that national governments, in their efforts to respond to the wide spectrum of special interests at home, transmit in their instructions to their representatives to that Council. In his brief analysis of the "national dimension" of European decision-making, John Fitzmaurice gives some idea of the scope of those interests and pressures that are directed upon national ministries and parliaments. For example, the somewhat eccentric behavior of Denmark on EU matters is explained partly by the great influence that a committee of the Danish Parliament has gained for itself in determining the country's policies towards the Union.

In some countries, in France for example, internal coordination among the ministries leads to relatively coherent EU policies. In many others (Germany would be an example), there has been coalition government in which smaller political parties sometimes exercise a disproportionate influence over those policies and sway them in ways to their liking (Fitzmaurice 1983, pp. 3–7). Because the Council of Ministers is at once a conduit for these pressures and a bulwark for resisting them (since, obviously, every government cannot always have its way), the Commission and now the Parliament, too, help Council members uphold the interests of the Union as a whole in enacting legislation. National leaders who are Europeanist in their outlook also give their high-level support to that approach.

If the foregoing analysis is valid, we have a European Union that is confederal by necessity but cast in a mold in which confederal institutions have been modernized and greatly strengthened in comparison to earlier models. Behind the complicated constitutional verbiage and complex decision-making procedures of the frequently revised Treaty of Rome, a relatively straightforward modus operandi may be perceived. It is that Commission, Parliament, and Court each assists and prods the two Councils to carry out, in a collegiate yet forward-moving manner, those functions that the member governments have agreed should be centralized. The institutionalization of this assistance (and of this pressure) has turned out to be a valuable asset for Europe, for without it little progress, or much slower progress, would have been possible. On the other hand, too much pressure is risky because no union of states can move forward at a faster tempo than its foot-dragging members such as Denmark or Britain are ready to tolerate.

The ways in which the three institutions assist and prod the Council of Ministers are of interest. Having the exclusive right to draft and revise legislation, the Commission is automatically involved in the wheeling and dealing of its enactment. The Parliament is also increasingly involved in that process, with many categories of legislation either requiring its assent or subject to its veto power. Finally, the European Court of Justice acts as a Supreme Court with jurisdiction when states and "natural and legal persons" (or any combination thereof) seek to circumvent or to ignore the EU treaty provisions and statutes that apply to them. This saves the Council from having to discipline one of its members. Serious crises may be sidestepped when such problems can be "solved" by nonpolitical bodies.

This, then, is the "confederal balance," one quite different from the federal balance that the founders of the United States invented in the late eighteenth century. It requires states still jealous of their sovereignty and semi-autonomous institutions to work together in managing a union that ministers to their common material well-being and competitiveness in the world economy. The states must concede some of their sovereignty in this cause, and the institutions must accept the fact that their authority is more limited than it would be in a full-fledged federal state. Whether one calls this new balance "modern confederalism" or "neo-federalism" matters less than whether it will attain the purposes for which the Union/Community was formed.

Mandate of the Union

The mandate of the Union falls into two spheres. In one, the Council of Ministers may take actions that are legally binding on member-state governments. In the other, it may only adopt and send them its recommendations. In the first sphere, it exercises a kind of joint sovereignty; in the second, it seeks to negotiate voluntary "consensuses." In our terminology, the first sphere is "confederal" or "proto-federal," the second "IGO." The first sphere now encompasses most of the economic, monetary, and external/internal trade relations of member states, as well as affiliated areas, such as agriculture and transport in which governmental policies need to be unified if there is to be a single internal market. The second sphere includes many of the other areas of governmental activity.

The Union's Treaty provisions do not always make it clear to which sphere the various functions belong. Accordingly, it is necessary in each case to determine the extent of the Council of Ministers' powers. For example, with regard to foreign affairs, the Council's powers seem to hover between IGO and confederal status. This probably reflects the drafters' uncertainty as to whether or not confederal treatment of this function was feasible. In fact, experience has shown how difficult it is for the member states, particularly the great-power member states, to pursue common foreign policies with regard to divisive and troubling issues such as the warfare among the Yugoslav successor states.

The Union's broad objectives are set forth in the Maastricht Treaty. They include "the creation of an area without internal frontiers," "the establishment of economic and monetary union," "the implementation of a common foreign and security policy," "the protection of the rights and interests of the nationals of its Member States through the introduction of a citizenship of the Union," and "close cooperation on justice and home affairs" (Article B). Two of these objectives, the implementation of a common foreign policy and close cooperation on justice and home affairs, were introduced in the Single European Act and the Maastricht Treaty, respectively, and fall largely within the IGO sphere in practice if not always in legal terms (see Articles J–J.11 and K–K.9).

The other broad objectives derive from those enunciated in Article 2 EEC. In the following Article 3 EEC, they are expressed as 20 areas of activity but without indicating which ones fall in the confederal and which in the IGO sphere. An attempt has been made to make this allocation for indicative purposes. The following are the activities that seem to fall predominantly in the confederal sphere of the Union's mandate:

1. Elimination of customs duties between member states (Articles 12–17);

2. Setting of the common customs tariff (Articles 18–29);

3. Elimination of quantitative restrictions in the trade between member states (Articles 30–37);

4. Common agricultural policy (Articles 38–47);

5. Free movement of workers (Articles 48–51);

6. Right of business establishment (Articles 52–58);

7. Right to provide services (Articles 59–66);

8. Free movement of capital (Articles 67–73h);

9. Common transport policy (Articles 74–84);

10. Rules to ensure free competition (Articles 85–94);

11. Harmonization of national taxation laws (Articles 95–99);

12. "Approximation" of national laws (Articles 100, 100a and b, 101 and 102);

13. Common visa requirements (Articles 100c and d);

14. Convergence of economic policies (Articles 102a–104c);

15. Common monetary policy (Articles 105–109m);

16. Common commercial policy (Articles 110, 112, 113, 115);

17. Consumer protection (Article 129a).

The following are the activities that appear to fall predominantly in the IGO sphere of the EU's mandate:

1. Social provisions (Articles 117–125);

2. Education, vocational training, and youth (Articles 126–127);*

3. Culture (Article 128);*

4. Public health (Article 129);*

5. Trans-European networks in transport, communications, and energy (Articles 129b–d);

6. Industrial cooperation (Article 130);

7. Economic and social cohesion (Articles 130a–e);

8. Research and technological development (Articles 130f–130p);

9. Environment (Articles 130r–t);

10. Development cooperation (Articles 130u–y).

To these 10 areas must be added the two areas of "foreign affairs and security" and "justice and home affairs." In most of these 27 activity sectors, the member states are also entitled to carry out many functions on their own.

The first list of activities confirms that the legally binding sphere of the Union's mandate is almost wholly focused on improving the material well-

*These areas are specifically excluded from "any harmonization of the laws and regulations of the member states," and thus from any mandatory law-making.

being of the new citizens of Europe. Thus, it impinges minimally on social and cultural relationships in their respective homelands. In fact, it is made quite plain that the Union will not intrude into areas such as education, culture, health and justice, and home affairs.

For the first three of the activities just cited, the exclusion clause protects them against it, while "cooperation," rather than any locking together of sovereign powers, is the goal of the other activities on the second list. For example, in justice and home affairs, the matters of common interest are carefully defined (asylum, border controls, immigration policy, drug trafficking, international fraud, judicial cooperation in civil and criminal matters, customs cooperation) (Article K.1). These are areas where voluntary cooperation among the national officials concerned is likely to prove both feasible and useful. In addition, some of these areas are the subject of international cooperation under United Nations auspices.

A glance at the first list shows the extent to which the EU remains in essence an economic union of states, even though the word "economic" was deliberately dropped from the title of the former "European Economic Community." The central thrust of the Union is the common economic policy "based on the close coordination of Member states' economic policies, on the internal market and on the definition of common objectives, and conducted in accordance with the principle of an open market economy with free competition" (Article 3a EEC).

These words were inserted not at Rome but at Maastricht where the Union's member governments agreed that there was a compelling need for much closer coordination of their economic policies and that sanctions should be applied against any member that did not take this obligation seriously.

The list of sanctions available to the Council appears in Article 104c (11) EEC of the Treaty. It should be noted that the Council, exceptionally, is allowed to act alone, i.e., without any proposal from the Commission, in applying them. Thus, compatible and convergent economic policies were correctly perceived as a *sine qua non* for monetary union, which is in turn a prerequisite for any full-scale economic confederalization of "Europe." The main thrust of both the SEA and the Maastricht revisions of the Rome Treaty was to provide for the single, borderless internal market without which there cannot be even a full-scale confederal economic union.

Finance and Taxation

In IGOs and confederations, it is up to the member-state governments to determine how much money will be raised and how it will be spent. In federations, popularly elected legislatures usually perform those functions.

The procedures of the European Union, while mixed, remain more confederal than federal.

Raising of Funds. Initially, the Union obtained the funds it needed entirely through assessments of its member states. But in Article 201 EEC of the original Treaty of Rome, the Commission was asked to study the possibility of replacing this assessment system by one that would give the EC its "own resources," in plain language, the power to tax its member states. Under that Article, there were two stages: first, the Council had unanimously to "lay down provisions relating to the system of own resources of the Community." Then the member states had to adopt them "in accordance with their respective constitutional requirements."

It had been understood that the common customs tariff might be allocated for that purpose. However, by 1970, when the new arrangements foreseen in Article 201 EEC were actually introduced, the customs revenues fell far short of the amounts needed. This shortfall was covered by the EC being given 1% of the value-added tax (VAT) collected at the national level. During the 1980s, this figure rose as high as 1.4% (Freestone and Davidson 1988, p. 117). In the prototype federations, as indicated in Chapter 1, central governments exercise a preponderance of the taxing power; hence the constituent states or provinces must look to them for donations. Contrariwise, in the Union, under Article 201 EEC, the member states have kept a tight rein on how and to what extent they will permit themselves to be taxed.

The Union's funds are now obtained from a variety of sources. In 1995, 53% of its budget was financed from VAT receipts (now only 1.2% of the total); 17% by customs receipts; 21% by assessments based on per capita GNP; and 9% by other means. The total amount budgeted for 1995 was Ecu 76.5 billion (or roughly $96 billion at September 1995 exchange rates), much of which was for transfer payments to individuals within the member states, which otherwise would probably have had to be included in national budgets.

Spending of Funds. Effective control over the EC's budget is complicated by a tug of war between the Europeanists who would like the control over the Union's budget to be exercised by the Parliament and the nationalists who would prefer to have that power left with the member states and the Council of Ministers. This disagreement has led to a series of compromises as a result of which Commission, Council, and Parliament are now involved in a relationship so complex that it is not easy to tell where the final authority over the budget rests.

The procedures are mind-boggling in their complexity. First, the Commission sets the growth rate for each year's overall expenditures on the basis of agreed-upon indicators, the growth of Community GNP, the movement of prices, and the expenditures of national governments.

Later on, however, both Council and Parliament may make amendments that have the effect of reducing or increasing that rate. Like the executive in IGOs, the Commission prepares the budget, but before doing so, it must consult both the EP and the Council of Ministers. Then, in late July of the preceding year, the draft budget goes first to the Council, then to the EP with the Council's changes, then to the Council with the EP's changes, and finally back to the EP with the Council's reaction to the EP's changes. These four steps have to be carried out in the last five months of each year.

There is another complication. Every budget is composed of two elements, the "compulsory" expenditures needed to carry out Treaty provisions as well as earlier legislative decisions and "noncompulsory" expenditures that are subject to review and adjustment. The Treaty gives the Council the upper hand in determining the level of "compulsory" expenditures such as agricultural subsidies. In its turn, Parliament has the upper hand in determining voluntary expenditures, though it is somewhat limited by the growth rate set by the Commission. Yet under Parliament's pressure, the proportion of the budget regarded as noncompulsory rose from 3% in 1973 to 25% in 1986. Parliament also has the power to reject the budget in toto and has exercised this power in 1979 and 1984 (Freestone and Davidson 1988, pp. 120–25; Articles 203–204 EEC).

In order to deal with the impasses that this system sometimes produces, a tripartite "Interinstitutional Agreement on Budgetary Discipline and Improvement of the Budgetary Procedure" was adopted in 1988 which, according to Noel, "fixed new rules for co-operation between the institutions and opened the way to a 'lasting peace' in the area of annual budget procedure." It must have worked tolerably well, for the Agreement was renewed in 1993 (Noel 1994, p. 38).

The Union would have fewer money problems if it were involved only in financing its own operations. However, as described earlier, it has become enmeshed in redistributing resources from taxpayers to farmers and from taxpayers to poorer regions. These agricultural subsidies now absorb about half of the Union's budget, and the regional funds absorb about one-third of what is left.

To sum up, the Council of Ministers and the member states substantially control the sources and levels of funding, while the Council shares control of the budgetary sphere with the Parliament. This leads, inevitably, to financial crises during which either expenditures have to be scaled back to match receipts or additional sources of revenue have to be found. Such financial crises also reflect the pressures that the EP and/or the Commission can bring to bear on the Council to finance existing activities adequately or to introduce new activities that fall within the scope of the Union's mandate. At the same time, there is a limit to which individual member states can be pressed for funds without creating a crisis like the one involving Britain in the 1980s. So long as there are member states that consider themselves to be sovereign, the ultimate financial control is likely to be exercised at the intergovernmental level.

Legislative Procedures

In the final three sub-sections of this chapter, the focus will be on the ways in which the legislative, executive, and judicial branches may handle their respective functions in a modern confederal setting. These functions need to be organized in such a way that the legislative power can ensure that the executive and judicial functions of government are conducted "in ways that are unthreatening to the sovereignty of its member states" (see confederal feature number 14). This means that it will guard them against the pressures towards centralization that are so commonplace in federal governance.

At the same time, the executive and judicial branches have to be given sufficient latitude—and sufficient resources—to carry out the important functions that the Treaty and the state partners have assigned to them.

In the European Union, each of the three branches is bound by the rules of its treaty-constitution. But the underlying partnership of sovereign states continues to exercise an ultimate supervision over the well-being and smooth functioning of the Union. Thus, anything seen as threatening to the future of that partnership quickly attracts the attention of the leaders of those states, who tend to give the preservation of their Union top priority.

Both in dealing with such crises and in its less dramatic decision-making, the European Council, in confederal tradition, seeks to work out consensuses among its members. When this proves impossible, the equally confederal technique is either to postpone action or to allow a leader to remain aloof from steps that he or she opposes. For example, Britain was allowed to opt out of the actions taken at Maastricht to establish a common currency and a common central bank for the Community as a whole. The other members, of course, hope that Britain will reconsider and join the European Bank and monetary system once it comes into being.

The survival and ultimate success of the Union depends heavily both on the ability of national leaders to steer it through such crises and on the capacity of those in the three other institutions (Parliament, Commission, and Court) to distinguish between pressures that will produce positive results and those that may jeopardize the interstate alliance on which the Union rests.

The detailed institutional arrangements of the Union are in line with this modus operandi. In the realm of legislation and decision-making, its supreme body is, as we have seen, the European Council, composed of the leaders of its member states and the President of the Commission. The Council's semi-annual meetings, which are free of institutional formalities, have become major events in the Union's ongoing evolution. The national leaders meet without civil servants and experts present, and the "Conclusions of the Presidency" are followed up by the foreign ministers (meeting in the Council of Ministers) and the Permanent Representatives of EU member governments (Noel 1994, pp. 30–31).

The European Council has lately been given a somewhat vague but obviously far-reaching mandate—to define the Union's "general political guidelines" and "to provide it with the necessary impetus for its development." The only other specific mention of it in the Maastricht Treaty is in its revised section on foreign affairs and security in which, among the guidelines it is asked to provide, are those that determine whether a foreign policy issue should be the subject of joint action. Beyond that, it is asked to "define the principles of and general guidelines for the common foreign and security policy" (Articles D and J.3, J.8).

These powers are broad and vague enough to allow the European Council to steer the Union in almost any direction that its members wish. Moreover, as the leaders of their respective sovereign member states, their predecessors exercised these powers from the time of the EC's creation in 1958, either from their capitals or at informal meetings. But by institutionalizing the European Council and its broad mandate, the SEA and the Maastricht Agreements gave legal standing to procedures that enabled these powers to be exercised more effectively in regularly scheduled face-to-face meetings.

As if to highlight their sovereign status, the members of the European Council do important things that are not mentioned in its mandate. For example, where steps are to be taken "by common accord," they reach, or occasionally fail to reach, such accord. Also, the members of the Council have the final say on who serves on the Commission and on who is named as its President. Once it is set up, they will also determine who will serve on the Executive Board of the new European Central Bank and who will be named as its President (Articles 109a and 158 EEC). Each leader's veto power over the choice of the Commission's President was exercised (albeit exceptionally) by Britain at the June 1994 session held in Corfu. The national leaders must also approve the entry of new members and determine the cities in which the main organs of the Union will have their offices.

Under the Maastricht Treaty, they are also to decide whether and when the Monetary Union will be established plus an even more delicate matter—which members will at that time "fulfil the necessary conditions" to join it. They are to take this crucial step, not as the European Council, but simply as "the Council, meeting in the composition of the Heads of State or Government." This brings them for the first time within the Union's formal decision-making system and empowers them to take this step by a qualified majority (Article 109j EEC).

While the guidelines laid down by the European Council do not have the force of Community law, this may not matter very much in practice because of the high level from which they emanate. Thus, it has provided political impetus or guidelines on such matters as the reform of agricultural policy, the accession of new members, the completion of the internal market and, of course, the new economic and monetary union. It has also been particularly involved in establishing common foreign and security policies (European Council 1993; Noel 1994, p. 30). As Juliet Lodge observed, "from 1974, European Councils have assumed a 'motor' role in integration" (Lodge 1989, p. 49).

At the next lower level, the Council of Ministers is the Union's most active power center. It is the nexus at which its member states interact with one another through face-to-face meetings of their plenipotentiaries. All are well aware that no step of importance can be taken without its concurrence.

Because of the central position of the Council of Ministers, and perhaps also because of the inherent weaknesses of intergovernmental bodies, member states have been at pains to increase its capacity. Institutionally, they have established levels above and below it. The European Council now occupies the upper level. At the lower level is the Committee of Permanent Representatives (widely known as COREPER), which acts as the Ministers' preparatory committee and links them with the many other parts of the EU's institutional structure. Stanley Henig stresses "the crucial role" of COREPER in the Union's legislative process, even though it lacks any formal decision-making competence. The press of business became so great that it is now operated at two levels: COREPER II, composed of the Permanent Representatives themselves, which deals with external questions and any matters having significant political aspects; and COREPER I, composed of their deputies, which tends to focus on internal EU matters. At the next lower level, there is a whole range of specialist and ad hoc committees whose members usually come from the member governments or from the offices of the Permanent Representatives. It is COREPER, and not the Council of Ministers, that supervises these committees (Henig 1983, p. 14).

The Council of Ministers itself is a body of many memberships that meet separately. The foreign ministers meet when it deals with matters falling within their purview or general policy questions, and have a coordinating function vis-à-vis the "sectoral" Councils. These sectoral Councils tend to act independently. For example, when the Ministers of Agriculture take farm support decisions involving large expenditures, they are usually responding to agricultural pressure groups and may not be acting in the overall interest of their member states. But once they have acted, it is not so easy for foreign ministers or even heads of state to overrule their decisions. There are many sectoral Councils of this kind, and the problems of getting them to act in the general rather than the narrow sectoral interest are so great that, according to Pinder, it has undermined the Council's effectiveness as a legislature (Pinder 1991, pp. 86–94).

Effective or not, the Union's decision-making organs have been very busy. In the early 1980s, the two Councils were meeting for more than 100 days each year and COREPER was in session for another 100 days. Thus, most days, either one or the other was sitting. In addition, a plethora of Committees and working groups filled any gap (Henig 1983, p. 17).

It should be added that while more than half of the sectoral meetings involve three groups of ministers—those responsible for foreign affairs, agriculture and finance—most of the other groups meet from time to time. Accordingly, while the Council of Ministers may be the modern-day successor of the earlier confederal decision-making bodies, nothing that took place in them prepares us for such a beehive of activity. In this respect, the Council of Ministers illustrates the evolutionary potential of confederal-type political institutions.

The Presidency of the Council of Ministers is an office of importance. Each member state is so eager to hold it that it must rotate rather than remain in the hands of a natural leader. Member states take turns providing the President for periods of six months each. When, once every seven or eight years, a state's time in the limelight rolls around, one of its ministers acts as President of the Council and its national leader acts as President of the European Council. The office of President has come to entail a number of executive functions, partly administrative, partly political, that make up what is called "the Council Presidency." This system works fairly well because each national leader is usually eager to make "his" or "her" Presidency memorable for its achievements.

In confederations, decisions are taken on the basis of unanimity or weighted voting. Also, the states rather than popular representatives are the voters. The Council of Ministers' decision-making is in line with these procedures. In most substantive matters, it now uses a weighted voting system and takes its decisions on the basis of "a qualified majority." That system provides that Britain, France, Germany, and Italy each has ten votes; Spain eight votes; Belgium, Greece, Netherlands, and Portugal, five votes each; Austria and Sweden, four votes each; Denmark, Finland, and Ireland, three votes each; and Luxembourg, two votes. This adds up to 87 votes in all. The qualified majority is 62 votes in favor; thus, any minority controlling 26 or more votes can block action.

In order to ensure that they command the needed preponderance of support, some decisions can be taken only if at least eight member states support them. Also, more than 30 categories of decision require unanimity. Two commentators wrote in 1987 that only 5% of decisions were being put to the vote (Freestone and Davidson 1988, p. 69). The Council clearly feels more comfortable when it can act on the basis of consensus rather than slender majorities.

The Council is also constrained by the complex yet constructive relationship it has with the Commission in the framing and enactment of legislation. The latter writes and sends forward its proposals, while the Council enacts or rejects those proposals but may not amend them unless its members vote unanimously to do so (Articles 155 EEC and 189a EEC). Thus, the Commission has been given a virtual monopoly on the right to initiate legislation, while the Council may reject the legislation submitted to it. The exception to this principle is typically confederal: Member states, when all of them combine their sovereign powers, may overrule the executive. But, in practice, this rarely happens. Finally, there is nothing to prevent member states from encouraging the Commission to come forward with proposals that they would like to see adopted.

As Emile Noel has pointed out, the Rome Treaty merely provided this framework and allowed the institutions to work out how they would work together within it. What has emerged is a "Commission-Council Dialogue . . . which begins between the ministers in the Council, who put their national points of view, and the Commission which seeks . . . to find European solutions to common problems." The dialogue is in fact a cooperative effort conducted on many levels by representatives of the Commission and of member governments to bring forth legislation that will be able to command a consensus, or at least a qualified voting majority in the Council. That the system works at least passably well is indicated by the magnitude of its product: The Commission in 1992 laid 651 proposals and drafts before the Council, which in the same time frame adopted 738 regulations, directives, and decisions (Noel 1994, pp. 25–30).

In its earlier years, the Council took the overwhelming majority of its decisions by unanimity or consensus (Freestone and Davidson 1988, p. 68). However, since 1986, with the adoption of the SEA, qualified majority voting has formed the basis for much of the Council's decision-making. Often the Council Presidency simply notes that the requisite majority in favor of a Commission proposal can be mustered, whereupon the members adopt the proposal. At present the requisite majority is 71% of the (weighted) votes (Noel 1994, p. 29). Not surprisingly, the level of this majority has become very important to member governments. For example, Britain and Spain sought unsuccessfully to step it up to 75% in connection with the EU's recent enlargement.

The European Parliament is the Union's second legislative organ, the one that Europeanists would like to turn into the "lower house" of a broader Parliament in which the Council of Ministers would become the "upper house." Nationalists fear that it might come to share the fate of most upper houses and fade away like the House of Lords or the upper houses in most federations (the U.S. Senate being the main exception). Eight years ago, however, we could be told that the EP was not really a parliament because it did not pass legislation or have the executive chosen from its ranks (Freestone and Davidson 1988, p. 71). But with the Maastricht revisions, this conclusion would need to be qualified. Of all the EU's institutions, the EP has seen the greatest expansion of its legal powers because, as Juliet Lodge has written, it "is an institution dedicated to increasing its powers" (Lodge 1989, p. 58). In constitutional terms, it has evolved from being a mostly advisory organ known as "the Assembly" into (in some situations) a full-scale legislative partner of the Council of Ministers. But the nagging question remains, Can it really occupy the constitutional niche that its promoters have won for it?

We shall not here trace the EP's evolution, but briefly describe its present structure and powers. As of July 1995, it was composed of 626 seats broken down as follows: Germany (99); Britain, France, and Italy (87, each); Spain (64); Netherlands (31); Belgium, Greece, and Portugal (25, each); Sweden (22); Austria (21); Denmark and Finland (16, each); Ireland (15); and Luxembourg (6). Representation is skewed slightly to give smaller members more, and large members fewer, delegates (e.g., Germany has one per 814,000 inhabitants compared to Luxembourg's one per 197,000 inhabitants). The others fall within those parameters, with relative representation increasing as total population decreases.

Since 1979, the EP's members have been elected by universal suffrage at five-year intervals, in 1979, 1984, 1989, and 1994. Britain uses its single-ballot majority voting by constituency; other members use systems involving a considerable degree of proportional representation (Noel 1994, pp. 6, 33–34).

The EP is organized not around national groups but on the basis of pan-European parties to which all but 32 of its members belonged in September 1995. The two main parties are the European Socialists (with 220 members) and a Christian Democratic Group known as the "European People's Party" (with 173 members). The remaining 233 members belong to seven smaller parties: the Liberal Democratic and Reformist Group, the Left Unity Group, Forza Europa, the Green Group, the European Democratic Alliance, the Right Wing Europe of Nations, and the European Radical Alliance. These parties are mostly affiliated with national parties occupying corresponding places in the political spectrum, though they are said to "guard jealously their independence from sister national parties." The political situation in the EP is complex. Lodge adds that

While MEPs sit in political party groups, the cohesiveness of each group varies. Although inter-party competition and rivalry are intensifying, cross-party voting is common, especially where issues of national interest unite MEPs from a given state regardless of their EP party affiliation. National party considerations do intrude into EP party politics for both political and technical reasons. (Lodge 1983, p. 28)

One problem is that the domestic implications for national parties of victories and defeats in contests for EP seats are likely to outweigh in the minds of voters and local political circles the effect that they may have on the EP's faraway legislative activities. The 1994 EP elections produced the lowest ever turnout of voters (56.4% down from 63% in 1979). *The Economist* concluded that "the electors chose either to stay away or to vote on national issues" (Lodge 1989, p. 60; *The Economist* 1994, pp. 55–56). In any event, the ties between voters and the members that they send to the EP seem to be much looser than their ties to their representatives in the national legislatures whose activities usually affect them more directly.

However that may be, Parliament's legislative role has been steadily expanding since 1958. With the SEA and Maastricht revisions, it is no longer restricted to a consultative role in the Union's legislative process. At least in many decision categories, it has become a coparticipant with the Council therein. For example, its assent must be obtained (1) before a new member may be admitted to the Union (Article 0); (2) before any uniform procedure can be laid down for EP elections (Article 138 EEC); and (3) before the Union can become a party to certain kinds of international treaty (Article 228 (3) EEC). It is also involved in cooperation and codecision procedures soon to be described.

Moreover, it can now initiate legislation by requesting the Commission "to submit any appropriate proposal on matters on which it considers that a Community act is required for the purpose of implementing this Treaty" (Article 138b EEC). Lastly, the EP is now involved in the complex procedures by which, once every five years, the Commission is reconstituted. It must be consulted before the President of the Commission is nominated, and it must approve the President and other members of the Commission as a body before they can be appointed (Article 158 EEC). It has always had the power to dismiss them as a body (Article 144 EEC).

Until the late 1980s, Parliament was, except in the budgetary sphere, accorded a relatively minor advisory role in the legislative process. "Cooperation" and "codecision" procedures, introduced as part of the SEA and Maastricht revisions, have turned the Parliament into a junior legislative body for which there is no confederal precedent. Both procedures are complex because, like the budgetary process described in the previous section, they are the product of hard negotiations between Europeanists and nationalists. Both involve triangular movements of proposals from Commission to Council to Parliament in a bureaucratic maze of procedures that is too intricate to describe in detail.

In the cooperation procedure, the Commission in effect acts on behalf of Parliament as an intermediary between it and the Council. It does so by screening the EP's comments and amendments with regard to proposals adopted by the Council. Presumably, it weighs these comments and amendments on their merits and their capacity to attract the requisite support among Council members. If an amendment passes both tests, the Commission revises its proposal accordingly. The EP's amendments can then piggyback on the pressures that the Commission brings to bear on the Council's decision-making. While it may seem somewhat strange that Parliament's proposals should have to be approved by an international executive, rather than the other way around, it is an ingenious way of enhancing the EP's influence over the legislative process. Since 1986, this cooperation procedure has been applied to 14 categories of decisions (see Articles 6, 75, 84, 103, 104a and b, 105a, 125, 127, 129d, 130e, 130o, 130s, and 130w, all EEC).

The "co-decision procedure" makes the EP a full partner in the adoption of legislation, and provides for conciliation when the two bodies cannot reach agreement. In such cases, a Conciliation Committee is jointly convened by the Presidents of the Council and Parliament. That Committee is composed of equal numbers of Council and Parliament members plus Commission representatives in order to negotiate a text that will pass muster in both bodies. If either institution rejects the text, the proposal is lost and the procedure is over *unless* the Council confirms its common position while incorporating some of Parliament's amendments if it wishes. The proposal then stands adopted *unless* Parliament, by an absolute majority of its members, rejects it (Noel 1994, pp. 39–40; Article 189b EEC). This procedure now applies to 16 categories of decisions, with the expectation that it will be extended to other categories if it works well (see Articles 49, 54, 56–57, 66, 100a, 100b, 126, 128–129, 129a, 129d, 130i, 130s, all EEC).

Is such a process too complicated? It would appear that earlier conciliation machinery for legislation did not work very well. Lodge states that it was "excessively time-consuming and ill-managed," and that "it took the Council, for example, four years to transmit a common position" on one Commission proposal (Lodge 1989, p. 76). It also gives both Parliament and Council many opportunities to block or delay legislation. Thus, it remains to be seen whether a union of states can be properly governed by two quite separate legislative bodies forced into a state of uneasy coexistence. It may be added that, under both procedures, no legislation that is unacceptable to the Council can enter into force.

The Union's Executive Capacity

While the earlier security confederations got by with little in the way of executive capacity, IGOs from the outset could not manage without it. Given general welfare mandates, they had to have the capacity to address them. Intergovernmental bodies might decide upon the activities to be undertaken jointly, but usually their staff had to carry them out. This was as true for the post-Napoleonic Rhine Commission and the Universal Postal Union in the nineteenth century as it is today for, say, the World Health Organization and the United Nations. Economic confederations also need an energetic executive with the capacity to offer expert advice on what should be done and to assume responsibility either for carrying out the courses of action that may have been decided upon by governments or for ensuring that these courses of action are carried out by others.

A principal problem arising from this situation is that of maintaining an adequate level of executive accountability. From the time of the Rhine Commission, the executive, within the limits of the monies made available to it, has tended to become a power unto itself. This problem has always faced IGOs, and it now emerges for modern confederations.

The founders of the European Community deliberately established in the Commission an executive that would be a power unto itself. In addition to being the Union's executive arm, it is supposed to serve as the guardian of the treaties, the initiator of Community policy, and the defender of the Community's interests in the Council of Ministers (Noel 1994, p. 15). The Commission that shoulders these heavy responsibilities is composed of twenty members, including two nationals from each of the five larger member states and one each from the other ten. They are now appointed by "common accord" for five-year terms that begin and expire simultaneously. Thus, the entire membership is renewed at regular intervals, though each individual member may be reappointed. In practice, "common accord" has meant that each government is allowed to select which of its nationals will serve on the Commission.

One of the Commissioners serves as President. Under the procedure formalized at Maastricht, he or she is nominated in advance, also "by common accord" of the member states. Next, the member governments are supposed to designate the other Commissioners in consultation with this nominee, presumably so that the latter may try to discourage the appointment of unsuitable candidates. However, nominee-Presidents are not likely to offend governments by rejecting their candidates, especially since the latter may be appointed anyway.

Once appointed, commissioners are supposed to act independently of their governments during their periods of service. The Rome Treaty provides that they "shall, in the general interest of the communities, be completely independent in the performance of their duties," and that in performing them "they shall neither seek nor take instructions from any government or from any other body." (Article 157 EEC)

The Commission as a corporate body has sought to maintain its independence by keeping aloof from political pressures. It has also acquired a good deal of sophistication in making a union of states function as effectively as possible. From the outset, the Commission's President has been chosen with great care by the governments. As Henig points out, "the coherence and effectiveness of the Commission depends greatly on the personal prestige and authority of the President and his power of leadership" (Henig 1983, p. 10). While they have no independent legal powers, the Commission's President and the President of the Council of Ministers play key roles in keeping the Community on an even keel. Moreover, a tactful Commission President who is sensitive to the wishes and fears of national leaders has an opportunity to play a leadership role both inside and outside the European Council. Whether the President succeeds in doing so depends mainly on his or her talent for leadership under the rather novel conditions of confederal governance.

The Commission takes its decisions secretly as a collegiate body. That means that the whole Commission shares responsibility for every decision taken. It also means that no Commissioner can be singled out for any position that he or she may or may not have taken. Presidents wanting to establish their leadership must begin by winning the "followship" of their fellow Commissioners.

In carrying out its main functions, the Commission is adapting itself well to the requirements of a confederal setting:

Guardian of the Treaty. The Commission's "watchdog" responsibility requires that it monitor the compliance of all concerned with the Treaty's provisions. It has the duty of enforcing those provisions against defaulters, whether member states, companies, or private persons. Needless to say, this function is a delicate one. However, in a union of states, it may be more prudent to assign it to a secretariat-type entity because, if one state begins to make charges against another, ugly disputes are likely to ensue. In situations when this does happen, the Treaty also provides that the charge must be submitted to the Commission for its "reasoned opinion" before being passed on to the Court of Justice (Article 169 EEC).

Freestone and Davidson have summed up the Commission's role:

States do not relish being arraigned in public for acting illegally, hence, the Commission, as the representative of the Community interest, is given this role so that member states are not left to police each other. This ensures that a consistent policy can be pursued and avoids the political damage that can be done to Community relations by inter-state actions. (Freestone and Davidson 1988, p. 62)

Initiator of Community Policy. The Commission carries out this function through its power of legislative initiative. Its monopoly over the drafting of the Community's laws eliminates the inconvenience of the Council being forced to choose between rival texts submitted by member states on the basis of their opposing positions. The Commission's sole right to revise the texts that it has submitted enables it to fashion compromise wordings capable of obtaining the widest possible member-state support.

The Commission is itself entitled to act independently under a few provisions of the Treaty of Rome. For example, Article 90 EEC calls upon it to address appropriate directives to member states in applying competition rules to nationalized or state-financed industries. But, mainly, it issues followup regulations under the direct authority of the Council's legislation. Of the 12,081 instruments it produced in 1986, less than half required the Council's approval (Freestone and Davidson 1988, pp. 64–65).

Executive Functions. The Commission also carries out many purely executive functions. These include implementing the Council's decisions and, as already noted, drafting the secondary legislation often required in this connection. In this latter task, the Commission is assisted by management committees composed of representatives from each of the member states but chaired by the appropriate Commission official. As in the legislative process, the Commission is involved in a close working relationship with member governments in joint efforts to attain the Union's goals.

The Commission does not directly implement the Council's legislative acts. While regulations do not require reenactment at the national level, directives must be followed up by national legislative action. It falls to the Commission to ensure that member states adopt, in due course, the necessary legislation.

Promotion of Community Interests. The Commission's President is an ex officio member of the European Council, and there is always a seat for the President or his or her representative at meetings of the Council of Ministers and its subsidiary organs. Confederal-type bodies composed of members representing their own governments need someone who will remind them of the broader (in this case European) interests that are often involved in their decision-making.

These broad powers of the Commission are offset, as they have to be in what is primarily a union of states, by certain structural and financial counterweights. The power of appointing and reappointing Commissioners remains in the hands of member-state governments. Commissioners are surely aware that their reappointment will be less likely if they act in ways that unnecessarily irritate their own countries' authorities. A Commissioner may also be retired for cause by the Court of Justice if he "no longer fulfils the conditions required for the performance of his duties or if he has been guilty of serious misconduct" (Articles 158–160 EEC). It is also within the Council's exclusive authority both to "alter," by unanimous vote, the number of Commissioners and to determine the salaries, allowances, and pensions of the President and the Commissioners (Articles 154, 157 EEC).

Above all, the broad latitude given to the Commission is counterbalanced by the fact that in a confederal setting the member states still hold the upper hand. As a result, the Commission has to exercise restraint in utilizing its powers. Like IGO secretariats, it can ill afford to be insensitive to the wishes of its member governments. On the other hand, to the extent that it is perceived as contributing to the attainment of the Union's common goals, the Commission usually attracts their goodwill and support. In particular, it will find natural allies in the national leaders that are sympathetic to, and supportive of, European goals. At the same time, those leaders cannot move much faster toward Europeanization than the voters who elect them.

The Union's Legal Capacity

The Commission is closely linked with the other institutions of the Union, particularly the Council of Ministers and the Parliament. In sharp contrast, the European Court of Justice executes its legal mandate in isolation. It is not answerable to any other body for its decisions and has been deliberately insulated from any form of political pressure from member states or the other institutions. Moreover, its mandate is straightforward and far-reaching: to ensure that "in the interpretation and application of this Treaty the law is observed" (Article 164 EEC). Its interpretations can be reversed only by amending the provisions of that Treaty. But, in a confederal setting, it is best if these interpretations adhere closely to the letter of the law, because there is always a risk that even a whiff of judicial activism may upset member states.

The Court is empowered by the Treaty to act in many capacities. In disputes between member states or between the Commission and member states, it acts as an international court (Articles 169–170 EEC). When there are allegations of illegal action or inaction by the institutions, it acts as an administrative court (Articles 173–176, 178, 184 EEC). And when it hands down preliminary rulings to national courts on the interpretation of the Rome Treaty or the statutes adopted under the treaty, it becomes a trans-national constitutional court (Article 177 EEC; Freestone 1983, p. 44).

The Court of Justice is at present composed of 15 judges, who are appointed "by common accord" for six-year renewable terms. These judges must be persons "whose independence is beyond doubt and who possess the qualifications required for appointment to the highest judicial offices in their respective countries or who are jurisconsults of recognized competence" (Article 167 EEC). The fact that they are not appointed for longer periods or for life is important, for governments thereby retain more control over the Court's membership. In practice, the Court now has one judge from each of the member states.

The Court's decision-making procedures are secret. Like the Commission's decisions, its judgments are collegiate, that is to say, individual judges are not allowed to hand down separate or dissenting opinions or to reveal their differing positions on controversial issues. Consequently, many of the Court's judgments have been described as having a "laconic unanimity." They certainly lack the detailed argumentation that is a distinctive and most useful feature of the opinions handed down by most national high courts and by the International Court of Justice. According to Freestone, the reason for this is to avoid any basis for political pressure on members of the Court (Freestone 1983, p. 13).

To some extent, this disadvantage is offset by a system of six Advocates-General having the same qualifications as the judges. Their duty is to make, in open court, "reasoned submissions" on the directions that the Court's decision might take with regard to each case assigned to them (Article 166 EEC). While these submissions are usually scholarly and comprehensive, it is usually unclear whether the arguments made in them have, in fact, swayed the judges.

The ability of the Court to function effectively in a confederal setting has been demonstrated by its rapidly rising caseload. By the end of 1992, the Court had had 5,405 cases brought before it. Moreover, the Court's caseload has been growing. In 1988, it received 373 new cases; in 1989, 401; in 1990, 443; and in 1991, 440. These figures compare with a 36-year average of about 150 new cases per year. Such a rapid growth in judicial activity suggests that a far-reaching and effective legal system is fully compatible with a modern union of states (Noel 1994, p. 45; Weiler 1993, p. 441).

To cope with this workload, the Court is empowered to form chambers of three or five judges to undertake preparatory inquiries or to adjudicate certain classes of cases. And since October 1989, the caseload has been shared between the Court and a new Court of First Instance, to which 446 cases had been assigned by the end of 1992 (Articles 165–168a EEC; Noel 1994, p. 45).

The Court plays its international role when it becomes seized of disputes that member states have with one another or with Community institutions over nonfulfillment of their Treaty obligations (Articles 169–170 EEC). Disputes between member states may jeopardize the interstate alliance on which the Union was founded. Up until 1988, only one such dispute ever got as far as court proceedings (a controversy between France and Britain over fishery legislation) (Freestone and Davidson 1988, p. 153).

Probably, this dearth of state vs. state cases only signifies that, ordinarily, one or another of the parties has preferred that the dispute be settled by other means. Governments have been equally reluctant to bring their more serious disputes before the International Court of Justice. Thus, serious interstate disputes are more apt to be resolved by negotiations among national leaders.

The other channel for compelling member states to adhere to Community law has been used much more frequently. When the Commission becomes convinced that a member state is obstinately refusing to fulfill one or another of its obligations under the Treaty, it may bring the matter before the Court. By December 1981, it had brought 165 actions against member governments in this context. In 22 of these cases, the Court found in favor of the applicant, i.e., the Commission. Only one case was dismissed on the merits. Most of the other cases were quietly dropped when defendant governments decided to comply with the Commission's demands. In cases when the Court has ruled against the national governments, the matter may be brought before the Court a second time if the governments concerned do not comply with the Court's judgment (Freestone 1983, p. 46).

Since the cases brought by the Commission usually involve clearcut violations, the governments that have been named are often reluctant to face what will almost certainly be the Court's adverse decision against them with the attendant bad publicity. Especially in countries where the rule of law is widely accepted, this prospect is not one to be taken lightly.

But in recent years, the effectiveness of this system has apparently been in decline. The Maastricht Treaty now empowers the Court to fine any government that refuses to comply with its judgment. Such a step has been required by member states' "diminishing fear of being exposed as one of the bad pupils of the class, and perhaps also by the indiscriminate use the Commission has made of the infringement action in recent years." The number of unimplemented judgments against member states had reached 44 by 1990 (Articles 169, 93, and 171 EEC; Koopmans 1991, p. 19).

Under the foregoing procedures, the Council of Ministers is spared direct involvement in prickly cases in which its members might feel compelled to support their country's claims regardless of their merits. But the recent difficulties in securing compliance reveal some of the limitations on the rule of law in a confederal union. In the long run, the two Councils need to find new ways of compelling their members to abide by the Court's rulings.

In addition to ensuring that the Treaty's provisions are duly applied, the Court is deeply involved in interpreting those provisions. The Treaty itself gives the Court far-reaching powers of interpretation, directly in Articles 173–176 EEC (when, in its administrative capacity, it reviews challenges to acts adopted by other EU institutions), and indirectly in Article 177 EEC (when, in its transnational capacity, it formulates preliminary opinions). If some of the Court's interpretations have displeased them, governments have had opportunities—so far never used—to cut the ground out from under the Court during their frequent revisions of the Rome Treaty.

Article 173 EEC begins by stating flatly that "the Court of Justice shall review the legality of acts adopted" by the Council, the EP, and the Commission. To accomplish this, the Court has jurisdiction over actions brought by member states, the Council, the Commission, and (since Maastricht) by Parliament on four grounds: lack of competence, infringement of essential procedural requirements, infringement of the Treaty *or of any rule of law relating to its application,* and misuse of powers. In Article 174 EEC, it is provided that if the action is well founded, the Court "*shall* declare the act concerned to be void" [emphases added].

Finally, under Article 175 EEC, if any institution "in infringement of this Treaty" fails to act, member states and other institutions may bring an action before the Court to have the infringement established. These are extensive powers that exceed those granted to many national supreme courts. For example, in Britain, legal decisions of its highest court (the House of Lords) can be reversed by an Act of Parliament even with retroactive effect (Freestone and Davidson 1988, p. 137).

As of December 1981, 268 actions questioning the legality of acts adopted by the institutions had been brought under Article 173 EEC, and 16 complaints of their inaction under Article 175 EEC. Of the 35 actions brought by member governments, 19 were dismissed by the Court on the merits, and only four were decided in favor of the complainants (Freestone

1983, p. 46). In carrying out this function, the Court not only established its authority vis-à-vis those governments; it was given 284 opportunities to interpret Community law.

It is under these same provisions that "natural and legal persons" (i.e., corporations and individuals) are brought within the Court's jurisdiction. They, too, are entitled to bring proceedings, though only against decisions addressed to them or against decisions and regulations addressed to others of "direct and individual concern" to them (Article 173 EEC). By the end of 1981, 229 actions had been brought by such persons. Of those that the Court agreed to hear, 33 were decided in favor of the applicant and 105 were dismissed on the merits. By 1992, one in five actions had been brought by individuals (1,099 of 5,405) (Freestone 1983, p. 46; Noel 1994, pp. 44–45). Thus, individuals and enterprises can, even in a confederal setting, receive legal protection against wrongful actions by the central authorities who oversee their activities under the Treaty.

As a consequence of the division of sovereign functions between central and state governments, a new legal system had to be created for the functions being centralized. That system needed to be coordinated with the national legal systems that remained in place beside it. In the Union, the broad rules for such coordination are provided for in Articles 100–102 and 189 EEC of the Treaty itself. Article 177 EEC also provides that the Court shall assist national courts, at their request, by clarifying the provisions of the newly emerging Union law.

This system of preliminary rulings provides the Court with an opportunity to interpret not just the provisions of the Treaty but also the acts of the Union's institutions. Under Article 177 EEC, any court or tribunal of a national member state, if it concludes that it needs an authoritative interpretation of almost any rule of European law (or on its constitutional validity) before deciding on a case before it, may request the Court of Justice for a ruling thereon. And, in the same circumstances, the highest national courts *must* seek such rulings. By December 1981, the Court had received 841 requests for its interpretation of, and 124 requests for its opinion on, the constitutional validity of the acts concerned. Eleven years later, the combined number had reached 2,547 (Freestone 1983, p. 46; Noel 1994, p. 45). In handing down such preliminary rulings, the Court clearly acts as a transnational forum, and the rulings themselves provide the main judicial avenue for dovetailing the European and national legal systems.

Modern unions of states have the same need as full-scale federations to determine the relative status of central and member-state law in situations where these may be conflicting. In the Rome Treaty, for example, the superiority of Community law in the sphere allotted to it was implied by the empowerment of the Council to adopt regulations that go directly into national statute-books and to take decisions that legally bind member governments. Even in the case of directives, the superiority of the Council's mandate is demonstrated by the fact that national legislation has to be harmonized with them rather than the other way around. Such harmonization is limited, however, as logically it should be, to the realm where members' sovereign powers are to be exercised jointly, the common market or, as it is now known, the internal market (see Articles 100 and 100a EEC).

But nowhere in the Treaty is this superiority of Community over municipal law specifically stated. It remained for the Court to remedy this situation in a series of landmark decisions, in one of which (Minister of Finance v. Simmenthal) "the Court imposed a *duty* on a national court to apply Community law in preference to national law" (Freestone and Davidson 1988, p. 161).

Has the Court been seeking to steer the Community/Union into a federal harbor through their interpretations? Perhaps, but it seems more likely that the justices have merely been shoring up the proto-federal ("modern confederal" in our terminology) balance that has been emerging in successive revisions of the Rome Treaty.

One might have thought that such intrusive activities would be impossible in a confederal setting; yet, the Court is now well into its fourth decade of judicial decision-making. Insofar as it has been serving the economic goals for which the member states created their Union, they have every reason to be pleased with its work. At the same time, even more than the Union's other institutions, the Court is exploring the outer limits of what is open to modern confederal governance. It is doubtful that the member states would continue to tolerate its activities with the same equanimity if they were to extend very far beyond the Treaty's agreed goals.

In his article, "Journey to an Unknown Destination: A Retrospective and Prospective of the European Court of Justice in the Arena of Political Integration," J.H.H. Weiler warns of the risks that may now face the Court (Weiler 1993). In the first part of the article (which he calls a "Retrospective"), Weiler describes the first three decades of the Court's life as an "extended honeymoon" in which it managed "to persuade, co-opt and cajole most, if not all, of other principal actors [other EC institutions, governments, transnational interest groups, etc.] to accept the fundamentals of its doctrine and of its position in making the constitutional determinations for the Community" (Weiler 1993, pp. 418–20, 434).

Among the reasons for governmental acquiescence, Weiler cites the Court's noninvolvement in the Council's decision-making combined with the assistance it renders in the post-decisional stage by supplying a legal apparatus that can enforce the decisions and compromises reached in that decision-making. So long as the member states can maintain their monopoly over the initial process, they have an interest in ensuring that their decisions are not disregarded or violated. The Court's powers of enforcement spare those states from having to rely on the classic enforcement devices of international law, reprisals, countermeasures, trade wars, and the like. In fact, what Weiler seems to be describing is how a legal system has come to be operated in a modern union of states in which an intergovernmental body rather than a popularly elected parliament acts as legislator.

At the same time, in his "Prospective," Weiler speculates that the judges may soon find themselves on a collision course with the other actors. He worries that the poorly drawn lines between what we have described earlier as the Union's confederal and IGO spheres of competence, and the vaguenesses inherent in the concept of subsidiarity, may be minefields (Weiler cites the forthcoming case on whether or not the Union can ban cigarette advertising) that will often place the Court in "no-win" situations in clashes between Europeanists and nationalists. He also foresees that national supreme courts may become less accepting in the future than they have been in the past of the European Court's attempts to establish the superiority of its law over theirs. He points out that the Court may become more widely visible in the future as a result of an increasing number of cases that capture media and public attention, sometimes in contexts that may mobilize opposition against it. Finally, Weiler warns that the caseload and judicial burden on the Court may become too great and exceed "the ability of the legal community to follow and digest appropriately the jurisprudence of its highest courts" (Weiler 1993, p. 442). Judge Koopmans' article "The Future of the Court of Justice of the European Communities" is also of interest in this connection (Koopmans 1991).

It is in the realm of legal interpretation that these dangers loom largest. In a confederal setting, the justices would be wise to approach their task cautiously, i.e., without any hint of activism. Certainly, such a course would help preserve their reputation for political impartiality and thereby help ensure that the Court remains a noncontroversial bulwark of the Union during the crucial and perhaps difficult times that lie ahead.

(3) CONCLUSIONS

Does the European Union belong to the class of federations or that of confederations? Let us recapitulate the main differences between the two classes. A federation is a union of peoples in a single state, whereas a confederation is a union of states (and secondarily of peoples) that locks together carefully specified sovereign functions under an intergovernmental treaty-constitution. In a federation, therefore, the member states and their governments are soon overshadowed by the new central institutions that they have created. In confederations, on the contrary, the member states and their governments not only refuse to fade away, they continue to dominate the new central institutions. Their dominance is manifest in their continuing control over decision-making at the center and in the joint exercise of sovereign powers within intergovernmental organs by delegates bound by the instructions that they receive from member-state capitals.

In all these respects, the European Community/Union has always been, and even after Maastricht remains, more in line with confederal than federal models. Its typically confederal modus operandi, far from fading away, has become entrenched as the Union's intergovernmental control mechanism has grown from the original Council of Ministers into a network of inter-governmental organs that now includes, in addition to that Council, a top-level European Council, the two COREPERS and a multiplicity of other committees.

At the same time, the European Union, while clearly falling within the broad class of confederations, differs in fundamental ways from earlier con-federal models. It has legislative, executive, judicial and financial capabilities that they did not have and that allow its institutions to operate much more effectively. While, like its predecessors, the Union remains in Murray For-syth's "halfway house" between the interstate and the intrastate realms, there is also some sense that, in its unique evolution, confederal governance may at last be finding a place of its own.

Federation has been a mechanism by which smaller states have turned themselves into great powers or at least middle-sized states. Confederation may now be emerging as a form of governance by which like-minded states, large and small, can form limited-purpose partnerships that bring a higher degree of economic and political order to entire regions of the world with-out, however, imperiling the sociocultural heritages of ethnic groups who live in the nation-states that they unite. If this is true, the modern confed-eration may no longer be just a way station, but a form of governance that both meets the need for higher-level political and economic unity and pre-serves the diversity of the world's peoples.

To this end, the Maastricht Treaty pledges that the Union will "respect the national identities of its Member States, whose systems of government are founded on the principles of democracy" (Article F). It sets up the principle of "subsidiarity," which promises that the Union's "institutions" will not intrude into areas where policies and activities are better carried out at the national level (though leaving it vague as to what "better" actually means). It would, however, be better to agree in advance upon the spheres that are *not* to be confederalized, that is to say, the areas where national governments will retain the right to act on their own. The lines between the two spheres need to be drawn with a precision that would enable the European Court of Justice and national supreme courts to settle any disputes that may arise between the Union and its member states over which of them has the com-petence to act in given situations. In the absence of such agreements and clarifications, the crises between states with minimalist and maximalist views on the nature of their Union may be disruptive and could even lead to a break-up of the Union.

However, such an outcome seems unlikely because the spheres to be confed-eralized have always been more or less agreed. They are the economic and monetary spheres and, to the extent that it proves possible, the foreign affairs and military spheres. In other spheres, there would only be intergovernmental cooperation of the kind that the United Nations promotes at the global level.

While Parliament's new legal powers combined with those it already had are impressive, it is still too soon to know whether its members will be able to exercise them effectively. Even on the legal front, the Council of Ministers remains the senior legislative partner. It can still block almost any important decision, while Parliament's power to do so is limited to a smaller range of decisions.

Indeed, efforts to vest the EP with powers that parallel those being exercised by member state legislatures may be impractical. The ultimate question is not so much whether a popularly elected body should be allowed to bring effective pressures to bear on a conclave of government representatives. Rather, it is whether, in what is still primarily a union of states, it is reasonable to expect the EU's "parliament" to function like the parliaments of federal and unitary states.

The Council's de facto strength lies in the fact that it is the agent of powerful governments, whereas the popular support behind the EP does not yet run very deep. Except among the Europeanist elites and other activist groups, that support still seems thin. Also, it may be that national electorates, if they fully understood what was involved, might not be too eager to have important powers transferred from their own legislatures to one in which their delegates are greatly outnumbered by those from other member states and in which most decisions are taken by a simple majority of those present and voting. Does it not seem likely that they will welcome such a transfer only when their allegiance to the European Union becomes stronger than their allegiance to their present homelands?

In these circumstances, it may be better for the EP to remain what it has always been, a pressure group whose main role is to reflect as best it can the wishes of the peoples whom it represents and to press national leaders and intergovernmental bodies to heed their wishes. If undertaken seriously, this approach may help counter the special interest groups, such as the farmers, that so often dominate governmental policies. In the carrying out of this more modest role, the "cooperation procedure" may prove a sounder instrument than the new "co-decision procedure," because it allows the Commission to mediate the inherent rivalry between Parliament and the Council of Ministers.

While the time may come when the peoples of Europe will wish to form a more integrated Union, that time is still not at hand. Indeed, the question whether it is either practical or desirable to form such huge federal states has many ramifications that need to be carefully weighed. The experience gained with confederal governance may eventually lead to one of two conclusions: It may show that there is no need for the Union to become a full-scale federal state or it may point the way to the gradual transformation of its present confederal or proto-federal institutions into federal ones.

Finally, the political evolution of "Europe" has shown that many nation-states can join together in forming wider unions and communities to attain very important economic goals. The question now arises whether some of the procedures and institutions that helped build the European Union may be adapted to the formation of another modern confederation—this time a global collective security confederation—to prevent the use of weapons of mass destruction.

NOTES

1. Judge Paul Kirchhof of the German Federal Constitutional Court stated: "The European Union is a confederation of states which is not legitimized by a single European people but rather by the people of the states which together form the Community" (*Eurecom* 1995, p. 3).

2. In this section, I have relied heavily on D. Swann's *The Economics of the Common Market;* John Pinder's *European Community: The Building of a Union;* and Derek Urwin's *The Community of Europe, A History of European Integration Since 1945.*

3. The dropping of "Economic" from the European Economic Community was apparently designed to remove a verbal barrier to the formation of a broader political union.

4. The successive constitutional conferences of the members of the European Community (Union) have created a confusing plethora of legal texts which create major problems of referencing. The original Rome Treaty adopted in 1958 "the Treaty Establishing the European Community" has been greatly revised and amended over the years while keeping the original format and subject matter of the 246 original articles unchanged. Where new articles have been added, they have been inserted with letters following the earlier number, e.g. Article 130 is now followed by Articles 130a–130y. The article references in this book with the additional "EEC" added after them refer to the latest version of that treaty. At Maastricht in 1992, another treaty, the Treaty on European Union, was superimposed on the Rome Treaty, but its articles are expressed in capital letters rather than numbers, i.e. Articles A–S. However, in some cases, several articles are assigned a single letter and expressed as K, K1–K8. Both the Treaty on European Union and the Treaty Establishing the European Community may be found in a single volume published in 1993 by the Office of Official Publications for the European Communities which is located in Luxembourg and is cited among the references to this chapter.

REFERENCES

Act Concerning the Election of the Representatives of the European Parliament by Direct Universal Suffrage, 1976. In *Treaties Establishing the European Communities, Treaties Amending These Treaties, Single European Act.* Luxembourg: Office for Official Publications of the European Communities, 1987.
Calingaert, Michael. *The 1992 Challenge from Europe: Development of the European*

Community's Internal Market. Washington, DC: National Planning Association (British), 1988.

Cavazza, Fabio Luca, and Carlo Pelanda. "Maastricht, Before, During and After." In *Daedalus,* Spring 1994, pp. 53–80.

Cecchini, Paolo, with Michael Catinat and Alexis Jacquemin. *The European Challenge, 1992 The Benefits of a Single Market*. Gower, 1988.

Constantinesco, Vlad. "Who's Afraid of Subsidiarity?" In *Yearbook of International Law,* 1991, 1, pp. 33–55.

Crouch, Colin, and David Marquand, eds. *The Politics of 1992, Beyond the Single European Market*. Oxford/Cambridge: Political Quarterly Publishing Co., 1990.

The *Economist,* June 18, 1994, pp. 55–56; July 8, 1995, p. 46a (1995a); May 20, 1995, p. 50 (1995b); August 29, 1995 (1995c).

Eurecom (periodical published by the European Commission), September 1995.

The European Council, Presidency Conclusions, October 29, 1993.

Fitzmaurice, John. "European Community Decision-Making: The National Dimension." In Juliet Lodge, ed. *Institutions and Policies of the European Community*. New York: St. Martin's Press, 1983, pp. 1–8.

Forsyth, Murray. *Unions of States*. Leicester: Leicester University Press, 1981.

Freestone, David. "The European Court of Justice." In Juliet Lodge, ed. *Institutions and Policies of the European Community*. New York: St. Martin's Press, 1983, pp. 43–53.

Freestone, David A. C., and J. S. Davidson. *The Institutional Frame-work of the European Communities*. London and New York: Croon Helm, 1988.

Henig, Stanley. "The European Community's Bicephalus Political Authority: Council of Ministers-Commission Relations." In Juliet Lodge, ed. *Institutions and Policies of the European Community*. New York: St. Martin's Press, 1983, pp. 1–7.

Hoffman, Stanley. "Europe's Identity Crisis Revisited." In *Daedalus,* 123 (4), Spring 1994, pp. 1–23.

Koopmans, T. "The Future of the Court of Justice of the European Communities." In *Yearbook of European Law,* 1991, 11, pp. 15–32.

Larsen, J.A.O. *Greek Federal States, Their Institutions and History*. Oxford: Clarendon Press, 1968.

Lister, Frederick. *Decision-Making Strategies for International Organizations: The IMF Model*. Denver, CO: University of Denver, 1984.

Lodge, Juliet, ed. *Institutions and Policies of the European Community*. New York: St. Martin's Press, 1983.

————, ed. *The European Community and the Challenge of the Future*. New York: St. Martin's Press, 1989.

Noel, Emile. *Working Together—The Institutions of the European Community*. Luxembourg: Office for Official Publications of the European Communities, 1994.

Pinder, John. *European Community: the Building of a Union*. Oxford: Oxford University Press, 1991.

Shonfield, Andrew. *Europe: Journey into an Unknown Destination*. Hammondsworth, UK: Penguin Books, 1973.

Swann, D. *The Economics of the Common Market.* Hammondsworth, Middlesex, UK: Penguin Modern Classics, 1970.

Treaty on European Union, Treaty Establishing the European Community. Luxembourg: Office for Official Publications of the European Communities, 1993.

Urwin, Derek M. *The Community of Europe: A History of European Integration Since 1945.* London: Longman, 1991.

Weiler, J.H.H. "Journey to an Unknown Destination: A Retrospective and Prospective of the European Court of Justice in the Arena of Political Integration." In *Journal of Common Market Studies,* 31 (4), December 1993, pp. 417–46.

Chapter 3

The United Nations: A Collective Security Confederation in the Making?

INTRODUCTION

The European Union is a continental community at some middle point on the heterogeneity–homogeneity axis. The United Nations, a universal political association open to all the world's states and to all its peoples, lies by definition at the heterogeneous end of that axis. The main issue before the European Union is: Can a regional community still in the confederal sector of that axis successfully adopt federal governmental institutions and eventually merge its member states in a federal union? The corresponding issue for the United Nations would seem to be: Can the world community confederalize its interstate relations in time and to the extent required to save itself from being overwhelmed by its weapons of mass destruction?

There is, of course, one obvious difference between the four prototype confederations mentioned in Chapter 1 and global security associations of states such as the League of Nations and the United Nations. Specifically, those confederations were "permanent" alliances of groups of states designed to protect themselves against a great power. Further, they were small "in-groups" of allies defending themselves against much larger "out-groups."

Contrariwise, the goal of both the League and the UN has been to minimize rather than to sharpen in-group/out-group polarization. Now, more than ever, the threat posed by the coming widespread availability of weapons of mass destruction requires all states, all peoples, and all ethnic groups, in the interest of their common survival, to learn how to coexist with one another in peace.

Despite this major difference, the smaller confederations and the United Nations share a common rationale: Both are founded on the notion that the security of states and peoples requires long-term alliances that gradually metamorphose into permanent associations of those states and into permanent communities of their respective peoples. In the prototype confederations, these associations were directed against external enemies. The association created by the United Nations is directed against rogue member states that engage in, or threaten, acts of aggression against the states that, in the words of the Charter's Preamble, "[are ready to] live together in peace with one another as good neighbors."

The practical problems involved in establishing an effective worldwide collective security system remain formidable. The prototype confederal unions could more easily command support and allegiance because their peoples and their forms of government (oligarchical, princely or democratic[1]) possessed elements of homogeneity. A global union, on the other hand, requires highly heterogeneous peoples and governments to learn how to cooperate closely and systematically with one another over the long term. Further, the earlier confederal unions, each formed in response to a common threat to its security, could more readily persuade members to exercise their military and foreign policy functions jointly because few of them could do so with equal chance of success on their own. By contrast, the many members of a global association (the UN now has 185 members!) usually face no such common threat or inducement.

In a global collective security system, states entrust the commonality with responsibility for their defense: They create what amounts to a common police force. Smaller states, which have always had to rely on powerful allies or on neutrality for security, usually welcome such a system. On the other hand, the states known as "great powers" have traditionally prided themselves on being able to take care of their own security and on exercising an influence that makes itself felt far beyond their own borders. Thus, it is much more difficult to persuade them to give up their freedom of action and to be legally bound by pre-agreed rules of procedure and action that limit their options even in times of political and military crisis.

Moreover, in any collective security system, these states usually insist upon playing the same dominant role that they have always played in their relationships with other countries. Their insistence upon having a privileged position is bound to create serious tensions between them and the other members of the system—a problem that the UN began to face at its founding in San Francisco and has had to face ever since.

Furthermore, the leaders and peoples of confederating states cannot escape the fact that in collective security systems each member has the duty of coming to the aid of any other member that may be attacked. This is clearly a burdensome duty; it requires governments to be ready and willing to put their citizens in harm's way in confrontations where their immediate interests may not be directly involved.

In the prototype confederations, it was plain to see that any successful act of aggression against one of the members threatened the security of all. In our present nuclear age, this is probably also true on a global scale. But the linkage is not so immediately apparent. Even when confronted with flagrant acts of aggression, therefore, peoples and their elected leaders are likely to be reluctant to intervene militarily unless they are convinced that key national interests are at stake. This is particularly true if the state under attack is far away or has an "unattractive" government.

But those who insist upon the national interest criterion fail to recognize (1) that in any collective security system, a state being overrun has a right to expect the military support of other members; and (2) that allowing aggressors to prevail in one place encourages aggression elsewhere and undermines the credibility of the system as a whole. In fact, the world community is not likely to attain any truly dependable collective security until the very notion of one state invading and annexing another is widely seen by governments and peoples alike as an intolerable offense calling for automatic intervention by the international "police force."

The protection of member states against aggression is just one aspect of maintaining international peace and security. Many less serious interstate confrontations may at times erupt into violence. These include not just legal disputes, but tensions, rivalries, and old scores to be settled. In many such situations, it is difficult to determine who is right and who wrong. Over the past 50 years, the Security Council has had a mixed record in dealing with these situations. During the next 50 years, the Council's success rate will need to be much better.

Its chances of achieving a better success rate will be minimal if its member states remain as ready to use force against one another as they have been in the past. Disputes and tensions among member states are apt to remain commonplace. The main question is whether they will be ready to resolve them peacefully, that is to say, by arbitration or adjudication instead of force.

Have the United Nations and its member states reached the point where a full-scale confederal relationship is or may soon be feasible for them? Actually, the UN's past record in countering obvious acts of aggression is pretty good: The statehood of both South Korea and Kuwait was preserved against powerful aggressors, and none of its member states has so far suffered the fate of Ethiopia and Czechoslovakia under the League of Nations. But it may be that prompt action in these cases happened to coincide with what the United States and its NATO allies saw as their direct national interests. The still-evolving situation in Bosnia has revealed the vulnerabilities of our post–Cold War collective security system.

Unfortunately, the UN's record in dealing with endemic tensions and rivalries is a very mixed one. The Security Council was soon marginalized when the Cold War broke out. And many regional crises, such as those in the Middle East and the Asian Subcontinent, were punctuated by brief wars that the Council was unable to prevent. If the commands of that Council, issued under Chapter VII of the Charter, are regularly ignored by the member states to which they are directed, there is no way that the UN can cross the threshhold of confederation.

The present chapter is focused on the UN's collective security role and on how it might eventually carry out that role (1) by explaining how its collective security system came into being and what happened to it during the Cold War; (2) by briefly analyzing the UN's present structure and procedures in terms of the seven features that have already been applied to the European Union; and (3) by weighing the long-term prospects for its collective security system and for the production of confederal-type ties among its member states. It will not address the many other elements in the UN's mandate.

(1) THE ORIGINS OF THE UN'S COLLECTIVE SECURITY SYSTEM

A careful distinction needs to be made between the constitutional framework provided for the United Nations by its Charter and the United Nations that has actually emerged during the past 50 years. The Charter provided for a UN that was mostly IGO, but had one confederal-type component. That component was the Security Council and its global collective security system. In 1944–1945, immense importance was attached to that component by those who wanted to make sure that there would never be another world war. The present section tells the story of how that confederal component came to be part of the Charter and how the attempt to establish a working collective security system quickly collapsed.

In 1945, the general problems just described were accompanied by a serious specific problem for which no answer could be found—the widely shared suspicion that the Soviet Union would turn out to be a maverick great power. Should that happen, there could be no global collective security system. As Winston Churchill later wrote, he felt "bound to proclaim [his] confidence in Soviet good faith in the hope of procuring it" (Churchill 1953, p. 400).

In retrospect, it seems remarkable that right through the San Francisco Conference, the three leading powers (the United States, Britain, and the Soviet Union) clung together. Their often bittersweet relationship was maintained as long as they faced common enemies in Germany and Japan. At President Roosevelt's insistence, the Charter was adopted before their collegial relationship could be destroyed in the aftermath of World War II.

In describing the framing of the Charter's confederal-type features, we shall draw heavily upon Ruth Russell's authoritative account of how they came to be the way they are (Russell 1958, pp. 92–124, 133–37, 154–65, 188–93, 206–15, 227–302, 349–68, 394–408, 424–32, 440–77, 497–506, 531–44, 599–610, and 646–776).

At the outset, the world community was confronted with preliminary questions. Should all the functions being carried out globally be confided to a single organization, or should there be one for collective security and another (or others) for the remaining functions? Should the body responsible for collective security include just the leading states, or should it include other states that would make it more representative of the various regions of the world? And should the collective security function be handled centrally, regionally, or divided between the two?[2]

During the early years of the World War II, Roosevelt seems to have thought in terms of a separate entity for peace enforcement composed solely of the great powers, with all other states totally disarmed. When Eden visited Washington in March 1943, Roosevelt and Sumner Welles "were very emphatic . . . that the real decisions should be made by the United States, Great Britain, Russia and China, who would be the powers for many years to come that would have to police the world." At the Teheran Conference in late 1943, he expatiated upon this idea while talking to Stalin, proposing that there be a four-power enforcement body, "the Four Policemen," with power to deal immediately with any threat to the peace or any sudden emergency. In countering a major threat of aggression by a "large power," "the Four Policemen would send an ultimatum to the threatening nation, and if the demands were not immediately met, they would subject that nation to bombardment and, if necessary, invasion" (Sherwood 1948, pp. 717, 785–86).[3]

At one point, the British Foreign Office carried matters even further, suggesting that the supreme direction of a postwar organization be entrusted to a council composed of the Big Four powers. However, Churchill was more sensitive to other countries' wishes and foresaw the creation of Scandinavian, Danubian, and Balkan "confederations" that would also be represented on the Council (Churchill 1951, pp. 636, 717). Neither the moral dubiousness nor the practical problems of subordinating all other states to the wishes of a great power alliance or "concert" (as it used to be called in the nineteenth century) seem to have been noticed at that moment when the Four were desperately staving off Axis domination.

Roosevelt expected that the Four Policemen would be supplemented by two other bodies, a worldwide assembly of representatives from all of the UN's member states to discuss world problems and make recommendations for their solution, and a smaller executive committee, composed of the four major states together with representatives of various other groups of countries to "deal with all nonmilitary questions—such as economy, food, health, etc." The Soviets, at first, did not agree that the new organization should deal with more than security enforcement (Sherwood 1948, p. 785; Russell 1958, p. 422). Thus, in the early planning stages, what were to become the UN's confederal and IGO functions (though they were not, of course, thought of in those terms) were to be carried out in separate entities.

Churchill's qualms with regard to the sensitivities of other countries came soon to be shared by Roosevelt and accepted by Stalin. The idea of a separate entity for enforcement purposes run exclusively by the leading states was soon dropped in favor of a more widely acceptable proposal for a Security Council composed of permanent and elected members. At the same time, however, the main thrust of the earlier proposal was retained: The Security Council was to be dominated by the great powers, and their domination would be greatest in the realm of sanctions and enforcement.

The decision to include elected members was of fundamental importance. It determined that the UN's collective security system was not to be run by the great powers alone; rather, it was to be a joint enterprise of those states and the UN's other members. Perhaps even more important, the balance of influence between the two groups might be modified by Charter amendment.

It was first assumed that the number of elected and permanent members would be the same, and the ultimate decision to have one more elected than permanent member was regarded as a major concession. What should be noted, however, is that the Charter authorized the great powers and six (later 10) other member states (i.e., a manageable number) to operate jointly a collective security system on behalf of the world community as a whole.

For a time, it looked as if the UN's collective security system might be given a strong regional orientation. Churchill, for example, supported the creation of regional councils for Europe, Asia, and the Americas. He argued that the experience of the League of Nations had demonstrated that "it was only the countries whose interests were directly affected by a dispute who could be expected to apply themselves with sufficient vigor to secure a settlement" (Russell 1958, p. 107). He thus drew attention to what was bound to be once again a major weakness in any global security system. Moreover, he was initially able to persuade Stalin, who was obsessed by fears of a German revival, of the wisdom of this approach. The proposal also enjoyed the support of Under-Secretary of State Sumner Welles and the Latin American states. But Roosevelt came to share Secretary Cordell Hull's preference for a fully centralized system, and Stalin, mindful of the USSR's major interests in the Far East, switched his position. The regional approach to collective security remained, but as one that would remain under the Security Council's ultimate control. (See Chapter VIII of the Charter.[4])

It would be hard to exaggerate the importance of this decision. It meant that the world was to have one supreme collective security system. The regions could have their own systems, but they would be subordinate to the one run by the Security Council. Even when they were carried out by regional entities, enforcement actions had to be authorized and controlled from the center (Charter, Article 53).

Creation of the UN's Collective Security System

The main features of the Charter's collective security system may be traced to the lessons learnt from the performance of the League of Nations and the political and military experience gained just before and during World War II. The League had not been able to cope successfully with aggressor-states, and the intensity of World War II had shown that effective enforcement of sanctions was not likely to be achieved with half-way measures.

Under Article 10 of the Covenant, Members of the League had undertaken "to respect and preserve as against external aggression the territorial integrity and existing political independence of all Members of the League," which made it a collective security pact. But, in that article's second sentence, it was provided that, when a state was attacked, the Council could only "advise upon the means by which this obligation shall be fulfilled" (Covenant 1958). While the Covenant did provide for compulsory economic sanctions against an aggressor, it empowered the Council only "to recommend to the several governments concerned what effective military, naval or air force the Members of the League shall severally contribute to the armed forces to be used to protect the covenants of the League" (Covenant 1958, Article 16 (1) and (2)). These powers proved woefully insufficient both to deter aggression and to bring meaningful assistance to its victims.

Furthermore, as three distinguished commentators have pointed out in comparing the Covenant and the Charter, the former "had emphasized the legal approach to the prevention of war by placing specific obligations upon members," whereas "the Charter approach was essentially political since in the last analysis the measures to be taken and their effectiveness were made to depend on the readiness of the major military powers to co-operate in defense of common interests" (Goodrich, Hambro, and Simons 1969, pp. 10–11).

The enforcement powers of the League of Nations had indeed proved sadly inadequate to cope with the crises it had faced. In framing the UN's collective security system, Britain, the United States, and the USSR agreed that they needed to be strengthened. To achieve this, the Security Council was set apart from the UN's other principal organs and given the power enjoyed by earlier confederal governing bodies to act on behalf of their member states. It was specifically authorized to determine when there had been breaches of the peace or acts of aggression, what sanctions should be imposed on the states held responsible for such acts, and what measures should be taken to enforce those sanctions.

Thus, rather than entrusting two bodies with identical powers of recommendation (as provided for the Council and the Assembly of the League in its Covenant), the three states planned for a Council having the sole power to summon the member states to military action and thereby to counter acts of aggression in a timely way. From the outset, it was envisaged that no other UN political body would be empowered to issue orders that would be legally binding upon member states, and even the Security Council's power to do so would be limited to serious crises that threatened international peace and security. For the most part, other states did not mind the Council being the principal body for maintaining international peace and security despite their doubts that it could really carry out such a challenging mandate.

This was the central concept around which the collective security system of the United Nations took shape, and the three great powers elaborated at successive stages what that shape should be. Chinese and French diplomats were successively admitted to their councils, but played peripheral roles. Most of the collective security provisions later included in the Charter were hammered out by diplomats representing the great powers at an old mansion in Washington, D.C. (Dumbarton Oaks), in the late summer of 1944.

Underlying the collective security system set up for the UN were seven implicit assumptions or premises:

1. The great powers would pledge themselves and would consider themselves morally bound not to go to war against each other, or against any other nation, and to cooperate with one another and with other peace-loving states in maintaining the peace;

2. Their unanimity must be preserved in all crucial matters since they alone were in a position to effectively enforce the Council's decisions;

3. Each great power would be willing to maintain adequate forces and would be willing to use such forces as circumstances required to prevent or suppress all cases of aggression;

4. No great power could be expected to commit itself to support an enforcement action that it had voted against;

5. If a great power disturbed the peace, action against it would be tantamount to war rather than to police measures, and would, therefore, have to be taken outside the Organization;

6. Accordingly, the military forces available to the Security Council needed only to be large enough to deal with international controversies that did not involve a great power;

7. To carry out the foregoing, the Security Council would need to be "predominant" in the UN's collective security sphere, and the great powers expected to counter acts of aggression would need to have permanent seats and the right of veto power over the Council's enforcement decisions (Russell 1958, pp. 245, 247, 260, 399, 403).

As events showed, these premises were far from being realistic in 1945. Some of them (especially (3)) seem equally unrealistic today. On the other hand, they seem to be conditions that a global collective security system must meet if it is to stand much chance of functioning effectively.

Anyone who reads Russell's account of the Dumbarton Oaks negotiations cannot fail to be impressed with the relative ease with which the main features of the UN's collective security system were agreed upon by the great powers.[5] For example, all were agreed that the Security Council should be given "binding power to determine threats to or breaches of the peace and to take any necessary action to maintain peace and security in such situations" (Russell 1958, p. 464). And, what is more surprising in view of their subsequent tense relations, they agreed readily on the general powers and procedures needed to enable the Council to fulfill those functions (Russell 1958, pp. 440–77).

There was some discussion of the practical questions of how military force was to be organized, perhaps more than is reflected in Russell's account. In their submissions, the Chinese and the Russians had proposed the creation of an international air force for use against aggressors, an idea that apparently also appealed to Churchill. The American counterproposal for earmarking military contingents in legally binding agreements for use by the Council in enforcement actions was adopted in its stead. The wishes of the Soviets and Chinese were, however, partly accommodated in what became Article 45 of the Charter: Air units were to be kept in special readiness while remaining under national control. The principal question that arose with regard to a proposed Military Staff Committee was whether it should be composed of representatives only from the leading states or from all members. The British, drawing from their experience with the Combined Chiefs of Staff (American/British) during World War II, urged the smaller number while the Soviet Union would have had all Council members represented. Since the Americans and Russians did not care much, the British view prevailed.

The guiding purposes and principles of the new Organization (Articles 1 and 2 of the Charter)—of great importance because they set the framework within which the collective security system was to operate—were apparently adopted with "little difficulty." So were the regional arrangements and the provisions for regulating armaments. The role that the Security Council was to play in the peaceful settlement of disputes raised more questions, particularly whether it would be limited to determining the procedures for settling disputes or would itself become involved in working out the terms of settlement. In hindsight, it appears that the framers would have been better advised to leave the Council the same broad latitude in dealing with disputes that they had given it in selecting enforcement actions (Russell 1958, pp. 455–57).

The only serious quarrel arose over the Council's voting procedures. Under Article 15 of the Covenant of the League, a party to a dispute had not been allowed to vote on its own case. Both the Americans and the British felt that this rule should be maintained in the Charter for all members, wishing to make the dispute-settlement procedures the same for all members, large or small. However, foreseeing its minority position in the Council, the Soviet Union strongly disagreed and could not be moved to change its view.

To lose its veto power in such situations meant that an unpopular great power might be publicly humiliated by its peers and their many allies and supporters. Moreover, in the dispute-settlement realm, any state was entitled to reject any recommendation it did not like, and a permanent member could veto any effort to enforce a decision that it had opposed. Thus, an adverse decision against one of them at the earlier stage would serve little purpose, while a better way of upsetting great-power harmony can scarcely be imagined. When discussion of the issue was resumed at Yalta in early 1945, Stalin warned that he would "never agree" to any Soviet action being submitted to the judgment of smaller states, and both Roosevelt and Churchill worried about finding themselves in the same position. Stalin later yielded on this issue, however, in return for getting Britain and the United States to agree to separate UN memberships for the Ukraine and Byelorussia (Russell 1958, pp. 445–50, 519, 531–34).

The compulsory abstention rule (which was ultimately adopted in Article 27 (3) of the Charter), if rigorously enforced, entails some other anomalies. For example, it would have made it very difficult for any proposal to get seven affirmative votes if the three Western powers had brought their complaint over the Soviet blockade of Berlin before the Council as a dispute with the Soviet Union. Similarly, in the 1951 Suez Canal dispute with Egypt, no less that five members of the Council were disputants. On that occasion, despite Egypt's strong objections, the five proceeded to use their votes, and a resolution was adopted anyway (Goodrich, Hambro, and Simons 1969, p. 229 (n. 122); Boyd 1971, pp. 85–87). A way around this difficulty was found; the Council no longer dealt with "disputes" but only with "situations" to which there were no parties and, therefore, no one to abstain. Thus, the most serious disagreement at Dumbarton Oaks was over a voting procedure that proved impractical and is now ignored for all Council members, large and small alike.

The San Francisco Conference

At the subsequent San Francisco Conference, the great powers, now numbering five, played a dominant role as the "sponsoring states." Over and over, the importance of their "unanimity" was dramatized by the lengthy caucuses that they held and the detailed consensus statements with which they sought to overawe the other participants. The many attempts of the latter to whittle away the special privileges that these states had carved out for themselves at Dumbarton Oaks could not prevail against this rare display of great-power unity.

However, the Five did submit their proposals for the global collective security system to the representatives of the 45 other participants and did make numerous changes of detail, many of them reflecting their own second thoughts after studying what they had wrought earlier. In listening to the other states, and trying to accommodate some of their suggestions, they went further than the founders of the League of Nations, whose Covenant had been adopted at the Versailles Conference by the great powers alone. Still, the system agreed upon at Dumbarton Oaks was, in its essential features, the one finally included in the Charter.

Quite naturally, the 45 states that had not taken part in the Dumbarton Oaks negotiations were not very pleased at what they quickly saw as the perfunctory treatment being accorded them. Boyd summed up that treatment as follows: "The San Francisco 'founders' were, in fact, summoned to that Californian city to approve a basic structure for the U.N. that had already been privately agreed between the Big Three. . . . [The latter] overrode protests; and the 'founders' had no choice but to countersign the great powers' plan" (Boyd 1971, pp. 54–55). In fairness, it should be added that this was true only of the collective security provisions. Even those of Chapter VI on the settlement of disputes were much changed, while the provisions on economic, social, and human rights and on the trusteeship plan were fully negotiated at San Francisco by the leading states.

Russell's account makes it clear that many of the 45 came prepared to challenge the predominant role of the great powers in security matters. To do so, they sought to remove the veto power of those states over Chapter VI "Settlement of Disputes" decisions and to increase the General Assembly's powers in the Chapter VII collective security sphere. In the first effort, they got nowhere; in the second, they had only marginal success.

The reason for this lack of success was that the 45 were far from united. Their bargaining power was weakened by the fact that they stood to benefit greatly if the collective security system embodied in the Dumbarton Oaks proposals could be made to work effectively. More than the great powers, they needed protection against aggressors. And a world political order of the kind set forth in the Charter was what they wanted most. Those of them that had just emerged from German and Japanese occupation knew how much they had to lose if that order again broke down. There was, in fact, no real opposition of interests, at least not in the realm of collective security, between these middle-sized and smaller countries and the Conference's five sponsors so long as the latter remained zealous enforcers and did not themselves engage in acts of aggression.

Thus, they were not so much averse to President Roosevelt's vision of the major powers acting as global policemen to keep a universal peace as profoundly skeptical that those powers could be made to perform that role. The prospects for creating a new world order in which national armies would begin to take on the character of police forces seemed dubious at best. Until that time came, they wanted to play a more active role in collective security than the Dumbarton Oaks proposals had allocated to them.

It was against this background that many of the 45 sought, without much success, to modify the Dumbarton Oaks proposals at San Francisco. The following examples may be cited in this connection:

1. Proposals to increase the Security Council's membership by adding more elected members were rejected (Russell 1958, pp. 649–50).

2. The Security Council's unlimited right of intervention was maintained, i.e., it was allowed "to prevent fighting as a policeman does, deferring inquiry into the rights and wrongs of a situation until later, when the procedures of peaceful settlement would come into play and the principles of law and justice could operate" (Russell 1958, p. 656).

3. A proposal that the Secretary-General should be empowered to bring a dangerous situation to the Assembly's attention as well as to the Council's was rejected (Russell 1958, p. 658).

4. Many smaller countries, quite naturally, wanted to have included among the principles in Article 2 a guarantee that there would be automatic collective resistance to any act of aggression against any member, i.e., an undertaking similar to that in Article 10 of the Covenant. Somewhat embarrassed, the leading powers insisted that the Council must be allowed "to act flexibly and selectively." They took refuge in ingenuous explanations, e.g., the U.S. Senate would never agree to such a broad undertaking. The truth was that none of the Five was eager to accept such a duty as a binding obligation. The absence of such a provision in the Charter remains a serious gap in the UN's collective security system. Some satisfaction was given the smaller countries in the following "interpretation" of Articles 39–40 of the Charter adopted by the Committee concerned with this issue:

    The Committee is unanimous in the belief that . . . in the case of a flagrant aggression imperilling the existence of a member of the Organization, enforcement measures should be taken without delay, and to the full extent required by circumstances, except that the Council should at the same time endeavor to persuade the aggressor to abandon its venture. (Russell 1958, pp. 673–76; the quotation is from footnote 59)

5. A proposal to enlarge the Military Staff Committee was rejected (Russell 1958, p. 677).

6. The most serious confrontation both among the Five and between the 45 and the Five was over the voting formula for the Security Council. Demands by the Soviet Union that the veto power extend to placing questions on the Council's agenda aroused general opposition and came close to wrecking the conference. In the end, the Dumbarton Oaks provision that procedural questions would not be subject to the veto power was kept unchanged. At the same time, the Soviet view that a decision to include a question on the Council's agenda was not a procedural question was rejected by other members. Yet no clarifying provision was placed in the Charter itself. However, the five sponsors did adopt a statement

indicating that the Council would have to decide whether or not a decision was procedural and that in such voting the permanent members must be in concurrence, the so-called "double veto." (In the early years, the members of the Council did agree upon the categories of decisions to be regarded as procedural.)

A proposal that dispute settlement questions not be subject to the veto also led to heated discussion. While it was widely accepted at the San Francisco Conference that enforcement was mainly great-power business, there seemed at first glance no good reason why all members of the world community should not be involved on equal terms in the peaceful settlement of disputes. The Five, however, insisted that they should be able to veto decisions on disputes because they were often interconnected with maintaining international peace and security. When the 45—led by Australia—protested, they were told bluntly that unless the voting provision was accepted, there would be no organization (Russell 1958, p. 736). In the end, no such limit was placed on the veto power of the Five.

7. Another flashpoint of disagreement between the 45 and the Five was the Dumbarton Oaks provision for Charter amendment, which provided that no amendment could enter into force until it had been ratified by all five permanent members of the Security Council. A number of proposals were introduced to make it easier to amend the Charter. But the Five were concerned that they would make it possible for the collective security system to be modified in ways that they could not accept. The most that the 45 could win (and it was not very much) was a provision that any proposal to hold a conference to review the Charter would not be subject to the veto power, and that if no conference had been held by the tenth session of the General Assembly, the question would automatically appear on that session's agenda. However, any amendments adopted at such a conference would still require ratification by all five of the leading powers (Russell 1958, pp. 742–49).

8. Finally, the 45 attempted, and on the whole failed, to broaden the collective security powers allocated to the General Assembly. The Five were adamant about maintaining the sole jurisdiction of the Security Council within its field of action. Thus, proposals to associate the Assembly directly in enforcement decisions or to permit it to review actions by the Council were all rejected. New Zealand also proposed that the General Assembly's power of recommendation be broadened to include "anything within the sphere of international relations," which would be especially useful "if the Security Council should be paralyzed by use of the veto." The United States responded that if "concurrent authority were allowed the two organs, it would change the whole concept of Dumbarton Oaks and necessitate rewriting the Charter" (Russell 1958, pp. 751, 758–59).

While the Assembly was eventually permitted to discuss and make recommendations on all questions "within the scope of the present Charter," it was barred from intervening in disputes or situations that were before the Security Council. Thus, the Council's primary responsibility for maintaining the peace remained untouched since the Charter makes it clear that it alone has the legal power to act and to enforce its actions on recalcitrant states. What the Charter does not make clear is how long the Council can "sit on" problems, and thus prevent the Assembly from becoming involved in them.

To sum up, the Five maintained all of the main features of the collective security system that they had adopted at Dumbarton Oaks. They asserted their authority in a way that would not be possible in any contemporary IGO. Their language was often blunt and the realities of relative power positions much in evidence. But there is something to be said for their insistence. In the closing months of World War II, the close relationship between military power and any system of collective security was being graphically demonstrated on the battlefield. Any such system that lacked the full support of the great powers would have lost all credibility. Those eager to reform the present political procedures of the UN to reduce what is perceived as the undue influence of the great powers would be wise to move cautiously. Nothing compels those powers to continue to utilize the UN's machinery if they see an advantage in circumventing it. The interest of the member states that are not great powers, like that of their 45 predecessors in San Francisco, is to give the Five no excuse to take their business elsewhere.

The seven implicit assumptions for great-power relationships in a global security system will be reviewed further in the third section of this chapter. But their significance should already be clear. They form the basis for an upper-level "concordance" that may either sustain, or—if it breaks down—upset, the wider union of the UN's 185 members. The world's dependence on this smaller group for its security was revealed by the long crisis of the Cold War. We now know how essential it is for great-power relationships to be kept on an even keel.

The Collapse of the UN's Collective Security System

It would oversimplify matters to place the entire blame for the breakdown of the UN's security system on the Cold War, but it certainly bore a large share of that blame. World War II, as became evident in the years following it, had left behind only two great powers rather than the five for which the Charter provided. Britain and France struggled to remain great powers but never fully regained that status. China had never been a great power in modern times and was destined to approach that status only in recent years. For whatever reason, the two surviving great powers were elevated to a newly invented status, that of superpower. But in the old terminology, the number of great powers had shrunk to two.

Two is an unlucky number. History is replete with examples of two great powers confronting one another like pit bulls. Among the four classic confederal unions, only the Germanic Confederation faced a similar situation, and it survived only as long as Prussia was willing to play second fiddle to Austria.

The Soviet Union, long an outcast from the world community, was tempted by its military victories and its sense of ideological superiority to precipitate a full-scale confrontation with its rival. As we know, Stalin and his successors succumbed to this temptation. The United States responded in kind. This meant that the assumption of great-power cooperation on which the confederal segment of the UN had been founded came tumbling down at the outset. Very soon, the Security Council and other UN organs were being misused by both sides as propaganda forums for waging the Cold War.

Thus, the worst apprehensions of the smaller states were soon borne out. The collective security system envisaged by the Charter collapsed before it could even be set in place. Article 51 of the Charter upheld the inherent right of member states to individual or collective self-defense "until the Security Council has taken the necessary measures to maintain international peace and security." This provided plausible legal grounds for ignoring Article 2 (4)'s prohibition against the use of force when, as often happened, a permanent member prevented the Council from responding effectively to a crisis situation. For many reasons, efforts to strengthen collective security on a regional basis did little to fill the gap.

For a time, it was hoped that the Assembly might be made to take the Council's place as the protector of international peace and security. But, ironically, the Charter's framers had done their work too well for that. A 1950 "Uniting for Peace" resolution sought to transfer some of the Council's enforcement authority to the General Assembly (*General Assembly Official Records,* Resolution 377 (V) of November 3, 1950). The Soviets argued, however, that the Assembly could not assume the Council's primary responsibility for maintaining and enforcing the peace or overturn the Charter principle of great-power unanimity. Moreover, as has been rightly pointed out:

Instead of "decisions" by the Security Council, which members are obligated to carry out, collective action [was] to be based upon recommendations by the Assembly which, while they may carry great political or moral weight, are not legally binding upon members. (Goodrich, Hambro, and Simons 1969, p. 125)

In any event, it was clear that no reinterpretation of the Charter could produce a confederal-type union that included two superpowers having a prolonged head-on confrontation with one another.

Nonetheless the Security Council, while reduced to operating as an IGO body despite its confederal structure and mandate, served the world community surprisingly well during the Cold War. Though we shall not cover this period in detail, the UN, mostly through the Council's efforts, often managed non-Cold War crises skillfully by coming up with modus vivendi for the parties. A few examples: It acted promptly to forestall major wars between Greece and Turkey over Cyprus in 1964 and between India and Pakistan over Kashmir in 1965. It played a most useful role in the Middle

East by placing its peace-keeping forces between Egypt and Israel first in 1956 and then again in 1973. The second time, when the Yom Kippur war between the two countries threatened to precipitate a Soviet–American crisis that neither superpower wanted, it saved the day by interposing troops rushed from Cyprus between the Egyptians and the advancing Israelis. In 1968, the Council presided over a rare moment of great-power harmony when the Americans, British, and Russians promised, in connection with the adoption of the Nuclear Non-Proliferation Treaty, to come to the aid of any state without nuclear weapons that found itself threatened with nuclear aggression (Boyd 1971, pp. 337–38).

On three occasions, the Council even found ways to enter the enforcement field. Taking advantage of the absence of a Soviet representative, it set in motion the defense of South Korea against the North Korean aggressors. It conducted a blockade against Ian Smith's Rhodesians with the active support of the British. And, after the Cold War, it intervened on behalf of Kuwait against Iraq. When it acted against North Korea and Iraq, however, it did so in IGO fashion, "recommending" that the UN members proceed against North Korea and "authorizing" them to proceed against Iraq. Having taken this step, neither the Council nor its moribund Military Staff Committee became involved in the military sanctions it had recommended and authorized.

Now that the Cold War is history, the question arises whether the collective security system embodied in the Charter can be somehow resurrected, that is to say, whether the confederal segment of the United Nations planned with such pains at Dumbarton Oaks and polished up at San Francisco might at long last be brought to life. We shall explore that possibility in two ways, first by analyzing what may become the confederal component of the UN under the seven headings already applied to the European Union, and then by analyzing the structural and practical problems that need to be resolved before that goal can be attained.

(2) ANALYSIS OF THE MAIN FEATURES OF THE UN'S COLLECTIVE SECURITY BRANCH

Political Allegiance and Social Integration

The UN's governmental superstructure depends, as does that of the European Union, on its possessing a sufficient base of popular support and allegiance. The framers of the Charter gave the United Nations, in its collective security sphere, a legal framework that is confederal in both structure and mandate. But it was not within their power to underpin that framework with any reliable degree of popular support. As a result, the UN's governmental institutions rest on the flimsiest of foundations. While the Charter provides for the Security Council to operate the collective security system in a confederal way, that system has remained, in IGO fashion, an instrument that national governments and their leaders often choose to ignore.

Its position, therefore, remains very precarious. We know that national leaders, including those of the great powers, will continue to compete with one another as heatedly and sometimes as irresponsibly as they have in the past. To keep national and great-power competitiveness within peaceful bounds through a collective security system, governmental leaders must understand and support it themselves and take the steps needed to ensure that the people whom they lead come to understand and support that system. Both of these conditions are still far from being met.

In fact, the importance of collective security was better comprehended in 1945 when so many countries lay devastated by war, and when everyone saw, for the first time, in the ruins of Hiroshima and Nagasaki, what weapons of mass destruction could do. People had, as it were, a preview of what the rest of the world would look like if these weapons were widely used. The shock value of those pictures may be gone, but humanity nonetheless continues to live in the shadow of this growing risk.

At the same time, as the Preparatory Committee for the new Organization noted in 1946, "the United Nations can not prosper, nor can its aims be realized, without the active and steadfast support of the peoples of the world" (quoted in Goodrich, Hambro, and Simons 1969, p. 575). The absence of widespread popular allegiance is a principal reason why such subregional entities as the Caribbean Community are not yet able to attain full confederal status. The world community faces a proportionately greater challenge in surmounting the allegiance hurdle, since the heterogeneity of its peoples is obviously far greater than that of the peoples that make up those subregional communities. Clearly, social cohesiveness is unachievable on a world scale, and the United Nations is not likely to generate feelings of political allegiance, even of a secondary kind, in any predictable time frame.

Accordingly, since the world community cannot hope to rely on *feelings* of social solidarity or political allegiance toward the UN for some time to come, it needs meanwhile to attract widespread *intellectual* support. Such support may be gained if its primary role in helping the world community to minimize the use of force and to avert nuclear exchanges is more widely grasped by the publics in its member states. A main goal of the worldwide network of national UN Associations is to maximize such support for the world organization and its global collective security system.

General Structure of the United Nations

For only a few of the functions assigned to the UN, i.e., for those associated with its collective security system, are the popular support and allegiance outlined in the previous section indispensable requirements. Its other functions mainly involve promoting international cooperation in the political, economic, social, human rights, and other fields. In these spheres, the UN acts as "a center for harmonizing the actions of nations" and in IGO fashion serves as a vehicle or convenience that governments have created to help them carry out certain functions that are best handled transnationally (Article 1 (4)). Governmental readiness to carry out or abide by the UN's recommendations is the primary concern in these spheres though, of course, popular reactions may play some role in determining governmental responses.

Even in the dispute-settlement provisions of the Charter (Chapter VI), the Security Council merely makes recommendations to the parties. Thus, only disputes and "situations" that are likely "to endanger the maintenance of international peace and security" (relatively few in number) activate the Chapter VII side of the UN's collective security system. And only when the Council becomes involved in such cases is it entitled to act authoritatively. Not surprisingly, however, this task of managing world crises that threaten international peace and security has been widely regarded as the quintessential function assigned to the UN.

Accordingly, the governmental structure of the UN is an amalgam of two disparate branches. Its collective security branch was designed to be run by the Security Council, whose members are empowered by the Charter to take decisions of sovereign import that are legally binding on all of the UN's 185 members. In the other branch of its mandate, the UN operates in the traditional way of IGOs, that is by adopting widely supported resolutions that are usually not legally binding upon its member states. The intergovernmental bodies in this other branch fall hierarchically under the overall authority of the General Assembly.

The two branches coexist within the broad framework of the Charter and utilize common financial, executive, and legal services. They have become so intertwined over the years that few fully comprehend the many complexities involved in their coexistence, or even that the UN is composed of these two rather oddly matched arms.

The text of the Charter confirms that the Security Council was intended to act in a confederal way and was, for this purpose, placed in a carefully circumscribed sphere of its own. The Charter entrusted it with the UN's principal mandate of maintaining international peace and security, thereby giving it a primacy over the 185-member General Assembly. In the Charter, the Council's primacy in this sphere is set forth in a categoric way:

In order to ensure prompt and effective action by the United Nations, its Members confer on the Security Council primary responsibility for the maintenance of international peace and security, and agree that in carrying out its duties under this responsibility the Security Council acts on their behalf. (Article 24 (1))

The foregoing provision is complemented by another that bars the General Assembly from making any recommendation with regard to any dispute or "situation" on the Security Council's agenda unless the Council requests it to do so (Article 12 (1)). The Assembly's role is limited to considering and making recommendations on "the general principles of cooperation in the maintenance of international peace and security" and on specific questions not already before the Council. If "action" is thought to be required on any question not already before the Council, the Assembly is not permitted to take such action itself but is obliged to refer it to the Security Council for that purpose (Article 11).

The Security Council's structure is one of power-sharing between the Five and the 180 other member states. The 180 have 10 members on the Council, who are always in a position, whenever any seven of them join together to do so, to block any action that the Five may wish to take.[6] But judging from the way the Council has been functioning since the end of the Cold War, the combined influence of these five members is such that the others do not choose to exercise their ability to block actions very frequently.[7]

The structure of the United Nations is further complicated by other Charter provisions. It is not just in the realm of collective security that the special status of the Five makes itself felt. Any one of them can blackball the application of a state for membership in the Organization and protect any member state from being expelled from it (Articles 4 and 6). This power has been used many times; a number of applications for membership have been delayed for years by it. In addition, any of the Five may block: (1) regional IGOs from taking enforcement actions (Article 53); (2) actions by the Security Council to enforce judgments of the International Court of Justice (Article 94 (2)); (3) appointments and reappointments of Secretaries-General (Article 97); (4) proposed amendments to the Charter (Articles 108–109), including any change in the size and voting arrangements of the Security Council itself; and (5) proposed amendments to the Statute of the International Court of Justice (Article 69 of the Statute). These provisions give the UN's five senior partners a pivotal position in its IGO as well as in its collective security branch.

The Charter belongs to the group of treaty-constitutions that remain deliberately silent on the right of members to withdraw. However, that right is implicit in the voluntary character of all IGOs and confederations, a point of view reluctantly acquiesced in by the founders at the San Francisco Conference. As in the case of most voluntary unions, loss of members through withdrawal has not, as yet, posed a practical problem for the Organization.[8]

The United Nations, like other IGOs and confederations, has the character of a legal partnership based, as Article 2 (1) affirms, "on the principle of the sovereign equality of all its Members." It was agreed at San Francisco that sovereign equality meant (1) that states are juridically equal; (2) that they enjoy the rights inherent in their full sovereignty; (3) that the personality of the state is respected, as well as its territorial integrity and political independence; and (4) that the state must comply faithfully with its international duties and obligations (Russell 1958, p. 672). In operating the UN's collective security system, the Security Council is supposed to heed these rules.

This legal equality of the UN's member states goes hand-in-hand with the many inequalities in their size, population, and influence in the world community outside the Organization. That the UN should have senior and junior partners is unremarkable: All IGOs and confederations share this feature. What is unique to the UN's structure is the extent to which these inequalities have been recognized by the privileges granted by the Charter to its five senior partners.

The reasons for this were probably practical ones. Onerous duties were supposed to accompany these privileges. By limiting the membership of the Military Staff Committee to themselves, the Five implicitly acknowledged that the main burden of enforcement would be theirs. Russell writes that "in [the Security Council] the major powers would be conceded a preferential position in return for their burden of special responsibilities." These "special responsibilities" were the dirty job of enforcement in which the Five would be expected to lead the way and to play the major role (Russell 1958, pp. 440, 646; Lister 1991, pp. 5–6). Needless to say, the Five have usually insisted upon the privileges while often refusing to perform the duties that were supposed to accompany them.

The UN's Collective Security Mandate

The UN's principal mandate is to be the world community's guardian of international peace and security. We come now to the details of the collective security system by which the UN was supposed to carry out that mandate. Under that system, a number of duties were imposed upon member states and upon the Security Council. To begin with, member states had to agree to settle their "international disputes by peaceful means in such a manner that international peace and security, and justice, are not endangered" (Article 2(3)). These states are then told that they must refrain in their international relations "from the threat or use of force against the territorial integrity or political independence of any state, or in any other manner inconsistent with the Purposes of the United Nations" (Article 2(4)). The Charter imposes these duties on nonmember states, too (Article 2(6)).

This prohibition against the use of force by individual governments is paralleled by the authorization to the Security Council in Chapter VII to use force against state malefactors. As Hans Kelsen has pointed out, the purpose of these provisions is to give the UN and its Security Council a monopoly over the use of force (Kelsen 1966, pp. 39–51).

However, Article 51 provides that "Nothing in the present Charter shall impair the inherent right of individual or collective self-defense if an armed attack occurs against a Member of the United Nations until the Security Council has taken measures necessary to maintain international peace and security." This constitutes an important exception to the Council's monopoly of force.

While the right of self-defense is specified in some confederal pacts (for example, in Article VI of the U.S. Articles of Confederation), it opens up a far bigger hole in a global collective security system, when the Council, because of great-power disagreements or for some other reason, cannot come quickly or effectively to the aid of a state or states that have been invaded. As Hans Morgenthau has warned,

a full-fledged war will have started by virtue of the right of collective self-defense. The Security Council, far from being able to stop that war and substitute for it its own enforcement measures, can only participate in it on terms that will necessarily be subordinated to the strategy of the individual belligerent states already engaged in full-scale hostilities . . . it will hardly lose its initial character and be transformed into an enforcement action under the actual guidance of the Security Council. (Morgenthau 1966, pp. 306–7)

When it acts on behalf of the commonality, the Council must be supported by all. Member states are required to "give the United Nations every assistance in any action it takes in accordance with the present Charter" and to "refrain from giving assistance to any state against which the United Nations is taking preventive or enforcement action" (Article 2 (5)). Also, Article 25 specifies that "the members of the United Nations agree to accept and carry out the decisions of the Security Council in accordance with the present Charter." And at the end of the section on enforcement actions, Article 49 reminds members that they are obliged to "join in affording mutual assistance in carrying out the measures decided upon by the Security Council." Finally, the application of such enforcement measures under Chapter VII is specifically exempted from the provision that bars the UN from intervening "in matters which are essentially within the domestic jurisdiction of any state" (Article 2(7)).

Chapters VI, VII and VIII, Articles 33–54, elaborate the Council's duties under the collective security system.

Under Chapter VI, the Council is bound to do what it can to avoid the need for enforcement by promoting peaceful settlement of disputes. Briefly, its role in this sphere may be described as follows. The Charter advises parties involved in disputes that are serious enough to threaten international peace and security that they must seek to resolve those disputes by peaceful means. At this stage, the role of the Council is limited. It may call upon the parties to settle their disputes by means of their choice; it may investigate whether a dispute or "situation" is likely to endanger the peace; it may recommend appropriate procedures or methods of adjustment to the parties; and it may, if the parties fail to reach a settlement, recommend specific terms for such a settlement (Articles 33–38). The Charter reminds the Council that "legal disputes should as a general rule be referred by the parties to the International Court of Justice" (Article 36). These provisions are couched in mild terms, but over each dispute or "situation" looms the possibility that a frustrated or alarmed Council may at some point decide to switch from methods of quiet persuasion to the imposition of sanctions.

Under Chapter VII, the Security Council, with its "primary responsibility for the maintenance of international peace and security," assumes a sterner role. Thus, it determines when there is "any threat to the peace, breach of the peace, or act of aggression," what sanctions should be invoked against those responsible for them, and the military means that may be required to maintain or restore international peace and security. The Council's right to judge the actions of states is far-reaching and not subject to appeal.

However, by exercising their veto power, the five permanent members may prevent such a determination from being made with regard to any of their own acts or to the acts of states whom they wish to protect. This potential gap in the system becomes less serious whenever the Council's permanent members are able to work together constructively, or in the words of the first of the seven premises, "to co-operate with one another and with other peace-loving states in maintaining the peace."

Once it has determined that there has been a breach or a threatened breach of the peace or an act of aggression, the Council has available to it a broad range of steps that it may take. For example, it may temporize by calling upon the parties to adopt provisional measures "without prejudice to [their] rights, claims, or position." It may make recommendations to the state or states involved or it may adopt sanctions. It has the leeway to decide whether to negotiate with the party or parties or to proceed directly to the imposition of sanctions. If it opts for sanctions, it has a wide menu from which to choose (Articles 39–42).

These sanctions are divided into two classes, those that involve the use of military force (Article 42) and those that do not (Article 41). The latter include the "complete or partial interruption of economic relations and of rail, sea, air, postal, telegraphic, radio, and other means of communication, and the severance of diplomatic relations." The former include "such action by air, sea, or land forces as may be necessary to maintain or restore international peace and security" and "demonstrations, blockade, and other operations by air, sea, or land forces of Members of the United Nations." While the Council is not required to adopt these sanctions in any particular order, it may adopt military sanctions only after concluding that nonmilitary ones would be "inadequate." However, this decision may be made at the outset, as it was with regard to North Korea and Iraq (with the ordering of the blockade).

The framers of the Charter did not limit the Council's functions to determining breaches of the peace and acts of aggression and to imposing sanctions. By Articles 43–47, they intended to entrust it with the means to ensure that its sanctions could be enforced. By Article 43 each member state undertook "to make available to the Security Council, on its call and in accordance with a special agreement or agreements, armed forces, assistance and facilities, including rights of passage." These agreements, which were to have been negotiated between the Council and member states as soon as possible on the Council's initiative, were supposed to govern "the numbers and types of forces, their degree of readiness and general location, and the nature of the facilities and assistance to be provided." Provision was also made for groups of states, presumably groups of smaller states, to conclude joint agreements with the Council.

While such forces were to be earmarked for mobilization in time of crisis, the UN was not allowed to have a standing army. However, in order to permit it to take urgent military measures in emergencies, members were to "hold immediately available national air-force contingents for combined international enforcement action" (Article 45).[9]

The Charter also provides for the five-member Military Staff Committee that would "be responsible under the Security Council for the strategic direction of any armed forces placed [at its disposal]." The Committee was given broad terms of reference. It was to advise and assist the Council "on all questions relating to [its] military requirements for the maintenance of international peace and security, the employment and command of forces placed at its disposal, the regulation of armaments, and possible disarmament." Further, other member states would be invited to send their representatives to the Committee "when the efficient discharge of [its] responsibilities requires the participation of that Member in its work." Faced with the same problems involved in choosing commanders as their Swiss and German confederal predecessors, the framers of the Charter, similarly, left questions of command over the joint forces to "be worked out subsequently" (Article 47).

Under Chapter VIII, the UN's collective security system is given a regional dimension:

Nothing in the present Charter precludes the existence of regional arrangements or agencies for dealing with such matters relating to the maintenance of international peace and security as are appropriate for regional action. . . . The Security Council shall, where appropriate, utilize such regional arrangements or agencies for enforcement action under its authority. But no enforcement action shall be taken under regional arrangements or by regional agencies without [its] authorization. (Articles 52–53)

In addition, states that are members of regional agencies are asked to "make every effort to achieve pacific settlement of local disputes . . . before referring them to the Security Council" (Article 52). Thus, the regional agencies might be involved both before and after the authorization of enforcement actions but the power to grant permission to use force remains a prerogative of the Council. However, the escape clause, mentioned earlier, for individual and collective self-defense set forth in Article 51, can be used in this case, too, as a legal basis for eluding the tutelage of a paralyzed or timid Security Council (Goodrich, Hambro, and Simons 1969, pp. 342–53).

Finally, the framers of the Charter saw the regulation of armaments as an important part of the UN's collective security system. Articles 26 and 47 put the major responsibility for this in the lap of the Security Council and the Military Staff Committee. While the General Assembly's role is only to consider "the principles governing disarmament and the regulation of armaments [and to] make recommendations with regard to such principles to the Members or to the Security Council or to both" (Article 11), it has been more active than the Council in this sphere.

What is perhaps the linchpin of the foregoing collective security system was never activated. Before the special agreements could be concluded between the Security Council and member governments, the Cold War intervened. Thus, the Council has never had available to it earmarked national forces that it can call upon to enforce its sanctions. Also, the Military Staff Committee could never perform the role envisioned for it. After 50 years of disuse, these provisions need substantial updating, but until the Council has at its disposal forces strong enough to overawe at least petty aggressors, the UN's collective security system cannot be regarded as fully operative.

At the same time, the Charter's collective security provisions constitute a considerable improvement over those of the League Covenant. Even without the special agreements and an operating Military Staff Committee, the Council has been able to counter successfully the two cases of major interstate aggression. But the system as such still has a number of gaps, flaws and other weaknesses which will be described in the third section of this chapter.

Finance and Taxation

The regular budget of the United Nations and the assessment of member states to pay for its activities in both its confederal and IGO branches were placed by the Charter under the sole authority of the General Assembly. Under Article 17, it considers and approves the budget and determines the scale of assessments in accordance with which member states are charged for their respective shares of the expenses that it incurs. As in other IGO and confederal-type unions, its member states are obligated to pay the Organization whatever monies they have been assessed: In withholding payments of their dues, member states violate one of their most important treaty obligations.

The framers of the Charter foresaw that some member states might not make their payments on time. Therefore, they provided that if a member was more than two full years behind in its payments, it would lose its vote in the General Assembly. However, this sanction could be waived if the Assembly was "satisfied that the failure to pay is due to conditions beyond the control of the Member" (Article 19).

The veto power of the five great powers did not extend to the budget, nor was there any system of weighted voting that would have allowed the wealthier member states (that together pay about 85% of the UN's expenses) to hold down the level of its expenditures. After a series of financial crises, the Assembly has followed in recent years an extraconstitutional practice whereby the UN's budget is now adopted by consensus. The effect is to allow the Five and wealthier states in general to set a ceiling on what the Organization spends. Accordingly, these members no longer have any pretext for withholding funds.[10]

The UN has been kept on a financial leash by the tightfistedness of governments and by their refusal to grant it borrowing powers. Painful as this has sometimes been for the Organization's financial managers, it has a bright side. The rate of increase in the UN's fixed expenditures has been slower than that of some of the loudest complainants among national governments.

While its control of the purse strings brings the General Assembly into the collective security branch of the Organization, there has never been any problem of its appropriating whatever funds are needed by the Security Council to carry out its functions. At the same time, most of the UN's expenditure for collective security has been financed outside its regular budget. The Council has undertaken a growing number of peacekeeping operations, each of which has its separate budget and a scale of assessments that places a slightly greater proportion of the costs on developed-country members. Since these budgets, too, require the Assembly's approval, that body is again involved in the collective security side of the UN's activities. The sums required are large in UN terms and rise with the need for peacekeeping forces which is, of course, unforeseeable. The unpaid arrearages under those budgets have been rising in recent years and now place the Organization under mounting financial strains.

Particularly in its use of peacekeeping forces, the UN's collective security system has often been inconvenienced, and sometimes impeded, when member states, including the United States, have refused or failed to pay the full amounts of their assessments. It should be added that member states that voted in favor of these peacekeeping forces are sometimes among the delinquents.

In the enforcement sphere, the substantial funds needed to finance operations authorized by the Council against North Korea and Iraq were readily found. In those crises, the military actions were from the beginning financed directly by the states participating in them, or benefiting from them, and thus remained outside the UN's financial purview.

Despite the financial pettiness of some member states, lack of money has not interfered with the UN's occasional enforcement actions for the reason just given. And because many of the expenses of peacekeeping contingents are borne initially by the governments that furnish them, it has not until recently become apparent that shortages of money may greatly limit the Security Council's ability to utilize peacekeeping forces in dealing with crisis situations.

The total shortfall in payments of dues to cover both regular budget expenditures and those required for peacekeeping has been steadily growing, and the financial plight of the UN is increasingly imposing itself on the attention of member states. The sums involved are relatively small, and it is hard to believe that solvent governments, such as that of the United States, will not honor their legal debts. Still, the UN's financial situation has reached the point where the world's collective security system is now being undermined by it.

Participation in Decision-Making

Like other IGOs and confederations, the UN has intergovernmental decision-making bodies that meet at regular intervals. They are composed of representatives from their respective governments who are bound by the instructions that they receive from those governments. The UN has a great number of such bodies which, save for the Security Council, are organized hierarchically under the General Assembly and the Economic and Social Council. However, there are striking differences between the decision-making rules of the Security Council and those of the other UN bodies. These differences were introduced to reflect the fact that the Security Council is empowered to exercise sovereign functions with regard to the use of force. Its decision-making system was designed to ensure that its decisions are assured of a broad preponderance of support among member states, including all of the Five with their special role in enforcement.

Voting in its confederal body, the Security Council, takes place in the following manner: (1) Each member has one vote; (2) Procedural decisions require the affirmative votes of nine of the 15 members; (3) Decisions on all other matters require the affirmative votes of nine members including the concurring votes of the permanent members; (4) In decisions taken under the dispute-settlement provisions in Chapter VI, the parties (including any permanent member or members) to any dispute should (but in practice do not) abstain from voting; and (5) There is also a well-established practice whereby abstentions by permanent members do not block the adoption of a decision (See Article 27; Boyd 1971, pp. 88–90).

This is clearly a confederal-style voting system. It grants a veto power to great powers and provides for decision-making by special rather than simple majorities. It should be noted that, in general, abstentions block action as much as do negative votes. Furthermore, each permanent member may express opposition in two ways: It may veto resolutions that it wishes to kill or it may abstain from voting on resolutions from which it wishes merely to distance itself. In this situation, contrariwise, an abstention may facilitate adoption of the proposal concerned. Two trends are significant enough to be mentioned: In recent years, the permanent members have become increasingly reluctant to use their veto power, and serious efforts are made to reach decisions that can be adopted on the basis of consensus of all or almost all Council members.

In its IGO branch, most of the Organization's decision-making, except in the General Assembly and its main committees, takes place in smaller commissions, boards, and committees to which member states are elected for limited terms, usually of two or three years. Except in plenary meetings of the General Assembly where a two-thirds majority is required for the adoption of "important" decisions, almost all of the decision-making in those bodies is on the basis of a simple majority of those present and voting aye or nay. Under this system, relatively small minorities of members may secure adoption of their proposals, particularly when there are many empty seats and/or abstentions. However, the relative ease of securing passage of resolutions in these bodies is largely offset by the greater difficulty of ensuring their implementation.

These procedural differences in the way in which decisions are taken affect the seriousness with which the resolutions themselves are regarded after their adoption. Though the UN only occasionally monitors what happens to the hundreds of recommendations made to governments by the General Assembly and the UN decision-making bodies under it, implementation is largely on a voluntary basis. The knowledge that little is likely to happen if governments fail to abide by such recommendations leads many member states to acquiesce in the adoption of resolutions that contain provisions that they either oppose or do not intend to take seriously. On the other hand, resolutions enjoying broad or consensus support among the 185 members sometimes lead, as in other IGOs, to concerted action on a global scale.

The Security Council, for its part, adopts far fewer resolutions, to which governments do tend to pay more attention. While some resolutions may be defied by the governments towards which they are directed, the latter must reckon with the possibility that the Council may impose sanctions on states that defy it. For example, in its vigorous pursuit of the Iraqi government during the aftermath of the Persian Gulf Enforcement Action of 1991, the Council has shown a determination to have such sanctions carried out in every detail against a state guilty of a flagrant act of aggression.[11]

The UN's Executive Capacity

The UN's executive arm, the Secretariat, is composed of "a Secretary-General and such staff as the Organization may require." The former is "appointed by the General Assembly upon the recommendation of the Security Council" (Article 97). Since it was agreed early on that the Council need submit to the Assembly only one candidate [Goodrich, Hambro, and Simons 1969, pp. 581–82], the five permanent members of the Council have been allowed to play the leading role in the Secretary-General's selection. First they must agree on a candidate who has then to be endorsed by the Council as a whole and finally confirmed by the General Assembly. Both the full Council and the Assembly have a right to reject the choice of the Five, but so far this has never happened. However, when in 1951 the Five could not agree on any candidate, Secretary-General Trygve Lie had to be allowed to serve three more years.

Once appointed, the Secretary-General assumes an office having wide powers and, at the same time, holding great personal risks for its occupant. For to exercise these powers successfully, he (or she) must command and keep the confidence and support of the leaders of all groups of member states, and particularly the confidence and support of the leaders of the Security Council's permanent members.

The legal powers vested in the Secretary-General by the Charter are, in IGO/confederal fashion, nominal. He or she is the chief administrative officer of the Organization; the Secretary-General or his or her representative has a permanent presence and the right to speak in the four principal decision-making organs of the UN (and in all its other decision-making bodies). As chief executive, the Secretary-General must also perform the functions with which these organs entrust him or her (Articles 97–98).

This latter role is more far-reaching in its scope and importance than it may appear, for there is no one else to carry out the UN's many activities. To take just one example, the Secretary-General is entrusted with the responsibility of organizing and operating the UN's many peace-keeping forces, and makes the highly political choice of which states should be asked to send troops. In the Bosnian crisis, for example, he was even given the power to determine in certain circumstances whether force should be used or not.

The Secretary-General's de facto powers are far-reaching in another sphere. Because UN resolutions often contain vaguely worded compromises, he or she has to fill in the gaps. Secretary-General U Thant once informed members of the Security Council how he planned to carry out peacekeeping in Cyprus in order to give them an opportunity to complain if they wished (Boyd 1971, p. 285). In most cases, governments are obliged to allow the UN's executive considerable latitude in determining how best to carry out the tasks with which it is entrusted. When these tasks involve the maintenance of international peace and security, Secretaries-General bear a particularly heavy burden.

The Secretary-General's sole independent power is to "bring to the attention of the Security Council any matter which in his opinion may threaten the maintenance of international peace and security" (Article 99). The significance of this power is that it invades an important sphere that governments have kept to themselves, that of choosing which crises they will take up and which they will deliberately ignore. By and large, Secretaries-General have been most reluctant to employ it. In 1961, Secretary-General Hammarskjold used that authority for the first time with respect to the crisis in the Congo (now Zaire). At the meeting that followed his exercise of that power, the tensions that were to develop between him and the Soviet Government were foreshadowed in a brief procedural debate during which he and the Soviet representative on the Council discussed whether telegrams addressed to him by the Congo Government should be included on the Council's agenda as part of the Congo item already on the agenda or as a separate item. The fact that this niggling point was raised seems to suggest that the Soviets had not been very pleased to see him invoke his powers under Article 99. While initially their point was only raised as a matter of procedure, six months later when the leader whom the Soviets were supporting, Patrice Lumumba, was murdered, they accused Hammarskjold himself of being responsible for the crime and were soon refusing to deal with him (Goodrich, Hambro, and Simons 1969, pp. 589–90; Urquhart 1972, pp. 506–9).

This incident shows the risk involved in a Secretary-General taking an initiative that might displease, or lead to results that were displeasing to, one of the Council's permanent members. It also demonstrates the limits of the Secretary-General's real powers and throws light on an underlying reality facing all executives in IGO and confederal-type unions: He or she is legally and politically subordinate to the leaders of their member states.

In the UN, some of the powers being exercised are major ones over which state leaders keep sharp watch. It is, therefore, essential for its executive heads to move cautiously and to keep the confidence and support of their many bosses. As it turned out, Secretaries-General Lie and Hammarskjold could not function effectively once they had lost the confidence of the Soviet leaders. Hammarskjold had been warned. During a meeting with Krushchev in the Crimea, he had ventured to suggest that "if he took positions which were not agreeable to the USSR, he felt he could trust Krushchev not to misconstrue his motives" to which the latter "replied with a smile, 'Please do not do anything which will force us to criticize you' " (Urquhart 1972, p. 467). Other national leaders might not have spoken so bluntly, but they too would probably have been uneasy with a Secretary-General who took independent positions that they felt ran contrary to their countries' interests.

Part of the problem is that the office of Secretary-General confers a far-reaching, but contingent, power on its occupants. Much of the influence that Secretaries-General wield is not conferred directly upon them by the Charter: It stems from what have sometimes been called the "inherent powers" of the office. It is contingent upon the diplomatic and other skills that they show in helping the Council and the UN's other intergovernmental organs to manage international political crises and the UN's many other activities. The "Let Dag do it!" philosophy that prevailed in some Western countries once they saw his skillfulness made Hammarskjold's influence a little too visible. It is best if Secretaries-General provide a quiet nonpartisan leadership, which no government can provide on its own. On most occasions, if none of the Council's members can be persuaded to recognize a crisis, it will not be helpful for the Secretary-General to act under Article 99.

In this respect, Secretaries-General find themselves in a similar position to their counterparts in the League of Nations and the prototype confederations. Their predecessors also had to win and maintain the confidence of the leaders of sovereign member states that had formed confederal ties. For example, the seventeenth-century Dutch statesmen Johan van Oldenbarnevelt and Johan deWitt successively shepherded the Dutch Republic through troubled waters by virtue of their adroit leadership of the seven provinces in the States-General. George Washington (during the confederal era), after initial missteps, found his way to a constructive relationship with the Continental Congress in which he exercised his quiet and modest leadership not only in the military sphere, but also occasionally in the new country's foreign affairs. Metternich, the Austrian statesman, was unmatched in his ability to please his masters, the many princes of the Germanic Confederation. The first Secretary-General of the League of Nations, Sir Eric Drummond, understanding the risks, kept a low profile during the successful first decade of the League. This ability to serve and to satisfy many masters was shared by all of those mentioned, each in his own way.

The other members of the Secretariat are appointed by the Secretary-General under regulations established by the General Assembly. Every one in the Secretariat, including the Secretary-General himself, is forbidden to seek or receive instructions from any government, and those governments undertake "to respect the exclusively international character of the responsibilities of the Secretary-General and the staff and not to seek to influence them in the discharge of their responsibilities" (Articles 100–101). This does not mean, however, that the Secretariat is a civil service that functions independently of governments. Rather, it is a body that is strictly bound by the provisions of the Charter and by the corporate wishes of governments as expressed jointly by member states in the decisions they take within its many intergovernmental bodies.

It may be noted that the UN's Preparatory Commission rejected the notion that each main organ ought to have its own separate staff. However, in establishing the eight main departments in which the Secretariat would be organized, one was created for Security Council Affairs (Goodrich, Hambro, and Simons 1969, p. 603). The Department of Political Affairs was, in effect, designated to carry out the collective security and other political functions of the Organization. In view of the differences in status and powers of the two main branches of the UN, the Preparatory Commission was probably right in giving the branch responsible for collective security matters its own separate Department.

The UN's Legal Capacity

There was wide agreement that the United Nations, as the League before it, should have a judicial presence in the world community. In response to that general desire, the Charter provided for an International Court of Justice (ICJ) composed of 15 judges, no two of whom may be nationals from the same state. At the same time, the legal experts who drafted the Statute for that Court faced the very difficult problem of making the Court's presence effective in a community of states most of which continued to insist upon their sovereign status and doubted, with good reason, that the court would be in a position to uphold their rights and protect their security.

When the provisions of Chapter XIV of the Charter and of the Statute are analyzed, it appears that these underlying realities of a half century ago were well understood by those who prepared them. Thus, these provisions, which seem to give the Court a far-reaching authority, contain many "escape clauses."

At first glance, the legal system established by the Charter seems impressive in its scope. All the UN's member states are ipso facto parties to the ICJ's statute, and nonmembers may accede to it (Articles 92–93; Switzerland, early on, exercised that privilege). Each member of the UN has undertaken to comply with the decision of the ICJ in any case to which it is a party, and if one party fails to honor a judgment of the Court, the other party may bring its grievance before the Security Council (Article 94). Furthermore, Article 36 of the ICJ's statute sets up a system that would give it jurisdiction over four very broad categories of legal disputes, namely, those that involve treaty interpretation, questions of international law, breaches of international obligations, and the nature and extent of the reparations to be made for such breaches.

However, the same Article 36 limits the jurisdiction of the ICJ to cases that the parties decide to refer to it or over which it is specifically given jurisdiction by treaties. While the Article contains an "optional clause" whereby any party to the Statute may declare that it recognizes the *compulsory* jurisdiction of the Court over *all* disputes in the four categories, this provision is also included: "The declarations referred to above may be made unconditionally or on condition of reciprocity on the part of several or certain states, or for a certain time" (Article 36 (3)).

Less than one-third of the UN's member states have deposited declarations still in force, and they now include only one of the five permanent members of the Security Council. Moreover, many of these declarations contain reservations that carefully circumscribe and limit the jurisdiction being conferred on the Court. Thus, most cases are brought before it on the basis of treaty obligations or of special agreements between the parties, i.e., only if both parties wish to use the Court's services. Disputants with weak legal cases are usually not too eager to submit them to the Court.

While most of the parties in cases dealt with by the Court have carried out its judgments, the Security Council's power to enforce those judgments is couched in rather half-hearted terms. Thus, even though states that fail to abide by the Court's decisions may be brought before the Security Council's dock, that body is told only that it "may, if it deems necessary, make recommendations or decide upon measures to be taken to give effect to the judgment" (Article 94 (2)). However, in the two most notable cases in which the Court's judgments were flouted, little would have been gained by calling upon the Council for assistance.[12]

While there was little support for giving the ICJ exclusive jurisdiction of the kind enjoyed by national courts, the Charter seems to go out of its way to stress the multiplicity of channels that member states are free to use in the adjudication of their disputes. For example, Article 95 of the Charter reads: "Nothing in the present Charter shall prevent Members of the United Nations from entrusting the solution of their differences to other tribunals by virtue of agreements already in existence or *which may be concluded in the future*" (italics added).

In the list in Article 33 of the methods by which parties may wish to settle their disputes, the Court is not designated by name, but only the method of "judicial settlement." In Article 36, the Security Council is not empowered to refer cases directly to the Court; this preserves the right of every state, even when it is involved in a dispute threatening the peace, to determine whether or not it wishes to bring it before the Court. Thus, while its Statute was made an integral part of the Charter and the Court was proclaimed to be a "principal organ" of the United Nations, the framers underlined by these provisions the modest role that they expected it to play.

The limited role that the Court has been playing in dispute settlement may have obscured the more rapid progress that United Nations law has been making on many fronts. As Oscar Schachter has pointed out, this is particularly true on the legislative front (Schachter 1994, pp. 1–6, 16–23). While the General Assembly was denied legislative power, it could and did adopt multilateral treaties binding on those states that became parties to them as well as declarations of law, often on the basis of consensuses that had been reached previously by its member states. The same technique is employed by other intergovernmental bodies, including the assemblies and conferences of the many specialized agencies that make up the UN system. In another area, the International Law Commission has made good progress in its Charter function of codifying and progressively developing international law (Article 13a), thus transposing much of the old customary law into treaty law and simultaneously updating it to make it more coherent and relevant to current needs.

In the latter part of his article, Schachter provides an interesting overview of the growing body of jurisprudence that has been created under the UN's aegis. The covenants on human rights and the conventions on the Law of the Sea are examples of this process that may be familiar to many readers. A draft statute for a permanent criminal court is now under review. Also, there is a widening international jurisdiction in many sectors of the general welfare sphere, for example, in such areas as international economic, financial and trade law, and international environmental law.

Both the judicial and legislative capabilities of the UN are limited by its continuing IGO status. A confederal UN, on the other hand, would pave the way for a stronger international legal system. In the first place, it would strengthen the law of peace and security and thus help the Security Council centralize the enforcement process in spheres where considerations of state power have generally prevailed over those of law. It would create a more secure basis for the rule of law since all states would have to reckon with the Council's greatly enhanced capacity to manage and resolve political disputes. This would, in turn, create a climate in which states might be less worried over their security vis-à-vis potential aggressors and malefactors.

The Charter and the Court's Statute provide, as they stand, a framework for resolving legal disputes that may readily be strengthened whenever the parties agree that it should be. The optional clause offers an open road towards a system of compulsory jurisdiction. If the UN could be upgraded to a confederal-type union, a new look might be taken at how to remove the following obstacles to giving the ICJ a more far-reaching role: (1) The uncertain enforceability of its judgments; (2) The heavily politicized procedures for selecting the Court's judges; and (3) Its relatively rigid and time-consuming procedures for handling cases. Moreover, as Jennings has pointed out, the Court is greatly limited by the fact that only states may be parties in contentious cases coming before it; the newer areas into which international law has been moving directly affect individuals and corporations—in other words, legal entities other than states. A number of reforms in the Court's statute would thus be needed before it can assume a role comparable to that of the Court of Justice of the European Union (Jennings 1995, pp. 504–5; Barton and Carter 1992, pp. 284, 292).

(3) THE PROSPECTS FOR ACHIEVING GLOBAL CONFEDERATION[13]

Of course, constitutions often fail to produce the governments that their framers had in mind. The risk of this is far greater in the case of a global constitution, which sets up rules intended to govern the behavior patterns of all sovereign governments. Even if there had been no Cold War, the UN's confederal-type collective security system might well have proved overambitious in terms of the duties it imposes upon its member states, and especially its great-power members. Also, the extent to which the Security Council could have succeeded in carrying out the broad functions and the heavy responsibilities entrusted to it by the Charter remains very uncertain.

In particular, it is not too likely that the great powers (and other states) would have been willing to carry out their enforcement responsibilities in situations where their immediate interests were not at stake. Even if there had been no Cold War, many of the same problems that had embarrassed and marginalized the League of Nations might well have reappeared to bedevil its successor. To understand why this should be so, it is necessary to review briefly some of the problems associated with global collective security systems and the ways in which an "ideal" system may need to be modified in order to make it viable in the real world.

Inis Claude has defined collective security as "the establishment and operation of a complex scheme of national commitments and international mechanisms designed to prevent or suppress aggression *by any state against any other state*, by presenting to potential aggressors the reliable promise of effective collective measures, ranging from diplomatic boycott through economic pressure to military sanctions, to enforce the peace" (italics added). He also cites other conditions: "It was conceived as a systematic arrangement that should serve, *with the highest degree of predictability that human contrivance could muster*, to confront would-be aggressors, *whoever they might be and wherever they might venture to strike*, with an *overwhelming collection of restraining power assembled by the mass of states* in accordance with clear and firm obligations accepted and proclaimed in advance" (italics added) (Claude 1971, p. 247).

Couched in these sweeping terms, this ideal model for collective security—especially in an era of weapons of mass destruction—is probably impractical. Even supposing that governments could be persuaded to adhere to it, it might often lead to unexpected and unwished for results. For example, it would be folly to apply force automatically against great powers. To take an obvious case, if the members of the League of Nations had, in the winter of 1939–1940, declared war against the Soviets (at that time, Hitler's allies) when they invaded Finland, it would probably not have helped the Finns and might have allowed the Axis powers to win World War II.

But, as Claude also points out, there are many possible systems of global collective security that meet some of the objections that can be easily raised against this "pure" system. For example, the Covenant of the League of Nations accepted the universal ban on all acts of aggression, but its provisions did not ensure "automatic response" nor did they provide adequately for the timely creation of an "overwhelming collection of restraining power." Yet while these loopholes may have made the system more acceptable to member states, they unduly weakened its capacity to respond to acts of aggression.

What is needed is a modified system (if one can be found!) that imposes duties on the great majority of law-abiding sovereign states that they are willing to accept while simultaneously giving the world community the means to overawe and deter would-be aggressors and to frustrate them should they harass or invade other states.

The lessons learned from the League's failed collective security system were, *inter alia:* (1) The nature of great-power relationships is crucial in determining whether the system works or breaks down; (2) Collective security systems usually cannot be applied successfully against a great power; (3) There must be institutional means for producing in a timely way large-scale military power for use against rogue states; and (4) In times of crisis, governments cannot be compelled to follow preordained procedures; they must be allowed to handle each crisis in the light of the particular circumstances surrounding it.

The United Nations Charter provides for a modified collective security system which shows that these lessons had been taken to heart by those who drew it up. All power of action to deal with crisis situations was centralized in the Security Council, whose composition and voting arrangements respond to points (1) and (2); Articles 43–49, never implemented, take into account point (3); and, with regard to point (4), Chapter VII, far from requiring the Council to react automatically to *all* acts of aggression, allows it great latitude in deciding how it may prudently respond to such acts. A fifth lesson, that serious steps toward global disarmament require as a prerequisite widespread confidence in the collective security system, was reflected in the cautiousness of the Charter's provisions that deal with that subject.

Yet each of these corrective steps has created a new problem or opened up a new gap in the system. Clearly, leaving the great powers outside the system creates a huge gap; and making the system dependent on great-power concurrence in the taking of decisions leaves it vulnerable to the kind of paralysis that occurred during the Cold War. Allowing for flexibility of action in time of crisis may be realistic, but it also means that some countries may be allowed to get away with acts of overt aggression and that the security of smaller states cannot be reliably assured. Finally, so far, the United States and other members have shown no interest in belatedly negotiating the Article 43 "special agreements" intended to provide the Security Council with "on-call" military forces that would give it automatic access to a military power likely to overawe and deter dictators such as Saddam Hussein. In these circumstances, it is hardly surprising that efforts to promote disarmament have not, as yet, been very successful.

On the other hand, the present configuration of power relationships in the world is favorable to the kind of system that the Charter has provided for. For the time being, a preponderance of military power resides with the United States, a country long uninvolved in territorial expansion. Moreover, the other great powers are mostly satisfied with the territorial *status quo,* and none has the kind of serious grievance that Germany had after World War I. The attention of Britain, France, and Germany is mainly concentrated on their economic/social/environmental interests as well as their increasing participation in the European Union, and none of the three has territorial claims against other states. Japan still wishes to have American forces in its midst and remains lightly armed in line with its postwar pacifist constitution.

Only China and Russia are or may be involved in territorial problems. In the case of China, there is the complex issue raised by Taiwan. Also, perhaps down the road, Russia will wish to reclaim the other successor states of the former Soviet Union. But these territorial issues do not bring them, at least not directly, into conflict with other great powers. Moreover, for the time being, the energies of both China and Russia are heavily absorbed in economic and industrial modernization as well as in coping with the serious internal political problems that they face in moving from autocratic to democratic forms of government.

If one adds to this lack of interest in territorial expansion the fears raised by the gradual spread (and possible future use) of weapons of mass destruction, the possibilities for great power cooperation on the world scene seem rather encouraging, at least as of January 1996. What may be evolving is a modified collective security system led by the kind of "concert of great powers" that kept the peace of Europe between the Treaty of Vienna (1815) and the outbreak of the Crimean War (1853). The foregoing political configuration seems to fit rather well with the Charter's provisions for collective security that presuppose and require great-power cooperation.

At the same time, what we have now may only be a window of opportunity that could be closed at any time should major governments become involved in angry confrontations. During the present period of relative calm, there is an urgent need to find a modus vivendi for rival ethnic groups and to develop confederal-type habits of solving *all* inter-state (and intra-state) disputes by peaceful means. Nonetheless, in a state system of almost 200 players, an effective collective security system will surely be needed for the foreseeable future to deal with rogue states. When armed with weapons of mass destruction (as Iraq almost was!), such states may threaten any other state, no matter how powerful or how far away it may be. As one delegate warned the League of Nations Council in 1935: "Great or small, strong or weak, near or far, white or coloured, let us never forget that one day we may be somebody's Ethiopia" (quoted in Claude 1971, p. 251).

Accordingly, what looks to be a fairly promising system may prove to be a weak reed if and when it is put to the test of nuclear blackmail. In particular, in the absence of confederal-type ties among the states forming the world community, any collective security system is likely to be precarious and may at some point collapse when confronted with the self-serving behavior of governmental leaders ready to exploit nationalist or ethnic prejudices.

The Present Situation

Now that we are beginning to discover what the post–Cold War world will be like, we need to make a balance sheet of the obstacles that still bar the way to global confederation and of the assets now available to us. But before doing that let us sum up, very briefly, the situation in which the UN now finds itself on the three levels—the legal level, the "affect" level (that is the level of popular support and allegiance), and the working level.

As has been shown earlier, the *legal* structure and mandate of the UN in the political sphere identify it as a security confederation so long as that class is defined broadly to include global unions of states formed to deter or foil rogue states that emerge within the world community. As noted earlier, the Security Council's confederal credentials are confirmed by the capacity of its members jointly to exercise sovereign powers and to take decisions that are legally binding on all states (Article 2 (6)). On the *affect* level, it is clear that the UN still has a long way to go before it can attract even a minimal political allegiance on the part of the peoples of its member states. It seems likely that until they see its collective security system working dependably, people generally will continue to regard the UN as one among many IGOs rather than as a union in whose successful operation they have an important personal stake.

On the *working* level, there are four structural problems and two practical problems that will now be described and briefly analyzed. The structural problems—gaps or flaws in the basic framework of the UN's collective security system—are the following:

1. *Great-Power Problem.* The special rights and complex relationships of the permanent members of the Security Council put the UN's collective security system under unique strains and stresses.

2. *Risk of Paralysis.* In specific situations, members of the Security Council may be unable to agree on what should be done and accordingly unable to protect a member state against an aggressor.

3. *Deliberate Inaction.* Nothing compels members of the Council to recognize or

respond to breaches of the peace or to clear acts of aggression when they do not choose to bear the burden of dealing effectively with those that have committed them.

4. *Incompleteness.* Other states that one of the Five may wish to protect can be placed, through exercise of its veto power, beyond the reach of the Charter's enforcement system.

These gaps and flaws spring partly from the great number, heterogeneity, and sheer geographical remoteness from one another of the prospective confederal partners. They also spring from the manner in which those partners have been divided into two groups with strikingly different legal rights and duties, the Five vis-à-vis the other 180.

The two practical problems involve the obsolescence of the military provisions of the Charter, which date back to the prenuclear age, and the need to overhaul many UN procedures and address its institutional shortcomings in the light of 50 years' experience.

Let us now briefly examine these six problems, which may keep the UN in its preconfederal stage for some time to come.

The Great-Power Problem

The starting point for examining this problem is the seven premises for the great-power partnership on which the UN's collective security system rests (see p. 120, this volume). Let us recapitulate them one by one:

1. The great powers would pledge (i) to cooperate with one another and with other states in maintaining the peace; and (ii) to refrain from waging war against one another or any other nation except through "enforcement actions" as provided for in the Charter.

2. As joint enforcers of the Council's decisions, they would need to preserve their unanimity with regard to all "crucial" matters.

3. Each of them would maintain (and be ready to use) military forces which would, in combination, be sufficient to deter or, deterrence failing, to put down acts of aggression by other states.

4. No great power could be made to support an enforcement action to which it was opposed.

5. The UN's collective security system, which would involve enforcement actions rather than wars, could not cover acts of aggression by a great power.

6. Accordingly, the combined military forces at the UN's disposal need only be sufficient to deal with breaches of the peace that do not involve a great power.

7. The Security Council would need to be predominant in its sphere, and the great powers having the main responsibility for enforcing its edicts would need to have permanent seats and the power of veto, at least over the Council's enforcement decisions.

These premises are either reflected in the Charter or flow from its provisions. They were probably as far as the great powers were prepared to go in 1944, and some of them are further than they would be ready to go today. However, they are, *mutatis mutandis,* very similar to the premises that underlie the smaller collective security systems of the prototype confederations, if one substitutes "member state" for "great power." The basis for all security confederations is a group of (leading) states that promise to settle their disputes by negotiation and compromise rather than by force. In all confederations, there have been inequities between the treatment of smaller and senior partners, at least in terms of practice. But if a confederation holds some prospect of protecting its members, such inequities are usually overlooked, as they were by the 45 at San Francisco and by the smaller states in the prototype confederations.

The world soon discovered that the seven premises could not be sustained. They may prove to be just as unsustainable today. It remains to be seen whether today's (or tomorrow's) great powers can move gradually towards such a confederal-type relationship in the decades ahead. Such a relationship, particularly among great powers, seems to run counter to deep-seated political behavior patterns that it will be hard to transform, at least in the short term.

On the other hand, most, if not all, of the seven premises will probably have to be met before any global collective security system will prove viable in practice. For example, it is difficult to imagine any such system surviving in a climate of open enmity among the great powers or even when those states are unwilling to come to the aid of law-abiding states being attacked by aggressors. Obviously, if a great power itself indulges in acts of aggression, the system would probably disappear in a general war, as we know from what happened to the Germanic Confederation in 1866 and to the League of Nations in 1939.

At the same time, if the leaders of the Council's permanent members behave rationally, there are a number of reasons why they may have a better chance now of establishing more stable relationships among themselves than in the past. They all have much to lose and little to gain from confronting one another. They all have the same interest in slowing down nuclear proliferation and in preventing the use of weapons of mass destruction. They all have populations more interested in economic growth than in territorial expansion. They all stand to benefit equally from the influence and prestige that their permanent membership and veto power in the Security Council give them. During the Cold War, they all saw how strongly the prospect of nuclear holocaust deterred the actual use of force by one great power against another. They all know how inordinately high the cost/benefit ratio of great-power confrontation has become. Finally, none of them has an active territorial dispute with another, and their divisive ideological confrontation seems to be a thing of the past. While the inevitable rivalries among great powers will certainly spring up again and may at times become disruptive, their leaders may be increasingly moved by these factors to conduct their relations in ways that do not recklessly endanger world peace.

Unfortunately, the logic of these arguments may be outweighed by the inevitable preoccupation of national leaders with short-term interests and narrow domestic concerns. It may even be that some aggressive leader like Hitler or Napoleon will again emerge at the helm of a great power. The limited capacity of governments to work together in coping with such threats remains, as it has always been, a principal obstacle in the way of stable great-power relationships and, therefore, of any dependable global collective security.

The Problem of Paralysis

One must distinguish between at least two types of paralysis. The first is the kind generated during the Cold War when the two superpowers were engaged in a full-scale confrontation with one another that would have probably been played out on the battlefield had nuclear weapons not made that prospect too fearsome. The second is the kind involved in any system where individual great powers or small groups of member states can block any course of action that they oppose.

The first kind of paralysis precipitated a long systemic breakdown in the Charter's collective security arrangements. The second does not involve systemic breakdown but only temporary blockages. It also necessitates a "lowest common denominator" approach, which may keep the system from performing well in a particular crisis, or at least from performing as well as it should.

For many reasons, this second type of paralysis is a particular liability for global collective security systems: the complexities of great-power relationships; the understandable wish of governments to avoid involvement in messy situations; the tendency to prefer postponement over immediate action; and the fact that many states are remote from, and may have little interest in, a crisis that is underway. The members of smaller confederations under attack were not so vulnerable to this type of paralysis because, usually, they could not delay their response to invasions.

Insofar as the Five are concerned, governments have dealt with this second kind of paralysis by discouraging use of the veto power while not challenging head-on the right to use it. Indeed, any collective security system depends upon the readiness of its members to exercise restraint and to negotiate in good faith. For example, neither Russia nor China was anxious to bring down Iraq over its occupation of a ministate having enormous oil wealth. But both bowed to the preponderance of opinion that felt otherwise. The Chinese abstained, and the Russians in the end joined the majority in upholding Kuwait's right, as a UN member state in good standing, to the UN's military assistance.

As stated earlier, an unwritten rule may be emerging that only vital interests justify a great power's use of the veto power. Nonetheless, there is always the danger that the Council will find itself powerless to deal with situations that call for prompt and forceful action.

The Problem of Deliberate Inaction, or of Ensuring an Automatic Response to Acts of Flagrant Aggression

As pointed out earlier, an act of aggression by a permanent member of the Security Council against another state cannot be countered within the framework of the UN's collective security system because the offending state would be entitled to veto any course of action directed against it. This does not mean that a great-power aggressor would not face retaliatory action, but merely that any such action would probably assume the guise of a full-scale war rather than an enforcement action undertaken by the Council and the world community.

In response to a clear act of aggression by any other of the UN's 180 member states, however, the collective security system ought to come into play almost automatically. If it does not, the system will rather quickly lose all credibility.

But, even when the aggressor is only a well-armed second-level state, this is obviously a burdensome and unpleasant duty. It requires governments to be ready and willing to put their citizens in harm's way even when their immediate interests are not directly involved. In the prototype confederations, this was not much of a problem because it was usually plain that any successful act of aggression against one of the members threatened them all. Now that we are well into the nuclear age, this is probably also true on a global scale, but the linkage is less self-evident.

In a global confederation, when the country being invaded by a neighbor with powerful forces is far away, perhaps on another continent, peoples and their democratically elected leaders are usually not very eager to come to its aid, especially when their own countries' interests are not directly involved. In such circumstances, the counterarguments that any collective security system must protect all its members and that looking the other way, or "appeasement," may merely whet the appetite of an aggressor do not carry much weight.

Since the collective security system adopted in San Francisco does not come into play automatically, it can only be activated by the leaders of its member states acting together in the Security Council. But nothing in the Charter compels the members of that Council to recognize breaches of the peace or acts of aggression to which they prefer to turn a blind eye. In this respect, the world community is once again confronted with the problem that brought down the League of Nations: Its members chose not to come to the defense of China, Ethiopia, or even Czechoslovakia, just as the UN's members have been reluctant to come to Bosnia's defense.

It must be again stressed that this kind of problem did not arise in the case of the four prototype confederations; the Swiss did not have the option of turning a blind eye to the Habsburg invaders, or the Dutch to the Spanish invaders, or the Americans to the British and Hessian mercenaries, or the Germans (in the 1830s) to the French threat to occupy and annex the Rhineland. Yet even if it is only a friendless small state that is being invaded, it sets a dangerous precedent when the world community abandons it to an aggressor. No self-respecting national state would dream of treating one of its provinces so casually.

Thus, assuring an adequate response to flagrant acts of aggression is a particularly sticky wicket for *global* collective security systems. How are small members of the world community to be reassured that, if and when they are attacked, the United Nations will come to their assistance promptly and with adequate force? As we have seen, Article 10 of the League Covenant did provide such an assurance, at least on paper. It was this duty, among others, that frightened members of the U.S. Senate into rejecting the Covenant. And the League's member states soon found themselves unable to honor it. The second sentence of Article 10 provided the escape clause that enabled them to renege on their duty of preserving China's and Ethiopia's territorial integrity; the Council's members simply could not agree upon the means by which the obligation would be fulfilled (Covenant 1958).

It will be recalled that at the San Francisco Conference, smaller states, remembering the League's abandonment of some of its members, demanded that a binding provision be inserted in the Charter that they would not be similarly abandoned to an aggressor. All they achieved, however, was an "understanding" whose content is given again because of its importance:

The Committee is unanimous in the belief that . . . in the case of a flagrant aggression imperilling the existence of a member of the Organization, enforcement measures should be taken without delay, and to the full extent required by circumstances, except that the Council should at the same time endeavor to persuade the aggressor to abandon its venture. (Russell 1958, p. 676)

It might be helpful if the Security Council were to adopt a formal declaration confirming this understanding.

While the framers of the Charter also sought to deal with this problem by providing the Council with readily available military force, such a capacity by itself does not guarantee automaticity of response. For example, a permanent member may be reluctant to permit a police action to proceed against one of its clients, as Russia was for a time in the case of Iraq, or against its ethnic cousins, as Russia has been in the case of Serbia. Other members may be afraid that if they authorize enforcement actions, they may themselves one day become the targets of such actions.

Thus, under the UN's collective security system, there is always the danger that the Council, even if it is not paralyzed by a great-power veto or too divided to act coherently, will be unable to come in time to the aid of victims of aggression. Moreover, if it takes charge of a situation but cannot act effectively, the victim state may not only lose its right to defend itself under Article 51 of the Charter; other states may be legally obligated to limit their assistance to the measures on which the Council has agreed.[14] These procedures need to be made more responsive to the requirements of the victims of aggression.

However, if the Council did have readily available military forces, it would be easier for it to respond to breaches of the peace and acts of aggression. While this would not ensure automaticity of response, it would remove a major obstacle to it. As already noted, the founders of the UN had provided for such forces in the never-implemented Articles 43–47 of the Charter. Secretary-General Boutros Boutros Ghali has pointed out that "the ready availability of armed forces on call could serve in itself as a means of deterring breaches of the peace since a potential aggressor would know that the Council had at its disposal a means of response"[15] (Boutros Ghali 1992, p. 25). This would be particularly true for petty aggressors eager to prey upon smaller neighbors.

The political and military obstacles that continue to stand in the way of the United Nations having an "in-house" enforcement capability are well-known. In the long run, however, and especially if weapons of mass destruction become widely available, the Council (or some successor body) will ultimately need such a capability if it is to have much hope of dealing with the megacrises that are likely to challenge humanity in the next century.

Before leaving this subject, attention may be drawn to a kind of mirror-image problem, which lies outside the area of collective security as such. In the last few years, the main concern of some observers of the Security Council has not been its inactivity but rather its hyperactivity and the nature of some of that hyperactivity. These critics have perceived an increasing tendency for the Council to use its Chapter VII powers to intervene in situations where the linkage to the criterion of a threat to international peace and security is at best dubious. During the years 1992–1995, for example, it invoked those powers with regard to situations in Somalia, Haiti, and Angola where there seemed to be little, if any, threat to *international* peace and security.

Matters have not been helped by the Council's increasing tendency to conduct its deliberations in private and to offer little explanation of how it has reached its determination that a given situation actually does threaten international peace and security. This inevitably feeds suspicions that the

Council has been exceeding the mandate given it by the Charter (Kirgis 1995, especially pp. 509–20, 537–39).

It would seem that the 170 UN members not represented on the Council are entitled to expect (1) that the far-reaching powers that they delegated to the Council when they became parties to the Charter will be exercised in accordance with the provisions that limit their use; and (2) that the Council will conduct its business with greater transparency so that they may follow its proceedings more closely.

In order to counter the tendency of great powers to dominate the Council's decision-making, it is important to have elected members that are capable of adequately representing the rest of the world community. In the past, too many of the Council's ten elective seats have been occupied by small states that do not carry much weight in international diplomatic circles. In 1995, for example, four of the ten seats were occupied by Botswana, Honduras, Oman, and Rwanda while populous secondary states such as India, Pakistan, Japan, Brazil, Mexico, and Egypt were not members. The need to allow all members to serve occasionally on the Council must be balanced against the need to have the most populous and the most influential states regularly involved in the Council's proceedings. For example, the Council's decisions would carry more weight if its members, at any given moment, represent a very large proportion of the world's people.

If the efforts now under way to alter the composition of the Council to make it more representative of the world community prove successful, it would tend to minimize the extent to which any single great power or any coalition of great powers could manipulate the Council's decision-making process on behalf of parochial interests.

Even if the Council is enlarged by six or seven seats as is now widely contemplated, the foregoing approach would reduce somewhat the frequency with which small states and mini-states could be represented in its deliberations. However, it must be borne in mind that only the larger states have the political clout and military superiority (when they act together) to dissuade a rogue state from bullying or invading other members of the world community. Furthermore, it would be harder to perceive a Council in which most of the world's more influential and populous states are voting members as acting on behalf of the parochial interests of one or two of them.

The Problem of Incompleteness

That the Charter's enforcement system cannot be applied to the permanent members of the Security Council constitutes a serious but unavoidable gap. This gap is enlarged, perhaps unnecessarily, by the capacity of each of the Five, by use of its veto power, to prevent sanctions from being imposed upon any of its client states and allies. So far, this secondary gap has not created major difficulties, perhaps because client states have not very often committed acts of aggression or, because when they have, they were not able to secure such protection (e.g., Russia did not in the end protect Iraq). On the other hand, Arab countries doubtless considered that the United States used its veto power in this way during their long confrontation with Israel.

There is a simple way to close this gap. Each of the Five might agree not to use its veto power to prevent the Security Council from imposing sanctions on any member state other than itself. By doing this, they would warn client states and allies that they could no longer protect them from such sanctions.

For the reasons already stated, the enforcement system cannot be applied against any of the great powers. But if any of the Five were to engage in an act or a series of acts of unprovoked aggression or commit any other egregious violation of the Charter, it would lead most likely to a new Cold War against the offending state, or worse. To this extent, if any of the Five engage in such behavior, their leaders already know that they would be running very serious risks.

Indeed, this apparent gap in the UN's collective security system may be more theoretical than real in an age when most national leaders seem more interested in stealing foreign markets than foreign territories. This is not only true of the Five, but of the two great powers in waiting, Germany and Japan. The risks and stigma of becoming a global outlaw would seem to greatly outweigh any possible advantages to be derived from following in the unlucky footsteps of Napoleon, Hitler, or Saddam Hussein.

Let us now flag the military and institutional obstacles.

Military Obstacles

The enforcement system adopted in 1944–1945 needs to be updated to reflect what are likely to be the military requirements for keeping the world's peace when weapons of mass destruction become increasingly available. In any event, the art of warfare has evolved during the past half century in ways that make it impractical to quickly form an effective multinational force out of disparate contingents from different countries and continents.

The United States has provided the nucleus for the two multinational armies that have so far been organized under UN auspices. In any serious military confrontation that the UN may face for some time to come, it will again have to rely heavily on American "cutting-edge" military expertise and American armed forces. This constitutes a serious obstacle because it imposes on Americans too great a share of the burden in policing the world, a burden that many Americans have made it known that they are not eager to assume. Alternatively, if the UN is ultimately given its own standing police force, it will not be easy to reach agreement on the many details of how such a force will be composed, where it will be based, and how it will be operated and led.

Institutional Obstacles

The United Nations faces the nagging problem that its institutions are very difficult to reform, even in the light of accumulating evidence that many of them are working rather poorly. Some of the weaknesses just pointed out in the collective security system might be removed by minor Charter amendments, but little is being done in that direction. Its highly politicized system for finding and appointing Secretaries-General has, on the whole, failed to produce the unique type of leadership that is needed for the world community's most important and challenging office. Its system for selecting other officials, firmly based on national quotas and security of tenure, has produced a secretariat that has been losing the confidence of national governments. The UN's arrangements for program planning have led to the steady addition of new activities and little or no phasing out of older ones that are no longer needed. The multiplication of specialized agencies and other autonomous organizations in the broader "United Nations System" has led to increasing duplication and overlapping.

In short, there is a sclerosis in the way that the UN operates in carrying out both its mandates that may result in its again being bypassed, as it often was during the Cold War. Without an adroit and widely trusted Secretary-General and a highly qualified staff to carry out its collective security responsibilities, the confederal powers provided for in its Charter are unlikely to be delegated to the UN by its member states.

THE ASSET SIDE OF THE BALANCE SHEET

Fortunately, the world community now has major assets that, to some extent, offset these many liabilities. In the first place, despite the flaws, gaps, and practical shortcomings of the UN's collective security system, the Security Council is by virtue of its mandate, structure, and voting rules a fully confederal body. Now that the Cold War is past, its great-power members have been able to concur, more often than in the past, on common courses of action. Such concurrence involves their increasing readiness to abstain on rather than to veto proposed courses of action against aggressor states.

Accordingly, for the first time, the Security Council has begun—intermittently at least—to function in the way that its founders intended it to. For example, it has effectively come to the aid of Kuwait, Cambodia, and El Salvador. In fact, as we have seen, the Council never lost its capacity to act occasionally, not even in the darkest days of the Cold War. Perhaps the presence of so many weapons of mass destruction is beginning to have the same steadying effect on all but a few rogue states that it had on the superpowers during the Cold War.

Especially if the Council is enlarged and made more representative of the world community, it will be in a better position to exercise its powers effectively in situations where joint action is clearly needed, say in the event that weapons of mass destruction become a serious menace in the next century. Yet to be effective in dealing with world problems, this enlarged Council needs to enjoy the confidence and willing support of most of the many non-member governments. It needs to acquire a capability for acting swiftly to deal with acts of clearcut aggression, which only ready access to the forces needed to put down aggressors will give it. Finally, when no state threatens international peace and security, it needs to act cautiously and within the parameters set for it by the Charter.

Second, a novel instrument, the peacekeeping force composed of small, lightly armed contingents from the armies of many member states, has been invented. Its original purpose was to separate hostile armies by placing neutral troops on mutually agreed cease-fire lines, for example, on a line separating the Egyptian and Israeli armies. Multinational forces of this kind gave the Council a nonthreatening presence on the ground that offered warring parties face-saving ways of stopping wars they no longer wished to wage. Its success in this capacity led to its wider use and attempts to adapt it to a great variety of situations. However, some of these efforts, e.g., to use such forces as a kind of backdoor method of enforcement through the establishment of "safe havens," have led to embarrassing results. Indeed, the Secretary-General has recently acknowledged that peacekeeping forces should not be used in situations where fighting is still underway (Boutros Ghali 1995, pp. 6, 9).

The UN's record in these places warns that peacekeeping and enforcement actions cannot be conducted simultaneously, and that peacekeeping forces cannot function well in the midst of hostilities. However, the peacekeeping force is still in the trial-and-error stage of its development. The Security Council's member states and Secretaries-General will probably, with longer experience, become better judges of when it can be used successfully and when it cannot. The peacekeeping force is likely to remain a valuable asset in dealing with future crises.

Third, most people, wherever they live or whatever their ethnic mix, have gradually grown aware that they inhabit a world filled with weapons of mass destruction from which they have an overriding need to protect themselves. The more thoughtful of them are already aware that a third world war fought with such weapons would be a catastrophe beyond any that humanity has yet experienced. The sense of immense relief at the ending of the Cold War is tempered, at least in some quarters, by the growing realization that the threat of this weaponry still hangs over everyone's head. Unfortunately, fear of these weapons is diluted by an ill-founded feeling that they will never be used. Sadly, the extent of our worldwide dangers may become compelling only after the TV screens have shown us the horrors of some new nuclear incident.

Fourth, the shifting focus of governmental attention is a major asset. Economic growth and social needs have been steadily replacing territorial issues as the primary concern of leaders and peoples alike. Today, with the new World Trade Organization and the IMF, with regional entities like the European Union and NAFTA, we are already providing some degree of central regulation to economies that are no longer congruent with national boundaries.

Other global organizations are focused on a whole host of international environmental, scientific/technological, and health problems. For many of the activities of these organizations, state borders and ethnic divisions are becoming irrelevant. To the extent that the ambitions of leaders and peoples become focused on such general welfare goals, arms races may gradually be sublimated into rivalries of a more constructive kind, particularly now that the gain/loss ratio of warfare has reached an all-time low.

Finally, the incidence of interstate aggression has remained very low during the past 50 years, particularly if the wars among the successor states of Yugoslavia and of the Soviet Union are, as they perhaps should be, excluded from the count. Aside from these, there have been very few cases of interstate aggression and even fewer of *successful* interstate aggression. The rarity of acts of flagrant aggression gives the Charter's distinction between wars and enforcement actions a validity and a viability that it would not otherwise enjoy. This change of terminology is based on the hypothesis that so few states are still willing to wage aggressive wars that it has become practical to treat those that do so as outlaws and thus proper targets for police action. With the ban on aggressive war widely accepted, it is now much easier to treat any state that persists in engaging in the unauthorized use of force as having committed a criminal act. This is, after all, a major step toward a working collective security system.

Let us look a little more closely at the conditions of enforcement. After all, police actions against individuals are quite different from police actions against sovereign states. When rogue states have powerful military forces, enforcement actions against them involve the world community in full-scale warfare, especially if the rogue state could retaliate with weapons of mass destruction. Collective police actions against well-armed governments become war under another name. The significance of calling it a police action is mainly normative; it characterizes the use of force by the UN in pursuance of the provisions of the Charter as lawful and ethically justifiable. While this distinction may be fundamental in terms of international law, it does not mean that there will be less bloodshed or that the UN-authorized forces will necessarily prevail over those of an aggressor state or states.

Our very limited experience with enforcement actions seems to demonstrate that the forces available to the central authorities need to be overwhelming if their operation is to assume the character of police enforcement. This was true, for example, of the operations conducted against Iraq where the preponderance of the enforcers' power was so manifest and so crushing that it broke the will to resist of the Iraqi soldiers.

Interestingly, confederal enforcement measures were also used by the Germanic Confederation. In its supplementary constitution (the Schlossakte of 1820), Article XXXI empowered the Confederal Diet to "have recourse to the requisite executionary measures" against its own member states once "all other constitutional measures had been exhausted." In extreme cases when a member of the Confederation persisted in defying the Bundestag, the regulations adopted under Article XXXI authorized the latter to place that member "under the rule of a commissioner supported by [confederal] soldiers, until the offense was corrected." Further, under Article XXXIII, the Bundestag could authorize "one or more governments not interested in the matter" to use military force against a recalcitrant member of the Confederation. This process was known as *Exekution* (Hurst 1972, pp. 158–159).

The Diet used this power on four occasions, against the City of Frankfurt; Hesse-Kassel (a middle-sized state); Holstein (in effect, Denmark); and finally Prussia. The first two were overawed and gave in quickly; the third resisted but was soon defeated by joint Austrian and Prussian forces; whereas Prussia quickly showed why it was futile to try to use the process of *Exekution* against a great power (Werner 1977, p. 24).[16]

How does all this play out in an era of weapons of mass destruction? It would seem to follow that there needs to be so great a preponderance of conventional, nuclear, chemical, and biological weapons at the enforcers' disposal that no rogue state will be tempted to challenge it. This brings us back to premise (2), "the unanimity of the great powers must be preserved in all crucial matters since they alone are in a position to effectively enforce the Security Council's decisions." Whenever they are able to act in open or tacit concert, the combined military power that they and their allies represent will usually be enough to discourage would-be aggressors.

(4) CONCLUSIONS

First, let me sum up the present position of the UN in terms of the 15 confederal criteria enunciated in Chapter 1:

1. It does unite states without depriving them of their statehood.

2. It does unite states whose populations are too heterogeneous to form viable federal-type unions.

3. In the United Nations Charter, it does have a written basic law whose collective security provisions are legally binding upon all of its member states.

4. It does have a raison d'être of overriding importance, that of protecting humanity against massively destructive wars.

5. & 6. Its confederal mandate *is* minimalist, leaving most governmental powers to be exercised independently by its member states.

7. & 8. However, the UN is still far from enjoying the wide measure of support and credibility among the peoples of its member states that would enable it to act authoritatively and effectively in dealing with megacrises. Worldwide popular support for the world organization is likely to increase substantially only as it proves increasingly effective in dealing with serious international crises.

9. There is no likelihood that popular allegiance to the United Nations will outweigh national allegiances any time soon.

10. The UN's member states *have* undertaken to "settle their international disputes by peaceful means in such a manner that international peace and security, and justice, are not endangered" (Article 2(3) of the Charter).

11. The Security Council meets regularly, operates under mutually agreed rules of procedure, and determines when it is necessary to impose sanctions on errant member states and which sanctions it will impose. Thus, it has become a vehicle through which governments can, and sometimes do, jointly exercise their "war and peace" powers.

12. The Council does have a voting system in which state entities are the voters, and in which decisions are based on broad collective support rather than on simple majorities of its members.

13. In the sphere of financing its activities, the United Nations has always had difficulties in getting its members to pay their assessed contributions. While in the past such problems have not kept it from carrying out essential activities, they are now reaching the point where its capacity to act on behalf of international peace and security may be increasingly compromised.

14. While the United Nations has been able to carry out the executive and judicial functions assigned to it in ways that do not threaten the sovereignty of its member states, the Secretariat's capacity needs to be enhanced through far-reaching reforms. Also, ways need to be found to induce member states to bring more of their legal disputes before the International Court.

15. Working solutions have been found for the problems arising from large state/small state inequalities that are widely accepted if not universally liked.

It may be concluded from this rundown that there is nothing in the present state of the UN's evolution that would disqualify it from being described as "a collective security confederation in the making." At the same time, the gaps and flaws in its security system, its military and institutional shortcomings, and its serious deficit in public support will probably keep the UN in a preconfederal stage for some time to come.

Does the United Nations have any reasonable hope of becoming a full-scale collective security confederation in the foreseeable future? The answer to this general question depends on the answers that may be given to a number of more specific questions. Will the peoples of the world eventually give the United Nations their support and allegiance? Can the great powers maintain their unanimity and thereby prevent the Security Council from becoming paralyzed in times of crisis? If the Five do remain able to act in concert, will they be willing and able to come to the aid of the victims of flagrant aggression in a timely way? Will each of them refrain from gross misbehavior and avoid using its veto power to shield its allies and client states when they behave unacceptably? And, finally, will they, and the non-permanent members of the Council, be able to manage successfully the great majority of disputes and confrontations in which the rights and wrongs are not clearcut?

Most of the major gaps and flaws in the UN's collective security involve, in one way or another, the great powers and the nature of their relationships with one another. It is impossible to exaggerate the importance of those relationships for the future of the world, for example, the importance of the three bilateral relationships among China, Russia, and the United States.

The world community's prospects for reaching confederal status depend upon positive answers being given to the five specific questions. I cannot help but be skeptical. In the balance sheet just drawn up, the liabilities seem still to outweigh the assets. While the establishment of a reliable collective security confederation is the goal that humanity should probably be pursuing, it is one that is only beginning to loom on the horizon as a realistic possibility.

It has come on the horizon only because the world community has successfully survived the Cold War crisis, successfully coexisted with weapons of mass destruction for half a century, and already has a Charter that provides the legal basis for confederation. But our species obviously has a long way to go before it reaches that goal. For the present, it must be concerned with what will probably be a lengthy and very dangerous transitional period.

The main items that need to be on the world's agenda during this pre-confederal period include the following:

1. The prevention of World War III by giving top priority to the avoidance or peaceful resolution of great-power confrontations;

2. The preservation of the state system (as the indispensable basis for confederation) while assisting, to the extent possible, in the reorganization of unstable states, often by finding ways of accommodating ethnic incompatibilities, such as those that plague the successor states of Yugoslavia and the Soviet Union;

3. The frustration of any acts of interstate aggression using the powers already available to the Security Council under Chapter VII of the Charter;

4. The augmentation of those powers by providing the Council with a standing military force, which would make it easier for it to come to the aid of victims of aggression in a timely way;

5. The promotion of confederal-type relationships among the great powers (which, in addition to the Council's five permanent members, may soon include Germany and Japan) on the basis of the seven premises listed earlier;

6. Restraint towards, and as possible assistance to, all states undergoing serious internal strains and stresses (at present, they include two permanent members of the Security Council—Russia and China);

7. Steps to inventory, monitor, and gradually reduce stocks of weapons of mass destruction and to prevent the manufacture of new ones; and

8. Creation in the United Nations and its specialized agencies of a greater institutional capacity that will enable them to play their respective parts in attaining these outcomes.

Even if global confederation remains a receding mirage on the horizon, a modest success in these spheres would enhance our prospects for long-term survival in the centuries to come.

In the last paragraph of his modern classic, *Federal Government,* K.C. Wheare wrote "federalism . . . is not the only device we need. . . . For the world as a whole, we need, I believe, different machinery, but it will be designed to secure the same general ideal, of making a combination of diversity and unity, independence and interdependence, safe and workable" (Wheare 1964, p. 245). One can only hope that this is an achievable goal.

NOTES

1. The Swiss Confederation was predominantly oligarchical; the Dutch Republic, oligarchical; the U.S. Confederation, democratic; and the Germanic confederation, mostly monarchical.

2. In this chapter, the words "region" and "regional" are used in the sense of large subdivisions of the world rather than as in Chapter 1, as the subdivisions of federal states.

3. In this book, Sherwood used Harry Hopkins' voluminous notes and papers to write the memoirs that Hopkins was prevented from writing by his early death.

4. All references to the UN Charter are to the *Charter of the United Nations and the Statute of the International Court of Justice,* published by the United Nations Office of Public Information, undated but including the amendments of 1965. Future citations will be to the chapter or article involved.

5. There had to be two separate meetings since the Russians refused to meet with the Chinese, not out of animosity but out of fear that the Japanese might use such a meeting as a pretext to attack them while they were still fully engaged in Europe.

6. The working majority required for adoption of most of the Council's decisions is nine; accordingly, in a 15-member Council, any seven votes can block action.

7. There is at least one precedent of small states rising up against great-power tutelage. For a brief time in 1864, a majority in the German confederal Bundestag, composed of resolute and angry German states, repeatedly rejected Austro-Prussian proposals and pushed through resolutions of their own in open defiance of the wishes of the two great powers that usually dominated their proceedings.

8. For a full discussion of this aspect, see Frederic L. Kirgis, Jr. *International Organizations In Their Legal Setting, Documents, Comments and Questions* (St. Paul,

MN: West Publishing Co., 1977), pp. 193–99. In 1965–1966, Indonesia withdrew temporarily from the UN, but soon resumed its membership.

9. The importance of this provision has been highlighted by the role of airpower in the recent enforcement actions taken against the Iraqis and the Bosnian Serbs.

10. The scale of assessments is revised once every three years; the percentage given is for the years 1992–1994. See General Assembly resolution 46/221 adopted on December 20, 1991, UN Press Release GA/8307, dated January 21, 1992, pp. 483–87. In the preparations at Dumbarton Oaks for the San Francisco Conference, the United States had originally proposed that "each member state should have voting power in proportion to its contribution to the expenses of the Organization." This provision would also have applied to the expenditures of the specialized agencies, but it was soon dropped (Russell 1958, pp. 378, 432, and 998).

11. The stipulations imposed on the defeated Iraqis may be found in Security Council resolution 687 (1991) on pp. 20–26 of UN document DPI/1104/Rev.5 of December 1994. The whole subject of the Security Council's powers vis-à-vis unrepentant defeated aggressors is fraught with legal uncertainties and political pitfalls. Some of the measures the Council took against Iraq, for example, rendering its debt repudiation null and void and imposing its determination of the Iraqi–Kuwaiti border on Iraq, can be easily criticized on the ground that it was exceeding the powers granted it under Chapter VII of the Charter (Kirgis 1995, pp. 528–32). It is also feared that the intrusiveness of some of the measures taken by the Council against a defeated Iraq may constitute a precedent for the taking of similar measures against other states in circumstances where they would be less justifiable.

On the other hand, it must be borne in mind that Iraq remains, in the light of its persistent efforts to arm itself with weapons of mass destruction, a major threat to the peace and security of the region. In this kind of situation, unforeseen by the framers of the Charter, it may be argued that the Council should be given some latitude in carrying out "its primary responsibility for the maintenance of international peace and security" under Article 24. However, when it treads on controversial legal ground, the Council needs to be careful that it does so with wide political support.

If weapons of mass destruction do become widely available in the next century, it may become necessary to give the Council (or some successor body) an even wider latitude to deal with the kinds of crises that may ensue. Such crises could, in fact, erupt before they are expected; indeed, in Iraq, we may be seeing the world community's first effort to deal with this looming problem.

12. The Soviet Union would doubtless have come to Albania's assistance in the 1949 Corfu Channel case to bar any enforcement of its finding in favor of Britain; and the United States would probably have vetoed any attempt to compel it to compensate Nicaragua in pursuance of the Court's judgment against it.

13. Relatively little attention seems to have been given to the question of how the UN's collective security system might be reformed to adjust it to the post–Cold War world's changed conditions, either in the main proposals for UN reform prepared for the UN's fiftieth anniversary or in the more general studies on security questions in the post–Cold War world. Perhaps because internal ethnic conflict has been much more common than acts of interstate aggression, UN reform studies have focused more on peacekeeping arrangements than on collective security and

problems of countering aggression. (See Boutros Ghali 1992 and 1995; American Assembly 1995; Independent Working Group 1995.)

A sampling of the voluminous literature on general post–Cold War security questions suggests that most writers have tended to ignore the UN's collective security system. (See, for example, the many articles in Allison and Treverton 1993; and Gaddis 1992.) There is an exception: Richard Gardner's article "Practical Internationalism" (Gardner 1992), which suggests the retention of the UN's collective security system and the adoption of agreements under Article 43 of the Charter that would give the Security Council a modest capacity to enforce its sanctions. Also, there is an article, "A New Concert for Europe," which would combine great power hegemony and regional collective security under a strengthened Conference on Security and Cooperation in Europe (Kupchan and Kupchan 1993). Their plan bears a family resemblance to that of the UN, but seems to reverse the 1944 decision to organize collective security on a global basis. Paul Kennedy in his *Preparing for the Twenty-First Century* allots relatively little space to security concerns of the kind that this book is focused on (Kennedy 1993).

14. Article 51 provides that the right of self-defense disappears once "the Security Council has taken the measures necessary to maintain international peace and security." In Article 25, the Charter is categoric in establishing the legal responsibility of all member states "to accept and carry out the decisions of the Security Council in accordance with the present Charter." The only way of legally escaping from this responsibility would seem to be to argue that a decision of the Council was not "in accordance with the Purposes and Principles of the United Nations" (Article 24 (2)).

15. The Secretary-General added that the option of taking military action is essential to the credibility of the UN as a guarantor of international security, and that this should involve not only negotiating the special agreements provided for in Article 43 of the Charter but activating the long-moribund Military Staff Committee. However, his proposal was not taken up by governments. Three years later, while acknowledging that governments were not yet ready to entrust the UN with carrying out major enforcement actions, he suggested that, alternatively, a "rapid reaction force" composed of "battalion-sized units from a number of countries" might be established, with its units stationed in their home countries in a high state of readiness. This force "would be the Security Council's strategic reserve for deployment when there was an emergency need for peace-keeping troops" (Boutros Ghali 1992, p. 25; 1995, p. 11).

The Secretary-General also expressed misgivings about the present system of entrusting enforcement actions to groups of member states, the procedure used in responding to the Korean and Iraqi crises. While agreeing that it was greatly preferable to the unilateral use of force by member states without reference to the United Nations, he felt that it raised a number of serious objections, such as its "negative impact on the Organization's stature and credibility" and the danger that the states so authorized might at times exceed the mandate that the Council had given them (Boutros Ghali 1995, pp. 18–19). He might have added that it does not address the underlying problem of how to respond to acts of aggression when there is no group of member states whose national interests impel them to come to the victim's aid.

16. In many respects, the Germanic Confederation provides a link between the other three prototype confederations (Swiss, Dutch, and American) and the League of Nations and the UN, particularly since it alone had two great-power members.

Its story is told in Chapter Seven of my unpublished *Confederation: Its Long History and Modern Revival,* pp. 397–508.

REFERENCES

Allison, Graham, and Gregory F. Treverton, ed. *Rethinking America's Security Beyond Cold War to New World Order.* New York: W.W. Norton, 1993.

American Assembly, 87th Sessions. *U.S. Foreign Policy and the United Nations System,* preliminary report. New York: UN Association of the U.S.A., 1995.

Barton, John H., and Barry E. Carter. "The Uneven, but Growing, Role of International Law." In Graham Allison and Gregory F. Treverton, eds. *Rethinking America's Security Beyond Cold War to New World Order.* New York: W.W. Norton, 1993, pp. 280–294.

Boyd, Andrew. *Fifteen Men on a Powder Keg: A History of the United Nations Security Council.* New York: Stein & Day, 1971.

Boutros Ghali, Boutros. *An Agenda for Peace.* New York: United Nations, 1992.

———. *Supplement to an Agenda for Peace: Position Paper of the Secretary-General on the Occasion of the Fiftieth Anniversary of the United Nations.* United Nations document A/50/60–S/1995/1, January 1995.

Charter of the United Nations and the Statute of the International Court of Justice. New York: United Nations Office of Public Information. Undated, but including amendments of 1965.

Churchill, Winston. *The Hinge of Fate.* Boston: Houghton, Mifflin Co., 1951.

———. *Triumph and Tragedy.* Boston: Houghton Mifflin Co., 1953.

Claude, Inis L., Jr. *Swords Into Plowshares,* 4th Ed. New York: Random House, 1971.

Covenant of the League of Nations. In Russell 1958, Appendix "E."

Forsyth, Murray. *Unions of States.* Leicester: Leicester University Press, 1981.

Gaddis, John Lewis. *The United States and the End of the Cold War.* New York: Oxford University Press, 1993.

Gardner, Richard N. "Practical Internationalism." In Graham Allison and Gregory F. Treverton, eds. *Rethinking America's Security Beyond Cold War to New World Order.* New York: W.W. Norton, 1992, pp. 268–277.

General Assembly Official Records, Fifth Session, Supp. 20 (A/1775).

Goodrich, Leland, Edward Hambro, and Anne Simons. *Charter of the United Nations,* 3rd Rev. Ed. New York: Columbia University Press, 1969.

Hamilton, Alexander, John Jay, James Madison. *The Federalist.* Modern Library Edition, undated.

Hughes, Christopher. *Confederacies.* Leicester: Leicester University Press, 1963.

Hurst, Michael. *Key Treaties for the Great Powers.* Devon, UK: David and Charles, Newton Abbot, 1972.

Hogan, Michael J. *The End of the Cold War: Its Meanings and Implications.* New York: Cambridge University Press, 1992.

Independent Working Group on the Future of the United Nations. *The United Nations in the Second Half-Century, Report,* New Haven: Yale University Printing Service, 1995.

Jennings, Robert Y. "The United Nations at Fifty: The International Court of Justice After Fifty Years." In *The American Journal of International Law* 89 (3), July 1995, pp. 493–505.

Kelsen, Hans. *Principles of International Law,* 2nd Ed. New York: Holt, Rinehart & Winston, 1966.

Kennedy, Paul. *Preparing for the Twenty-First Century.* New York: Random House, 1993.

Kirgis, Frederic L., Jr. "The Security Council's First Fifty Years." In *The American Journal of International Law* 89 (3), July 1995, pp. 506–539.

Kupchan, Charles A., and Clifford A. Kupchan. In Graham Allison and Gregory F. Treverton, eds. *Rethinking America's Security Beyond Cold War to New World Order,* New York: W.W. Norton, 1993, pp. 249–266.

Larsen, J.A.O. *Greek Federal States, Their Institutions and History.* Oxford: The Clarendon Press, 1968.

Lister, Frederick. *Decision-Making Strategies for International Organizations: The IMF Model.* Denver, CO: University of Denver, 1984.

———. "Thoughts on the Use of Military Force in the Gulf Crisis." Occasional Papers No. VII. New York: Ralph Bunche Institute on the United Nations, CUNY, 1991.

Morgenthau, Hans. *Politics Among Nations,* 3rd Ed. New York: Alfred A. Knopf, 1966.

Resolutions of the United Nations Security Council and Statements by Its President Concerning the Situation Between Iraq and Kuwait. 2 August 1990–16 November 1994. UN document DPI/1104/Rev.5, 1994.

Rousseau, Jean-Jacques. *Political Writings,* edited by C. E Vaughan, Vol. I. New York: John Wiley & Sons, 1962 (first published by the Cambridge University Press, 1915.

Russell, Ruth (assisted by Jeannette Muther). *A History of the United Nations Charter.* Washington D.C.: The Brookings Institution, 1958.

Schachter, Oscar. "United Nations Law." In *American Journal of International Law,* January 1994, 88, 1, pp. 1–23.

Sherwood, Robert E. *Roosevelt and Hopkins.* New York: Harper & Brothers, 1948.

Urquhart, Sir Brian. *Hammarskjold.* New York: Alfred Knopf, 1972.

Werner, George S. *Bavaria in the German Confederation, 1820–1848.* Madison, NJ: Fairleigh Dickinson Press, 1977.

Wheare, Kenneth C., *Federal Government,* 4th Ed. Oxford: Oxford University Press, 1964.

The Closing Argument

THE EMERGING NEED FOR GLOBAL GOVERNANCE

Senators Lugar and Nunn, during their hearings mentioned in the Opening Argument of this book, alerted us to the possibility that a new crisis, perhaps the most serious that humanity has ever faced, may be looming on the horizon. If their warnings prove correct, we shall need to find a way to get by in a world where, in the not-too-distant future, weapons of mass destruction will be widely available not only to countries with rogue leaders but maybe to terrorist groups as well. While we need to take immediate steps to counter or postpone that possibility, we must also reckon with the likelihood that the present policy of non-proliferation will break down. Indeed, it may already have broken down!

Assuming that these apprehensions are justified, we shall soon need to organize and conduct carefully coordinated joint actions in the international sphere and to have in place inter-governmental machinery capable of mounting these actions and of carrying them through effectively.

At the global level, however, there has been, until now, very little in the way of central governance. In earlier times, sovereign states' freedom of action was limited only by what each perceived to be its duties and obligations under international customary and treaty law. In the twentieth century, the League of Nations and the United Nations have sought successively to fill this gap, but neither has had, in practice, the political standing to fully exercise even the very limited authority contained in its mandate.

In fact, the League of Nations and the United Nations were both improvised institutions, created in the aftershock of the incredible damage that modern weaponry can inflict. Once that aftershock had worn off, their member states came to regard them more as IGO-type conveniences than as bodies for taking binding actions. Yet both were associations of states that sought to ensure the collective security of their member states, "proto-confederations" if you will. Whatever their limitations and shortcomings, they provide us with a valuable store of experience that could now be put to good use.

The need to create a more effective authority at the intergovernmental level may soon impose itself on us. The question may only be whether that new authority should assume a federal or a confederal form. As regards the federal alternative, it is difficult to visualize how, at the present time, a world federation, based on parliamentary institutions, could be organized and made to work effectively. The European Union, as noted in Chapter 2, has had great difficulty in introducing such institutions on a regional scale among peoples with longstanding common ties. For the foreseeable future, there would seem to be no realistic possibility of establishing a popularly elected global Parliament whose members would act on behalf of the world community over the heads of national governments.

This leaves the confederal alternative. Probably, the most that we can realistically hope for—and it is already a lot—is that our national leaders may succeed in establishing an effective union of states capable of securing our safety in the difficult times that probably lie ahead.

The confederal model is interesting in its own right because it can be introduced with the least possible disruption of the present state system. As has been shown, the UN Charter already provides for a world organization with confederal legal powers. Moreover, any confederal model would not require states to surrender their statehood, but merely to exercise certain powers jointly with others for certain carefully circumscribed purposes. And any such joint empowerment would be limited to the extent that may be required to bring weapons of mass destruction under dependable international control and to keep them from being made in secret, that is to say, only to the extent necessary to protect everyone from the use of those weapons. And decisions to do so would be taken in confederal fashion, i.e., on the basis of voting arrangements like those presently employed by the Security Council.

The purpose of reviewing and strengthening our confederal-type commitments and procedures would be to create a worldwide institutional base strong enough to support the complex and far-reaching global security measures and institutions that will probably be needed to deal with the emergency, or the series of emergencies, toward which we seem headed in the next century.

A LAST LOOK AT THE CONFEDERAL MODEL

The confederal model has been an option that, since Greek times, has been open to states wishing to join together in carrying out a limited range of functions without losing their separate identities. However, it is an option that, until now, has rarely been taken.

Perhaps this is because three conditions must usually be met first. First, governments must be friendly enough to negotiate, conclude, and adhere to a confederal pact, a kind of confederal "bargain," within the terms of which they will be able to maintain over many years an intimate cooperative relationship in carrying out certain sovereign functions. Second, the peoples of confederating states, particularly in democratic societies, must be ready— or persuaded—to give their support to such a relationship. Finally, there must usually be some overriding interest that imposes itself on governments and that impresses itself on peoples to generate the desire to form such wider unions.

These are the three conditions that I would juxtapose to those raised by Deutsch and others described in the Opening Argument.

The ultimate dangers presented by the widespread availability of the weapons of mass destruction in the next century meet this third condition. Collective security in such circumstances is bound to become an overriding concern. Such dangers seem likely to instill in governments and peoples alike a readiness to act jointly in response to them. Responsible leaders will wish to save their peoples from them, and the establishment of confederal-type relationships among governments would help to achieve that.

Moreover, confederal union, in its collective security form, offers a relatively simple political framework that, in the Netherlands and the United States centuries ago, was created quickly in response to emergencies. It requires, however, that the other two conditions of relatively friendly governments and sufficient popular support also be met. If these conditions are met and the emergency is serious enough, quite heterogeneous governments and peoples may be able to form confederal ties.

During the last 50 years, the idea of economic union has, for many reasons, been pursued more actively than that of security confederation. As is now revealed by what has been happening to them during the last few years, NATO and the Warsaw Pact were no more than long-term alliances of governments without any strong popular base. And, as we have just seen, the UN's collective security system is still far from being in full operation. While a network of regional and subregional economic unions (that may or may not be on its way) would help greatly in managing the "too many states" problem, it cannot deal directly with the security problems that seem likely to arise in the twenty-first century. For that purpose, we shall need to return to the collective security model set forth in the Charter and see how it needs to be modified in the light of the latest turn of events.

Finally, some may claim that confederal-type governance will prove ineffectual, particularly in a global context and given the problems mentioned in Chapter 3. But confederations, whatever their shortcomings, have generally worked tolerably well in times of serious emergency when people knew that their lives were at risk. Moreover, the alternative federal model has its own set of shortcomings as anyone who follows the domestic politics of, say, the United States and Canada knows full well. In any event, federal-type governance is not within the world's reach. And the confederal model is clearly a step up from an IGO association, which is all that the UN now offers.

THE GREAT-POWER PROBLEM REVISITED

The looming crisis brings us back to the key role of the great powers in any global collective security system. Their leadership will be essential, and in order to provide such leadership, they must first create and sustain a climate of peaceful coexistence among themselves.

With regard to the evolution of great-power relationships, Raymond Aron wrote an insightful chapter entitled "Enemy Partners" in his great work, *Peace and War.* On the eve of the Cuban missile crisis in 1962, he affirmed that "both [the United States and the Soviet Union] feared total war more than the limited advances of their rival." He added that "they have a common and vital interest *not* to resort to the use of the weapons they brandish. It is not only because they both risk being defeated together . . . but because the victor—absolute or relative—might not receive any benefit from the victory" (Aron 1968, pp. 536, 546).

Aron went on:

The two powers almost openly recognize their common interest in not fighting each other . . . And they act, to some extent, as though they admit the reality of this solidarity at the same time as the reality of the hostility of their principles. . . . Thermonuclear war is too horrible for the Kremlin to risk, either voluntarily or through imprudence . . . the major fact of the [1960s] remains the balance of terror, the desire of the two superpowers not to start the war for which they are preparing. (Aron 1968, pp. 547, 569–70)

His prediction was soon borne out during the Cuban missile crisis.

Elsewhere, Aron declared

I think, in fact, that the United States and the Soviet Union, despite the ravings of their propagandists and their Homeric challenges, have learned to know each other and no longer lightly impute bellicose intentions to each other . . . No longer disposed to doubt each other's desire to limit the conflicts, the two superpowers are less inclined to hysteria and panic when, through the fault of an ally or neutral, a crisis arises in which a country or regime runs the risk of changing allegiance. (Aron 1968, p. 566).

It may be surmised that the leaders of the superpowers were moved to act the way they did, not by brotherly love, but by fear and an ingrained instinct for survival.

Now that the circle of those in possession of large stocks of nuclear weapons has widened to include all five permanent members of the Security Council, the same considerations may ensure that the same degree of caution and prudence will prevail among them as prevailed between the superpowers during the Cold War, especially since rival ideologies and class confrontations are no longer major international issues. If they are capable of rational assessment of their national interests, the leaders of those states—and of most other states that may join the nuclear club—may be driven, by the same motives, to exercise the same restraint. Also, now that no great power can any longer guarantee its own security, the five permanent members of the Security Council may be readier to play their parts in the UN's worldwide alliance against rogue states and terrorist groups that threaten to resort to weapons of mass destruction.

THE ALTERNATIVE SCENARIOS AND THE NEED FOR POPULAR SUPPORT

We cannot assume that confederal governance is having more than a modest revival. Chapters 2 and 3 presented the evidence that such a revival has been taking place in the European Union and may be on its way in the United Nations. There is additional evidence of its revival in the Benelux Union and of its potential revival in the Caribbean union known as CARICOM. As yet, there is little assurance, however, that the confederal model will hold a wide appeal for governments or peoples. Moreover, even if this hurdle is overcome, no one knows the extent to which confederal governance will turn out to be widely replicable, and especially whether it will prove to be replicable on a global scale.

Yet the main alternative scenario is extremely ugly. It is one in which ethnic hatreds, religious fanaticisms, or the unrealistic ambitions of short-sighted dictators unleash the fury of our weapons of mass destruction and bring, in the poignant words of the Charter, "untold sorrow to mankind."

The horror of this alternative scenario is what may induce governmental leaders to decide eventually to pursue confederal governance in one form or another. But, especially in democratic countries, they cannot hope to succeed in that task without broad popular support. When the first atomic weapons were exploded in 1945, it became clear that if humanity hoped to coexist in the long run with such weaponries, the wars in which they might be used would have to be outlawed. This would require some minimal level of popular support for—even some level of worldwide solidarity on behalf of—the steps that would have to be taken to ensure that these weapons were brought under international control. Now that the strategy of non-proliferation is beginning to break down, the need to mobilize such popular support has become imperative.

As indicated in the Opening Argument, a main obstacle to the peaceful coexistence of states is the many incompatibilities and tensions among the various ethnic groups into which the human family has become divided. Like the states themselves, these groups, too, must learn how to coexist with one another in peace. As suggested in the Opening Argument and in the final pages of Chapter 1, smaller ethnic groups may find the requisite degree of political unity in economic confederations where their group rights will be fully protected. Other steps to persuade these many groups to maintain peaceful relations with one another should be actively pursued.

One response to the question "How can we learn to act together to eliminate war?" is as follows: Behavior of this kind cannot be learned; the need to eliminate it must be widely felt; and the feelings must be an outgrowth of the human instinct for survival. Thus, the model for the world is not America's great federal constitution, but its little-known Articles of Confederation, which achieved for 13 contentious states what we now need to achieve for humanity as a whole. The former colonies did not "learn" to act together; they were forced to do so if they hoped to maintain their independence. Likewise, the world's peoples, and their governments, may find themselves ready to act in concert once they "feel in their bones" that the alternative is too frightening to contemplate. When that moment comes, the confederal model may be the one that they will need to have updated and at their disposal.

REFERENCE

Aron, Raymond. *Peace and War: A Theory of International Relations.* Translated by Richard Howard & Annette Baker Fox. New York: Frederick A. Praeger, 1968.

Index

About the Author

FREDERICK K. LISTER is a veteran of thirty-four years of service in the UN Secretariat where he helped to coordinate the many interlocking activities of the UN and its fifteen specialized agencies. In his retirement, he has engaged in research on international organizations as a senior research fellow of the Ralph Bunche Institute at CUNY.

Edwards Brothers Malloy
Thorofare, NJ USA
September 16, 2014